T0154037

INVENTING LATIN HERETICS

Medieval Institute Publications is a program of
The Medieval Institute, College of Arts and Sciences

 WESTERN MICHIGAN UNIVERSITY

INVENTING LATIN HERETICS

Byzantines and the Filioque in the
Ninth Century

Tia M. Kolbaba

MEDIEVAL INSTITUTE PUBLICATIONS
Western Michigan University
Kalamazoo

Library of Congress Cataloging-in-Publication Data

Kolbaba, Tia M., 1963-
Inventing Latin heretics : Byzantines and the Filioque in the ninth
century / Tia M. Kolbaba.
    p. cm.
Includes bibliographical references (p.   ) and index.
ISBN 978-1-58044-133-9 (casebound : alk. paper)
    1. Holy Spirit--Procession--History of doctrines--Middle Ages, 600-1500.
2. Heresies, Christian--History--Middle Ages, 600-1500. 3. Orthodox
Eastern Church--Relations--Catholic Church. 4. Catholic
Church--Relations--Orthodox Eastern Church. 5. Orthodox Eastern
Church--Doctrines--History--To 1500. 6. Constantinople (Ecumenical
patriarchate)--History--To 1500. I. Title.
    BT123.K63 2008
    273'.6--dc22

                                        2008012896

        Printed in the United States of America
        C   5   4   3   2   1

CONTENTS

I did not set out to write this book. I set out to write—I still intend to write—a book about Byzantine views of Latin theology in the eleventh and twelfth centuries. I have, in fact, written the introduction to that book more than once. Nevertheless, what I present here is a study of the Byzantines and their anti-Latin writings in the ninth century, for reasons which shall become clear. I mention this in the preface for one simple reason: I owe many people thanks for the moral support I needed when it became clear that I was, in fact, writing a book on the Patriarch Photios and the ninth century. Anyone who has proposed a particular research project and been granted a year of leave to do it and then found him- or herself working on something entirely different will know what I mean.

First, my cohort at the Institute for Advanced Study in Princeton, New Jersey, 2003–4 (the year of the seventeen-year cicadas). This book was researched, conceived by accident, and partly written there, with the friendship and morale-boosting support of Cynthia Hahn, Emma Dillon, Alexander Lingas, Caroline Bynum, Giles Constable, Johannes Pahlitzsch, and other members of the "medieval table." Each of them listened to my monomania about Photios rather more than could be expected. Celia Chazelle joined the table and helped me after our meetings in invaluable conversations that took advantage of her erudition in the field of Carolingian thought. David Marsh helped out when editors' Latin was just too much for me.

A number of scholars responded to my e-mails and letters, especially in the early stages; they include Claudia Sode, Andrew Louth, Sarolta Takács, John Duffy, Alice-Mary Talbot, John Haldon, and Aristeides Papadakis.

Alexander Alexakis has stuck with the project throughout and may edit the *Mystagogia*, for which many of us will be eternally grateful.

To Lynn Jones, Maura Lafferty, Liza McCahill, and Molly Greene, friends beyond compare in their utterly different ways, I give thanks for moral support and friendship and laughter. Maybe I could have done it without you, but my life would be far less rich. Then again, maybe I could not have done it without you. Kevin Ferry knows me too well and tries to keep me honest; it turns out I do not work best at home.

Thanks to my colleagues in the Department of Religion at Rutgers, the State University of New Jersey for another step in restoring my faith in myself; to Susan Rosario, Administrative Assistant *extraordinaire*; and to the Dean of the Faculty of Arts and Sciences at Rutgers for research leave in spring 2006, which enabled me to complete the manuscript.

Most of all, love and thanks always to Jim Masschaele, who has heard more about anti-Latin polemic than any historian of England would ever want to know, and whose own second book has often languished in order to help mine go forward; to Cameron, who once asked me if a book about Photios was going to be a best seller and make me rich; and to Elodie, who keeps my office decorated. These three know best of all that I am *always* serious. They are my life.

This book is dedicated to the memory of Paul (Leopold) Masschaele, who died in March 2006, and to Madeline Marie Vandergunst Masschaele, who is still very much alive. These two extraordinary people, my husband's parents and my children's grandparents, worked harder than I can fathom to rear and educate five children, each unique and successful in his or her own way. Their love has embraced daughters- and sons-in-law, too; I am proud to be related to them. Some people express sympathy when I say my in-laws are visiting (be it the parents-in-law, or the brothers/sisters-in-law), but they are wrong. Those visits are one of the great joys in my life and in the lives of my children. Keep coming to the Masschaele-Kolbaba hotel, you lot; the attic futon is always available and the beer is always cold.

Ninth-Century Anti-Latin Texts

L ike all projects that take too long, this book has had many beginnings. Although it began as part of a project on the twelfth
century, in the end it focuses on crucial ninth-century texts—both technical
issues regarding their transmission and attribution and more theoretical
issues regarding their implications for definitions of orthodoxy and heresy.
In doing so, it reveals my own modus operandi, which is to move continually
from close studies of texts to broader studies that may help me understand
those texts, and then back again. My ultimate goal is to illuminate several
aspects of Byzantine thought—their self-definition; their theology; their
uniquely constituted state—based both on what they had to say for themselves and on modern approaches to the study of group identity, religious
conflict, and sociology of knowledge. This book moves toward that goal. If
its reach exceeds its grasp, it is because of certain characteristics both of
Byzantine theology (including heresiology)[1] and of modern research on the
subject.

If Byzantine literature is a "distorting mirror" that fools the modern
reader with its apparent timelessness and immutability,[2] Byzantine theology
is a maze with white walls, ceiling, and floor. Walking through it involves all
of the usual turns, blank walls, sometimes even reverses. But it always looks
pretty much the same; one could think that one had not moved at all.
Byzantine theologians help us—indeed helped themselves—believe in this
illusion, for it was essential to their faith that theology, like the God it seeks,
remain unchanged and unchanging.[3] Even when he says the most outra-
geously and obviously innovative things in new terms—or perhaps especially

1

when he says such things—a Byzantine theologian will assure his readers that his teaching is ancient and approved by the Fathers.

This position is not necessarily hypocritical nor ridiculous. It can have considerable internal consistency based on a fundamental belief that anything of this world is by nature imperfect and can be improved, including theological understandings of God.[4] Theological improvement, in terms of this belief, is not innovation, for it is, as Susanna Elm has put it,

> intended to move "backward" . . . in steadily improving mimesis. Orthodoxy in this conceptualization is thus quintessentially innovative, defined as improved *mimesis*. It is a continuous, dynamic movement towards the ideal prototype, the *eikon* as embodied in and elaborated by Scripture. It thus requires continuous reading, learning, understanding and explication of Scripture. This continuous process of scriptural interpretation permits, on the one hand, the preservation of the *mores* of the orthodox fathers whilst justifying, on the other, the interpretative innovations of the sons, made visible through their external appearance: ascetics as priests.[5]

Nevertheless, the maze can be discouraging. Moreover, most of those who have researched Byzantine theology have been writing a history of ideas, especially of the development of doctrine. Repetitive and derivative material, which includes the bulk of heresiological material, is irrelevant for this task, which seeks "progress," new formulations, evidence of new knowledge and new methods. Antiheretical texts, which are often encyclopedic collections of earlier material and only rarely original discussions, have been—quite understandably—neglected by historians of doctrine. Among the many consequences of this neglect is a lack of editions, precise dates, and in-depth analyses of antiheretical texts, including discursive texts of the kind presented in this study, florilegia compiled to refute heresy, catalogues of heresies, and lists of the errors of specific "heretical" groups.

In the particular case of Byzantine anti-Latin polemic, progress toward critical editions, more precise dating, and more context for individual texts is being made daily. There are, however, still some substantial and important lacunae. One of those is the subject of this book: the beginnings of Byzantine writings against the Latin addition to the creed, the Filioque. Such writings began, for reasons detailed below, around the middle of the ninth century. When I started researching a book on the twelfth century several years ago, I turned to the ninth-century material with confidence that these earliest texts, three-quarters of which were attributed to the eminent and well-researched Patriarch Photios of Constantinople (858–67, 877–86), had solidly established authorship, incontestable textual traditions, and firm dates. I was soon disillusioned. Far from being simple texts with a straight-forward history of composition and tradition, these allegedly Photian texts often looked like tangled balls of string, and string of many colors, at that. The most important of these works was the *Mystagogia of the Holy Spirit*, but recent scholars who had studied Photios and his writings in detail, including Frances Dvornik, Basil Laourdas, L. B. Westerink, Warren Treadgold, Nigel Wilson, and others, had had little interest in this text. Josef Hergenroether's enormous corpus of work on Photios, which included the only modern edition of the *Mystagogia*, was useful in innumerable ways, but his accep-tance of Photian authorship was broad and often uncritical—or perhaps one should say too critical, for he tended to believe that Photios would and did do everything possible to save his own career and undermine the papacy.[6] Moreover, Hergenroether lacked the advantage of over a century of work, including exemplary editions of other Photian texts, that is now available.

Reluctantly at first, I abandoned immediate plans for a book on anti-Latin theology in the twelfth century. Enthusiasm followed reluctance as I realized how important the ninth-century material might be and concluded that a study of Greeks and Latins in the last half of the ninth century was more than a chapter or an article. I seemed, in fact, to be writing a book on it. With that settled, it became necessary to look at the one other ninth-century text that addressed the Latin teaching on the Holy Spirit: a treatise on the procession of the Holy Spirit by Niketas Byzantios (fl. second half of the ninth century)—a figure primarily known for having written the first sura-by-sura 'refutation' of part of the Qur'an.[7] The reader will find chapters on each of the three Photian works and the work of Niketas below.

The book has developed simultaneously in two directions, reflected in those chapters. My primary interest is Byzantine anti-Latin literature as both one of many kinds of antiheretical literature and a window onto Byzantine mentalities. But I can only pursue that interest by providing a more precise and nuanced dating and context for these texts, which are the seminal texts for the history of Byzantine reactions to the Filioque. Two of the three texts on the procession of the Holy Spirit until now attributed to Photios raised textual questions that could not be ignored. One—the *Mystagogia of the Holy Spirit*—lacks a modern critical edition, and badly needs one. I have not answered all of the textual questions here; I hope to do so soon in an editorial collaboration with Professor Alexander Alexakis. While it contains much information on the texts, the current book is fundamentally an attempt to determine what Byzantines were saying about the Filioque in the earliest texts we have.

So this study moves back and forth between two complementary but different kinds of analysis. Chapter 1 is an introduction to heresiology in general. It defines terms, summarizes as much as possible a vast body of secondary scholarship, and brings the history of Byzantine antiheretical texts down to the ninth century. Chapter 2 introduces relations between Latin and Greek Christians before the time of Photios—another intellectual and political context for the these works by Photios and his contemporaries. Chapter 3 discusses Photios himself and his knowledge of Latin practices in the ninth century. Chapters 4 to 6 examine the transmission, form, and contents of the three anti-Filioque works attributed to Photios: Ep. 2, the *Mystagogia*, and Ep. 291. Nonspecialist readers, if I am fortunate enough to have them, will want to skim these chapters. Their arguments are crucial for scholars working with these sorts of texts, whether they are interested in the textual tradition or the history of ideas, but they are probably both incomprehensible and boring to those with more general interests. Chapter 6 is followed by an "Intermission," summarizing the conclusions of chapters 4 through 6 for those who take this option. Chapter 7 analyzes Niketas Byzantios's anti-Filioque treatise. Chapter 8 deals with an additional piece of evidence for what Byzantines were saying about Latin "errors" in the late ninth century, a letter of Pope Nicholas I dated to October 867. The "Conclusion" brings us full circle—back to heresiology, this time specifically focused on the late ninth-century texts.

NOTES

1. For what I mean by 'heresiology,' see chap. 1, below.

2. Cyril Mango, *Byzantine Literature as a Distorting Mirror*, Inaugural Lecture (University of Oxford, 1975).

3. The question of whether our (secular, post-Enlightenment, western, sometimes orientalist) faith also requires belief that Byzantine theologians were the ultimate keepers of the flame of Byzantine conservatism (thus projecting our own fear of change onto a safely "othered" society), is far too much to deal with here. Still, it is true that even those who know Mango's distorting mirror very well have been known to cling to the idea that the Byzantine Church was always a force for conservatism and inertia in the face of considerable evidence to the contrary. See also Averil Cameron, *The Use and Abuse of Byzantium: An Essay on Reception*, Inaugural Lecture,

King's College London, 15 May 1990 (London: The School of Humanities, King's College London, 1992).

4. For some interesting discussions of the development of doctrine as a theological matter, see the essays in Sarah Coakley and David A. Pailin, eds., *The Making and Remaking of Christian Doctrine: Essays in Honour of Maurice Wiles* (Oxford: Clarendon Press, 1993).

5. Susanna Elm, "The Diagnostic Gaze. Gregory of Nazianzus' Theory of Orthodox Priesthood in his Orations 6 *De pace* and 2 *Apologia de fuga sua*," in Susanna Elm, Éric Rebillard, and Antonella Romano, *Orthodoxie, Christianisme, Histoire. Orthodoxy, Christianity, History* (Rome: École française de Rome, 2000), 86. What Gilbert Dagron and John Haldon have said about Byzantine attitudes toward law is analogous to Elm's point about theology; see Gilbert Dagron, "L'Église et l'État (milieu IXe–fin Xe siècle)," in *Histoire du christianisme des origins à nos jours,* ed. Jean-Marie Mayeur et al., vol. 4, *Éveques, moines et empereurs (610–1054)* (Paris: Desclée, 1993), 167: "To restore the ancient order becomes an obsession of sorts—and sometimes an alibi that grants the freedom to innovate"; and John Haldon, *Byzantium in the Seventh Century: The Transformation of a Culture* (Cambridge: Cambridge University Press, 1990), chap. 7.

6. Josef Hergenroether, *Photius Patriarch von Konstantinopel. Sein Leben, seine Schriften und das griechische Schisma,* 3 vols. (Regensburg, 1867; repr. Darmstadt: Wissenschaftliche Buchgesellschaft, 1966). Hergenroether, *Monumenta graeca ad Photium eiusque historiam pertinentia* (Ratisbon: George Joseph Manz, 1869; repr. Westmead: Gregg International, 1969). Photios, Patriarch of Constantinople, *Logos peri tes tou agiou pneumatos Mystagogeas,* PG 102:279–396; hereafter cited as *Mystagogia.* For an example of a text Hergenroether attributed to Photios that has been convincingly reassessed and redated, see M. Gordillo, "Photius et Primatus Romanus. Num Photius habendus sit auctor opusculi 'Pros tous legontas os e Rome thronos protos'?" *Orientalia Christiana periodica* 6 (1940): 5–39.

7. *Works against Islam,* ed. and German trans. Karl Förstel, *Niketas von Byzanz. Schriften zum Islam* (Würzburg: Oros, 2000); Théodor-Adel Khoury, *Les théologiens byzantins et l'Islam. Textes et auteurs (VIIIe– XIIIe s.)* (Louvain: Nauwelaerts, 1969), 110–62; Khoury, *Polémique byzantine contre l'Islam (VIIIe–XIIIe s.)* (Leiden: Brill, 1972).

CHAPTER 1

Heresiology and the Invention of Heretics

Scholars are far from having a single method for analyzing anti-heretical writings from late antiquity, the Middle Ages, and later. I put myself firmly in the pragmatists' camp by opining that there will never be a single method or a single set of theoretical presuppositions applicable to all such texts and acceptable to all scholars. The texts and their contexts are too plentiful and too varied. Nevertheless, the last century has seen fascinating, suggestive, and often controversial attempts to redefine terms and reassess narratives about the church and Christian doctrine that had long been dominated by certain spoken and unspoken assumptions. In traditional histories of heresy, there tended to be an ever-developing but fundamentally unchanging entity called orthodoxy and its ever-innovating but fundamentally unchanging opponent, heresy. Orthodox believers were portrayed as pursuers of the truth, intent on preserving tradition, while heretics used underhanded means, lied about what they really believed, and innovated (often and paradoxically by going back to some ancient heresy, often by having relied too much on intellect instead of faith). Seeing some ages in which there was great concern about heresy, traditional historical accounts concluded that there are periods of more heresy and less heresy. They also posited or assumed that we can learn, if not everything we need to know, at least much that is true and important, from what orthodox writers say about the beliefs and practices of heretics.

All of these assumptions have been called into question in the last century, with important results. The vast majority of historians now view Christian sources with the kind of skepticism that used to be reserved for the sources of alien faiths. Given, however, that there are those who see the resulting work as fundamentally flawed by the (secular) scholars' unwillingness to admit that they, too, have assumptions; and given that some see this work as reductionist, it seems useful to put my own cards on the table. I am a historian, not a philosopher or a theologian. As such, I limit myself to pronouncing on matters that can be proved or disproved by another historian regardless of her faith or lack thereof. My claims are not metaphysical and should not be taken as such. My ongoing attempt to be as objective as possible—with willing admission that I do not always succeed—means that I cannot and will not pronounce on metaphysical matters. This does not make me reductionist, however.[1] Certainly a historian must "allow a weight" to such matters as "faith, spiritual aspiration, religious belief."[2] But allowing that the motivations of past human beings included spiritual and ideological ones is not the same thing as pronouncing on whether or not the things they believed were real or true or Real or True. I insist, moreover, that the matter is not as simple as saying that historians who claim to operate without faith-based assumptions simply have different, unacknowledged assumptions.[3] Certainly we make assumptions. But insofar as we strive to write history according to the current canons of the field, we do not assume that God does not intervene in history any more than we assume that he does. We simply insist that declarations about God belong to the realms of theology and metaphysics, not to history.[4] One of the things that this means is that ecclesiastical history should not be somehow treated differently from "general history."[5] The history of Christian doctrine, of the institutions of the Christian churches, and of the men who have led them must be written to the same standards as the history of any other set of ideas, institutions, and people.

It is necessary to say all of this because some Christians, firmly rooted in certain ideas about the historical nature of their faith, object to the methods and many of the conclusions of historians who work as I do. They may find their objections laid to rest much more effectively by David A. Pailin, Gotthold Lessing, or Alfred North Whitehead than by me, so I leave the references there. I hope it suffices to repeat that the assumptions of my work are historical ones, and that I see a vast and sometimes awkward gulf fixed between history and theology[6]—the former seems to me open to objective interpretation even if we never achieve absolute objectivity; the latter studies the divine which, as Jack Sanders puts it, has "proved itself most elusive of comprehension and analysis."[7] I am also certain that at times I have let my unwritten and unacknowledged assumptions affect my analysis, and I encourage my readers to point out my blind spots. I aim to illuminate some interesting aspects of the past. If some find implications for their personal faith and for contemporary doctrine and belief in them, that was not my intent.

To return to the subject at hand, this way of approaching the history of Christianity—indeed we should say Christianities—suggests that we deal with heresy, orthodoxy, and the very concept of religion in the western sense, as ideas constructed by specific human individuals in specific times and places, intended for specific audiences.[8] In other words, given that pronouncements on the correctness or error of any theological doctrine belong to the realm of theology and philosophy, historians seek as much as possible to explain the triumph of a particular group of men or a particular doctrine in terms of what we can say as historians. Thus we try to explain which of two competing theological views became orthodoxy and which heresy in terms of historical circumstances amenable to proof or disproof, rather than in terms of the inspiration of the Holy Spirit. Our interest in real changes in theology—changes that most Christian believers, but generally only Christian believers, can see as continuity—makes this work more accessible to the historian who wants to bracket questions of ultimate Truth. These approaches to heresy take as their subject not the heretics, but those who write about heresy. They seek less to understand heterodox groups and their teaching than to understand the self-proclaimed orthodox who write about them. In sociological terms, we are interested not in those who are labeled as deviants, but in those who do the labeling. We study antiheretical works in order to understand their authors, not to narrate what we consider an imaginary history of heresy, and therefore we tend to say that we are studying "heresiology." A neologism that may grate on some nerves, it is nonetheless a necessary distinction, for it makes clear the difference between real groups and their ideas, on the one hand, and the heresiologist's perceptions, on the other.

As Averil Cameron has recently pointed out, the focus on heresiologists rather than heretics has been for some time central in studies of the early Christian and late antique churches, as well as the Latin west in the twelfth and thirteenth centuries and the Protestant Reformation.[9] Although it is less common in Byzantine studies, Cameron also points to a few representatives among Byzantinists of the newer ways of looking at heresy and orthodoxy. Marie-France Auzépy, Gilbert Dagron, Paul Speck, and Cameron herself, for example, have provided crucial insights into the nature of Byzantine heresiology. In addition, many studies of subjects other than heresiology per se have shed light on how Byzantines dealt with "the Other," which included heretics.[10] Still, we have a long way to go before someone can write a synthetic study of heresiology in Byzantium that goes beyond the true, but uninformative, commonplaces: it is rarely original or creative; it is repetitive; it is never fair and balanced. It is, in a word, boring.[11]

My labors in writing not one but two books on the subject may reveal that I disagree with this last statement. Heresiology is not boring if we concentrate a bit less on its content and a bit more on its authors, purposes, and forms. Describing, defining, and refuting heresy were the obsessions of some Byzantines and of perennial interest to many. The logical conclusion, if we accept that they were not stupid and superstitious where we are clever and rational, is that there was something in this literature that mattered to them. Their political and ecclesiastic institutions, their education, and the power structures of their society differed from ours, and understanding the heresiological texts—in many ways the kind of Byzantine literature that is most alien to us—may be one of the keys to understanding Byzantium as a whole.[12]

Here, however, I run up against the crucial question that is not going to be answered in one book: what are Byzantine heresiologists doing, exactly, given that they rarely write to provide their readers with new, accurate, eyewitness information? As Cameron notes, much of the modern distaste for heresiology starts "from the premise that heresiologies are there as sources of information" when they are not.[13] Another part of the modern distaste for heresiology stems from the expectation that its arguments should somehow logically address the real positions of their opponents. The heresiologists themselves try to convince us of this by often presenting their works as dialogues or debates. In fact, with rare exceptions, heresiologists do not write for the other side of the debate, the heretics themselves. They write to persuade, reassure, and/or encourage people within the group they call "us." None of this is surprising in light of scholarship about heresy in late antiquity or the twelfth and thirteenth centuries in western Europe. Scholars of these fields have also advanced various theories to explain early Christian antiheretical writing, the antiheretical writing of the fourth through seventh centuries, or the antiheretical texts of the Latin west in the High Middle Ages. Among these I have found none that works entirely for Byzantium in the ninth century and for the anti-Latin texts of that period. Still, I am not sure that I believe in models that work entirely, and I have found some of this research in other times and regions useful.

Antiheretical Polemic before Constantine I

Some of the most useful developments can be found in studies of Christian and Jewish groups in the early centuries of the Common Era. This is not the place to rehearse the last half-century of seismic shifts in the study of varieties of Christianity, varieties of Judaism, and the varieties of relations between Christians and Jews in this period.[14] At the risk of doing the scholars who have contributed to these shifts an injustice (they deserve more nuanced coverage), I would note the following ways in which their work has helped me think about Byzantine anti-Latin polemic.

Recent scholarship on early Christianity and rabbinic Judaism stresses that, while church leaders "asserted and reasserted and reasserted again" that Judaism and Christian were incompatible, nevertheless "the incompatibility of Jewish and Christian 'ways' remained less than clear for others in their midst."[15] Christian writers who insist that Jews are Jews and Christians are Christians and never the twain should meet are not describing reality; they are attempting to construct reality as they would like it to be and to persuade others to accept their construction. In reality, many people frequented both church and synagogue, followed both the laws of Moses and the sayings of Jesus. Some who acknowledged Jesus as God's anointed nevertheless remained among the most Torah-centered of the many Jewish groups. In short, many characteristics that we think of as unique indices of Christianity or Judaism were not so clearly distributed in the first four centuries of the Common Era.[16]

Nevertheless, the Christian thinkers who wanted a clear separation between Christianity and Judaism *did* persuade many and did begin to make for themselves a world in which all important markers could be divided between Christians and Jews. *Logos* theology is ours/Christian; dietary observances are theirs/Jewish. Ironically, their most powerful allies in this process of creating separate religions called Judaism and Christianity, a kind of abstraction that had previously not existed, were their counterparts in the Jewish world. As Christian separatists worked on the wall from their side, powerful opinion-leaders within the Jewish community were adding bricks on theirs, composing the Talmuds, defining out of Judaism those who professed Jesus of Nazareth as the Messiah, those who believed in a separate entity in the Godhead (the Logos), and those who challenged other aspects of the rabbinic interpretations of Torah.[17] We know that many people fit into neither of the categories thus created: there were

Jews who believed in the Logos but not that Jesus of Nazareth had been the Logos made flesh; there were Pharisees who believed that Jesus was the Messiah but not the Logos. Such people who agreed with neither the rabbis of the Talmud nor the bishops of proto-orthodox Christianity were numerous, as the texts of the rabbis and bishops themselves remind us. Yet the strategy of those texts is always to deny the name of Jew or Christian to those who disagree. The resulting picture in the texts of the rabbis and the Apologists is of a world clearly divided between Jews and Christians. Scholars of earlier centuries accepted this picture not because they were blind, but because the separatists won in the end. Theirs were the texts scholars had as evidence. Much of the traditional narrative of church history alluded to at the beginning of this chapter was bequeathed to us by the same separatists.

The direct connections between the earliest texts to separate Jews from Christians and the beginnings of texts that separate heretics from the orthodox have often been noted. Again it is not my purpose here to rehearse all of those connections—merely to note that Christian heresiology develops in the context of the anti-Jewish material and adopts many of its categories and some of its language.[18] Like early anti-Jewish material, it constructs a particular world. Fundamental to this world is division—an absolute boundary and barrier between us, orthodox Christians, and them, heretics.[19] In that world, orthodox institutions are authorized by apostolic succession and characterized by harmony and agreement regarding the oikonomia[20] of God and his Son; by simple, straightforward doctrine; by obvious and clear biblical exegesis; and by clear boundaries separating right-thinking Christians from Jews and pagans. Heresy, on the other hand, is characterized by a diabolic succession of heresiarchs that goes back to Simon Magus; by wild diversity, innovation, and complexity in its teachings; by tortured exegesis of the Scriptures; and by the blurring of the lines between Christians, Jews, and pagans.[21] To accept the texts of these self-proclaimed orthodox is to write again that traditional narrative of early church history. Here again recent—and some not-so-recent—studies have broken down the narrative. Early in the twentieth century Walter Bauer challenged the notion of early Christian homogeneity, maintaining that early Christianity was not a primordial unity broken down by corrupting outside forces after the apostles were dead. Instead, it was a vast mosaic in which many of what would later be labeled heretical groups preceded many orthodox ones. Early Christianity actually narrowed, Bauer argued, from many forms to one, that one eventually gaining such hegemony that it could erase the stories of the others. Already when it was published, and then again after its publication in English in 1971, Bauer's work inspired interest in early Christianities that had not survived the fourth century.[22]

Nor was Bauer the only cause of this interest. The second half of the twentieth century saw the discovery and publication of the noncanonical early Christian documents from Nag Hammadi, the apocalyptic texts of the Dead Sea Scrolls, and a number of other noncanonical texts written by Christians and Jews of the early Common Era. As I write, a second- or third-century "Gospel of Judas" has been revealed to the public for the first time. These texts, written by opponents of the hegemonic orthodox, did more than confirm Bauer's initial hypothesis. They showed that he had, if anything, underestimated the number and variety of Jewish and early Christian sects. The field faced a paradigm shift. Instead of seeing the anti-Jewish and antiheretical polemicists of the first through fourth centuries as representatives of their entire religion, reporting the simple facts about hostility between Jews and followers of Jesus, heretics and orthodox, most historians now emphasize that the polemicists were describing the world they wished to see, and trying to persuade others to join them.

Take, for example, Christian heresiologists from Justin Martyr and Irenaeus of Lyon in the second century to Epiphanius of Salamis in the late fourth. Justin represents the many Christian leaders who were defining a new kind of institution with its own rules of succession, admission, and exclusion. They needed to define their own beliefs; to construct the other or others over against which they stood; to distinguish themselves from those others; to ensure cohesion within the group. Different kinds of literary endeavors did different parts of this job, although it is easy to see the overlap between apologetics (defining us against the pagans), anti-Jewish and anti-Judaizing polemic (defining us against the Jews), and antiheretical writing (defining us against heretics). In the last case, the goal was to ensure a certain kind of unity in the church—a unity in which the right people (all men) were the leaders, the other people (especially women) followed loyally, and authoritative texts limited the extent to which anyone could speak for God or Jesus. Heresiology enabled these formers of opinion to project everything they did not want in their institution onto heretics, thereby eliminating the unwanted from the church. Heretics have unfit leaders (including women), prophets (including women) who claim to teach new things, and falsified Scriptures.[23] Their scriptural exegesis is flawed by being somehow both too literal and too allegorical. They are, in short, not really Christians.

In this way recent studies of pre-Constantinian anti-Jewish and anti-heretical literature emphasize that heresiology is a literature of group identity. As such, it defines us, often by defining them in ways that they would never define themselves. That is, while there are literatures that deal mostly in positive statements about what we believe and how we ought to behave, heresiology is generally a literature of what we do not believe and they do, wrongly of course.

As a literature of group identity, heresiology is also meant for internal consumption. It may aim at persuasion, but only of those within the group who do not yet sufficiently understand that the heretics are wrong. It may also be performative, a way of acting out our difference from others, which is also a way of celebrating our harmony and community. The latter is especially prominent when heresiologists stress, as nearly all of them do, the tremendous variety and lack of cohesion among heretical sects.

Finally, heresiological texts regularly identify a real division in the world around them. As Daniel Boyarin puts it, "One might say that Judaism and Christianity were invented in order to explain the fact that there were Jews and Christians."[24] That is, given the existence of communities that in fact believed different things and practiced different rituals, and given an ideology that stressed the unity and community of all Christians, heresiological writers tried to compile a set of reasons why communities different from their own were wrong, misled, diabolically inspired.

It is important to stress two things here. First, we should resist any temptation to believe what members of one religious group tell us about the motives, beliefs, and practices of another. The Gospels and other early Christian literature do not give us real Jews;[25] the heresiologists do not give us real heretics; and Protestant descriptions of Roman Catholics are seldom full of unbiased facts. In describing the existence of different groups, heresiologists may be reporting facts, but in explaining the histories of the groups, the origins of the difference, the motives of their leaders, and their fundamental errors they give us a distorted view. For example, Epiphanius of Salamis thought that Origen's teachings endangered the souls of believers (he was especially concerned about monks) and fought them for that reason. Perhaps we can believe him when he tells us his own motives; we certainly must question him when he tells about Origen's.[26]

Second, this recognition of how very much our sources can mislead us does not imply insincerity or mendacity in the heresiologists. There are undoubtedly manipulative demagogues in the group, but in general I am convinced that they believe that the differences they describe are crucial. There really are, for our authors, heresy, heretics, and Judaizers, and the errors of belief and practice are stains on the church, obstacles to salvation, insults to God. The frequency with which heresiologists use various forms of the word *hubris/hubrizo* to describe heretics and their teaching is striking; the term's multiple meanings of insult, injury, betrayal, and pride, suit their purposes perfectly.

One further question must be addressed, even if it returns us to the realm of the ultimately unanswerable: Why the emphasis on unity through uniformity and conformity? It simply will not do to say that Christians emphasized this type of unity because their Scriptures and early traditions emphasized the unity of the church as the body of Christ. Those texts and traditions are reflections of the idealized unity, not causes of the ideal, nor do they describe the kind of uniformity of doctrine that characterizes later Christianity. Given that, in fact, there was great diversity among groups who followed Jesus of Nazareth, the triumph of this particular ideal, this particular concept of unity, may need to be explained. And the explanation may be different for different periods. I think it likely, for example, that Justin and others who lived through the period in which Christianity was still marginal and yet also important enough to have come to the attention of Roman authorities, promoted such unity as a matter of survival. The church could survive only by promoting a consistent message, and that message included the claim to be the true continuation of Judaism, loyal subjects of Rome, and not disturbers of the social order who had secret knowledge and did such things as reverse gender roles. By the end of the third century, however, Christian concerns to form a canon of Scriptures, to eliminate heresy, and to homogenize the credal statements of the liturgy closely parallel other developments in the Greco-Roman world. The beginnings of a cultural shift from an intellectual world that values debate and disputation to one that values ascetic authority can be found in pagan circles as much as in Christian ones.[27] Above all, from Diocletian onward, anxious to prevent the recurrence of the crises of the third century, emperors tended to emphasize very similar concerns. When the emperors and the proto-orthodox Christians combined forces, the pressures for conformity became irresistible.

Antiheretical Polemic in the Age of the Councils (325–682)

Justin, Hippolytus, Irenaeus, Clement, and the other early polemicists bequeathed to the newly imperial church and its theorists the paradigm of a world divided between orthodoxy and heresy. According to this model, orthodoxy is characterized by apostolic succession, harmony and agreement regarding the salvation of God, simple teachings, clear biblical exegesis, and separation from Jews and pagans. Those who do not understand every detail need not worry but should rather follow the lead of the bishops and presbyters, who follow directly in succession from the apostles. Heretics are in every way the binary opposite of the true church. They have institutions of their own, but, far from being apostolic, their succession is diabolic, reaching back to Simon Magus, Mani, or some other heresiarch. Like Simon, they are in fact rebelling against the apostles. They disagree not only with the orthodox but also with one another. Pride causes these disagreements, and pride also leads each of their leaders to make up his own outlandish doctrine, based on tortured exegesis, false Scriptures, and intellectual pride. Ironically, while they try to be creative in this way, their doctrines can be recognized as heretical because of their similarity to the teaching of earlier heretics. In the end, all heresies have a common, diabolical source. Finally, the second- and third-century heresiologists would have us believe that heretics are outsiders and have always been outsiders; if they ever seemed to be real Christians, they were lying.[28]

When one has been introduced to this paradigm, and once one understands that this is a description of what the heresiologist thinks should be more than a description of what is, it becomes possible to look at the next four centuries and the first six "ecumenical" councils in a new way. For example, the very labeling of most opponents of the First Council of Nicea (325 CE, only much later known as the First Ecumenical Council) as "Arians" adopts a familiar heresiological fiction: a heresy is the work of one man who teaches innovative ideas and is too proud simply to submit to the authority of tradition as represented by his bishop, successor of the apostles. The situation was much more complex, involving what Lewis Ayres has called "four broad theological traditions" that contributed eventually to the definitions of both Nicene orthodoxy and Arianism. The theology of Arius himself played a minimal role in the negotiations and conflict among proponents of these four views that followed Nicea 325.[29] The orthodox who refuse to yield or compromise on the decisions of this council, which condemned Arius, tell us that he was proud and rebellious, that he was a mere priest who refused to obey his bishop, that he spent suspicious amounts of time in the company of women, that he had intellectual pretensions that led him into error, that when his error was pointed out he refused to admit it, and that even when it was clear that the error recapitulated a number of ancient and condemned errors (especially Adoptionism) he still believed he was right. The reader might be suspicious of such claims even before Arius, according to his opponents, dies on the toilet, his bowels spilling out like Judas's.[30] The fit with the model of a heretic as it has been painstakingly constructed over a period of centuries is too close to be true. And if we dig a bit deeper, or even read the Nicene sources with a more jaundiced eye, we find evidence that before Athanasius went to work on Arius's biography Arius was known as a devout ascetic, a popular preacher, and a composer of hymns to help his congregation understand doctrine. Far from teaching a new and obviously blasphemous Trinitarian theology, his explanation of the relations between Father, Son, and Holy Spirit was traditional in many circles and easier for many people to accept than the innovative Nicene terminology of same substance (*homoousia*).[31]

Thus there is much that continues from the early Christian tradition of heresiology into the period of the councils. Starting in the fourth century, however, the continued formation of orthodoxy takes place under rapidly changing circumstances. Historians of late antiquity stress that this age valued "centralization . . . , standardization . . . , economic and political solidarity."[32] Richard Lim, among others, has shown how the "triumph of Christianity" over pagans and Jews and the "triumph of orthodoxy" over heretics were interwoven with and dependent upon particular changes in the uses and acceptability of theological speculation and the solidification of hierarchical structures in church and empire.[33] This is the period when Christians confronted the changes implied by imperial acceptance of and intervention in their religion. For more than a century—indeed for the rest of history—Christian leaders would struggle to agree about such complex issues as the incorporation of Hellenic *paideia* into doctrine, the role of ascetics in the community, the control of popular preachers, the role of the bishop in the imperially sanctioned church, and the relative power of the bishops of Rome, Alexandria, Antioch, and increasingly Constantinople.[34] Theoretically, there are myriad ways that the church could have responded to these challenges; it is not surprising that, in fact, it fell back on its experience and used the tools at hand. Those tools included, among other things,[35] the heresiological paradigm described above. In this context, many depictions of heresies and heretics look like projections of strains and anxieties within the newly accepted church. Further, we must remember that Christians within the empire shared many of their contemporaries' concerns, including a desire for order (even at the price of autocracy) after the political chaos of the third century.[36]

The antiheretical literature of this period has received a great deal of attention, but has not yet found someone to synthesize it in a way comparable to Le Boulluec's analysis of pre-Constantinian thinkers. Maybe it will never happen, for the material is not only more voluminous but also expressed in a wider variety of genres. What follows is not an attempt to cover that material in any detail but rather a sketch of the background for the later material that is the subject of the rest of this book.

The most famous heresiological piece of the era is Epiphanius of Salamis's *Panarion*. Continuous with the past in terms of genre, for it is a catalogue of heresies and heretics, the *Panarion* was also the end (at least for some centuries) of creative use of this genre. There is a long interval between Epiphanius and the next era in which cataloguing of this sort is one of the primary forms of heresiology. Even if it is more the culmination of past efforts than the beginning of new ones, however, Epiphanius's attitude toward heresy and his idea of orthodoxy owe a great deal to century in which he writes. Aline Pourkier has shown how Epiphanius's emphasis on the biographies of specific heresiarchs differs from earlier heresiologies: Epiphanius tells of several heretical teachers who began as irreproachable Christians but who experience "a sort of anti-conversion," changing markedly the portrayal of Justin, Irenaeus, and other earlier writers that would have heretics begin and end as outsiders.[37] Rebecca Lyman has noted that Epiphanius thus makes the heresiarch a kind of mirror image of the holy man who is another feature of the period.[38] Moreover, Epiphanius's work is a clear example of how heresiology changes as the church changes from being a sometimes-persecuted minority religion to being the religion of the emperors. Writing in the 370s, Epiphanius no longer sees the primary threat to orthodoxy coming from outside the church; his adult lifetime has been spent fighting battles within the church. Most strikingly, he gives us portraits of heretics, especially a portrait of Origen, in which the danger of heresy is entirely internal and even afflicts ascetics of otherwise outstanding virtue. In doing so, he reflects his age, a period in which it was no longer possible to deny that heretics had at least *begun* within the church. As Lyman puts it, "In the public doctrinal debates of the fourth century church, doctrinal division was revealed as an embarrassing and persistent problem of the Christian community."[39]

Another feature of Epiphanius's heresiology illustrates one of Lim's central points. The corrupting influence on many of Epiphanius's heresiarchs, Origen among them, is love of disputation and dialectic. Earlier heresiologists, including Justin and Clement of Alexandria, occasionally pointed to intellectual pride as a heretic's besetting sin, but they also often presented their own works as the recording of philosophical disputations. By the time Epiphanius wrote, in the late fourth century, many people saw disputation itself as the problem. The picture of the heretic as one who raises unnecessary issues and questions matters that ought to be left untouched is a product of this period.[40] When public disputation becomes an activity of heretics, histories of even the Council of Nicaea strive to remove any connection between the Fathers and such disputation.[41]

Other features of the heresiology of the period also differ from the earlier literature. The fourth and fifth centuries saw a diminution of the secular sphere in society, including a dramatic diminution of literature that was purely secular. As more literature came to be permeated with religious themes, written in religious contexts, and written by men of religious profession, heresiology ceased to be a separate genre and became simply one subject for different genres: persuasive treatises, encomia and invective, materials for catechesis and preaching, biographies of bishops and holy men, placards to post on the doors of the churches. Again to cover all of this would be a different book (or books), but a few of the ways that antiheretical writers express themselves in this period are worth highlighting.

After Constantine's conversion, and with increasing imperial involvement in the church, doctrinal disputes become public and political. As a result, heresiology becomes literature for public consumption. So, for example, placards, posters, and public sermons surround the councils of Ephesus in the early fifth century. The controversy, initially focused upon Patriarch Nestorius of Constantinople, begins when someone accuses Nestorius of reprising the heresy of Paul of Samosata—the accusation appears in a broadsheet nailed to the door of the Church of Holy Wisdom.[42] The results of the council that condemns Nestorius, led by Cyril of Alexandria, are posted throughout Ephesus and proclaimed by heralds, to which the imperial representative Candidian responds by publishing an edict against the validity of Cyril's council. Preachers from both sides regale the people of Ephesus for weeks.[43]

Meanwhile, Epiphanius was not the only fourth-century figure to realize that when the threat of heresy was within the church, different tools were required to combat it. Some way of distinguishing right from wrong doctrine that went beyond Scripture was needed. Many of the ultimate victors in the "Arian" controversy—victors who waited a long time for their final victory—"came to see [Nicea 325] as something more than a momentary expression of orthodox resolution against Arianism. It embodied some kind of supreme teaching authority after Scripture."[44] By the fifth century, when Nicea 325 had become a revered authority, and the idea had developed that some councils were ecumenical and uniquely important, the acts of councils themselves became literary products with heresiological elements.[45] So, as Helen Sillett and Evangelos Chrysos have demonstrated, the Acta of First Ephesus are not a neutral record of what occurred at the council but rather a careful composition by Cyril of Alexandria. Under Cyril's editing hand, they become "a polemical tool to defeat an alternative theology. The acts are a dossier of arguments and techniques which seek to create a new reality by demonstrating that an orthodox bishop is actually a heretic, and that only Cyril's theology properly articulates the Christian faith."[46] It is, in fact, hard to imagine how conciliar records could have been anything else given that they were only very rarely scribal transcripts of the actual proceedings.[47] Sometimes, when they are sufficiently inconvenient, the Acta even of ecumenical councils disappear.[48]

In many ways all of these developments are part of a wider phenomenon: the permitted sources for theology and the permitted authorities for dogma are being reduced and canonized.[49] The Arian controversy demonstrated that Scripture alone did not suffice to answer some theological questions and reinforced the hierarchy's sense that not just anyone could be allowed to speak on such questions. The words of certain leaders of the church and certain councils were authoritative; the words of others were not. Basil of Caesarea put together what is possibly the first collection of selections from "the Fathers" to refute Macedonius and the "Pneumatomachians." Both Chalcedonians and their opponents would claim utter faithfulness to the words of Cyril of Alexandria, who had claimed utter faithfulness to the words of Athanasius. By the fifth century there existed "a canon of particular individual writers of the patristic period who became known as fathers, and whose writings came to have authoritative status."[50] This canon would take a couple more centuries to solidify, but it had already become necessary to support one's theological positions with patristic arguments. The result was a multiplication of patristic florilegia, collections of short passages from the Fathers, not unlike the debater's card-file, that could be said to support one's position.[51] One of the interesting features of the emergence of florilegia is that they may have started largely as heresiological texts—that is, as ways of detailing what the heretics said, rather than as statements of orthodox doctrine. Cyril of Alexandria was partly responsible for and possessed a florilegium of Theodore of Mopsuestia's theology—in this case, a negative florilegium, which was used to refute Theodore's positions.[52] At the Council of Ephesus Nestorius's statements were tested both against a florilegium of orthodox fathers and against a florilegium of the heretical Paul of Samosata.[53] This new genre of heresiology deserves further study. For our purposes, it is sufficient to note again the narrowing of vision that exclusion of certain writers on the basis of mere selections from their works implies. It was a weapon that Cyril and others would use to great effect in the battle to remove most traces of Antiochene theology from the orthodox church.[54]

There is a kind of closure here, which has been often noted and explained, although never in terms on which everyone can agree.[55] Beginning in the fourth century, proto-orthodox Christianity gives way to orthodox Christianity: vague teachings of the church are made specific, unclear matters are either "clarified" in ways that narrow their meaning or placed out-of-bounds as matters that cannot be known,[56] biblical exegesis is given boundaries beyond which it must not go. Speculations that were once acceptable are labeled heretical: Origen is condemned posthumously, as are Theodore of Mopsuestia and other Antiochene theologians. Practices that were once widespread and unquestioned are now considered heinous: John Chrysostom inveighs against Judaizers and Augustine of Hippo against the Puritannical Donatists—groups for whom the loosely knit group of institutions that comprised the earlier church had room. Heresiology, then, changes with orthodoxy; as orthodoxy's binary opposite, heresy must both exist and mirror the stresses and concerns of the orthodox. Collections of the orthodox teachings of the Fathers are balanced by collections of the heretical teachings of the heresiarchs.

From the Age of Justinian to the "Restoration of Orthodoxy"

In his chapter of the *Cambridge Companion to the Age of Justinian*, Patrick Gray concludes that "[i]t was characteristic of the age, perhaps, to be haunted by a past it had, in large part, invented."[57] It was characteristic of the next age to be haunted by the same past, now not of its own invention—or, as Averil Cameron put it, this age engaged in "a dialogue with the real and imaginary spectres of the past."[58] Whatever the condition of the empire ca. 600—and there is considerable debate on that point—by 700 it was quite clearly neither the empire of Justinian nor the empire of Constantine. The profound changes of the seventh century led to an extended series of struggles over the past, present, and future identity of the empire. To complicate matters, Byzantine ideas of the golden past of the sixth century came from the written history available to them—a history that stressed the harmony of the past church and empire, and the tranquility of truly ecumenical councils. As if those were not sufficient complications, the writers of the seventh and eighth centuries had few classical texts and only remnants of classical education, yet they needed to form "a new cultural and intellectual identity from the wreckage of classical antiquity and its [Byzantium's] sense of continuity with the past."[59] In an age when everything was changing, the human search for security and knowledge continued. Some found security in additional solidification of the canon of orthodox fathers; this was the "golden age" of florilegia.[60] These centuries also saw repeated attempts at total knowledge, at saying everything that human beings needed to know in one summary work: think of Maximos the Confessor or John of Damascus.[61] All of this was a response to the seventh century, in which the very "nature of truth and the foundations of knowledge were themselves called into question,"[62] and we should not be overly surprised that the main task of the intellectuals of the era seems to have been to answer those questions, securely, once and for all. Whatever their differences, the "iconoclasts" and the "iconophiles" shared this desire for certainty and total knowledge, as well as the desire for "the security of a closed canon" of theological works.[63]

They shared also the conviction that the only secure answers were to be found in God. One portion of the elite of the empire sought the explanation for military defeat and geographic shrinkage in a specific religious transgression: they looked at the increasing use of images of the saints by the faithful and saw superstition and idolatry. Another portion agreed that military defeat and other tribulations of God's people were results of the sins of those people but disagreed about what constituted the punishable error of God's people. Whether or not they had a specific idea about what the flock had done wrong before the first emperor began to limit icon use, they soon found one: God's wrath was caused by emperors who exceeded their secular authority and interfered with the licit worship of God's people; by those who denied the reality of Christ's flesh; by those, in short, who condemned the veneration of icons as it had arisen in the previous centuries. To a great degree, the iconoclast dispute was immersed in and inseparable from a number of other seventh- through ninth-century developments in Christian understanding of the physical representation of God, the saints, the angels, and other heavenly matters. For discussion of these matters, I refer the reader again to Cameron, Brubaker, Charles Barber, and others.[64] For my purposes, it is the heresiologists of each side who are important. I will deal here primarily with those who wrote for the iconophiles, for it was they who won, and their explanation and history became our main sources.

In those sources, we see most of the traditional motifs of heresiology. Iconoclasm, the iconophiles claim, came from outside the church, or at least from those who had only seemed to be Christians, while hiding their real identities. The specific place outside the church whence the heretics allegedly came varied. Leo III was called "the Isaurian," although he was not in fact from the region of Isauria. Isaurians did, however, have a reputation as bandits and brigands, uncivilized barbarians within the empire's boundaries. It was not surprising that they should be wolves in sheep's clothing. Alternatively, one could emphasize that Leo III came from Syria, from the borderlands where contact with Muslims was the norm. Thus, clearly, he was "Saracen-minded" even if he claimed to be a Christian, and his iconoclasm stemmed from that. Other connections with the "Saracens" could also be claimed. And then there were the Jews. The iconoclasm of Leo III and others was ascribed to Jewish influence in more than one iconophile tract.[65] But these are not simply ahistorical repetitions of early heresiological motifs. They reflect the orthodoxy of their age, its internal tensions and its external enemies. It seems to be true, for example, that Christian veneration of the Cross picked up remarkably in the eighth century. With increased veneration came accusations of idolatry from the Jews. A new wave of anti-Jewish polemic thus preceded anti-iconoclast polemic. So, too, Muslims challenged Christian reverence for the Cross because their prophet denied that Jesus had really suffered on a cross. The heresiology of the age thus echoes the polemic against external enemies of the age.[66]

These claims that the "heretical" "iconoclasts"[67] came from outside the church and were influenced by infidel both within the empire and outside of it have a further distorting effect on the history. In fact, as mentioned above, a specific set of concerns, anxieties, and arguments about representations of Jesus and his servants, including representations such as the Cross or relics, as well as icons, was characteristic of the age. On the ground, considerable evidence indicates that the earliest leaders of the movement to restrict icon use were members of the hierarchy of the church. Throughout the movement, the majority of the clergy seem to have gone along with at least some restrictions legislated by the emperors and patriarchs. Even the monks were less monolithically iconophile and less inclined to martyrdom than some sources would have us believe.[68] The conflicts that continued to split the church for some time after the "Restoration of Orthodoxy" in 843 reveal the dilemma of the first patriarchs of this period: since most of the clergy, including almost all of the bishops, were tainted by association with the iconoclast regime, to expel all of them from the church without pardon would be to decimate the clergy. There would be too few left to perform the clergy's duties. As a result, patriarchs who would not compromise with repentant iconoclasts faced one set of problems, while those who were more conciliatory angered and alienated absolute iconophiles.[69]

Not only do the iconophile heresiologists tell us that the iconoclasts come from outside the church, they demonstrate for us how iconoclasm is the recapitulation of all the heresies that have gone before it. Somehow, for example, it can be simultaneously Monophysite and Nestorian. Ironically, the iconoclasts accuse the iconophiles of the same errors.[70] Still more ironically, many modern commentators have accepted the arguments of one side or the other, turning a controversy that began as a question of practice—specifically, about accusations of superstition leading to idolatry—into a straightforwardly Christological controversy.[71] On the contrary, as Sebastian Brock, among others, has noted, "specifically Christological arguments are absent from the opening phases of the controversy. In fact it is almost as if the whole issue of Christology had been introduced as it were out of habit, simply because that had become the traditional battle ground for controversy."[72] Cameron, Barber, Brubaker, and others have modified this view somewhat; they have clarified the extent to which iconoclasm and iconophilism were expressions of a wider concern about what Barber calls "the limits of representation." Nevertheless, Brock is correct in seeing a kind of habit of using patristic statements from earlier controversies to solve rather different debates. I would go further than Brock in this: the habit he refers to is in fact the expression of that codification and canonization of patristic and conciliar literature that we have been discussing. Risking overstatement, I would argue that the Byzantines of the eighth century could have expressed their worries about icons and representation in no other terms. The terms adopted from Christological debates were the only terms they had, and the iconoclasts used them every bit as much as the iconophiles did.

The utter discrediting of the heretics themselves by whatever scurrilous means available also continues to be a trait of heresiology. Arius may have died on the toilet, but the iconoclast emperor Constantine V surpasses him: he defecates in his own baptismal font. In fact, in the iconophile sources, Constantine is a monster in nearly every way one can imagine; it helps that the iconophiles could use a considerable body of anti-Constantine propaganda already compiled by his mortal enemy and rival for the throne, Artabasdos.[73] The atrocities Constantine allegedly committed against recalcitrant iconophiles are legendary, but most of these accounts are indeed legends composed long after the fact. In ninth-century manuscript illustrations, the iconoclasts are paralleled with the people who offered Jesus vinegar and gall on the Cross, with Jews bribing the soldiers sent to guard Jesus' tomb, and above all with Simon Magus.[74]

Finally, the latest studies of iconoclasm emphasize that the heresiologists, here as so often in the past, condemn as novelties beliefs that are quite traditional while defending as traditional practices and doctrines that are new.[75] In a general sense, much of the veneration of icons, especially the treating of icons as if they had the same status as relics, was relatively new. In the last few decades, Averil Cameron, Judith Herrin, Leslie Brubaker, John Haldon, and Charles Barber, among others, have shown that the seventh century saw considerable development in the ways that icons were used—and with that development came concern, even opposition. The iconoclasts were not demonically trying to destroy an ancient church custom; they were reacting to developments in practice and piety that seemed to them superstitious, even idolatrous.[76] The writings of the iconophiles themselves sometimes provide us with examples that support the iconoclasts' case. To give just one example: Theodore of Stoudios wrote to an acquaintance to congratulate him because, "We have heard that your Lordship had done a divine deed and we have marveled at your truly great faith, O man of God. For my informer tells me that in performing the baptism of your God-guarded child, you had recourse to a holy image of the great martyr Demetrius instead of a godfather. How great is your confidence."[77] This was not traditional practice, and many other ways in which people had begun to use icons as if they were relics—scraping paint from the icon, for example, to use as a cure for disease—had only a short history.[78]

Just as we have seen these weapons deployed consistently throughout Christian heresiology from the second to the ninth centuries, we have also seen that each age brought to the deployment some concerns unique to its context. One of these in the iconoclast period, Gilbert Dagron has argued, was a vigorous attempt by one group—those usually identified as iconoclasts—to consolidate and sacralize imperial power as it had never been before: "This is the epoch in which the imperial office is more sacralized than ever, in which it claims, as we will see, a quasi-sacerdotal character and sustains itself by references to the Old Testament."[79] Supporters of a sacralized emperor faced the vigorous resistance of another group—those usually identified by their commitment to the use of icons. The elevation of Leo III, the first iconoclast emperor, followed a time of considerable political turmoil and inaugurated a stable dynasty with a number of lengthy reigns.[80] To justify their rule these emperors relied heavily on invocation of Old Testament models of kingship. It is Leo who is said to have called himself "emperor and priest," a phrase which invokes the memory of Melchizedek. By using such Old Testament models of royal priesthood, Leo forced a confrontation between two features of Byzantine rulership that were in tension from the time of Constantine I's conversion: as Dagron puts it when describing imperial processions from the sacred palace to the heart of the Great Church, "an imperial Christianity that was Old Testament in tone was confronted by the more New-Testament oriented Christianity of the clergy."[81] Leo was hardly the first emperor to claim a right to legislate for the church; if the Justinianic Age was the ideal to which all dreamed of returning, then imperial involvement in church affairs was a given. Even if it is only part of the truth, it is nevertheless true that the goal of the iconoclasts was greater centralization of power. Among other things, this helps explain the cooperation of much of the secular hierarchy and the resistance led by monks. Consolidation of the hierarchy appeals to bishops and has historically been resisted by monasteries. Still, it is too simple to posit a dichotomy here—emperors and church hierarchy seeking order, monks not—and Dagron does not do so. He joins Cameron, instead, in seeing that we can explain more by understanding that *both* sides were seeking "the closer definition of the truth" through control of Christian behavior and doctrine.[82]

Sebastian Brock has proposed another way to look at this struggle, complementary to Dagron's and Cameron's. He pointed out some time ago that "[t]he Iconoclasts wished to confine the sphere of divine 'interference'—to put it that way—to certain given areas, in particular the Eucharist, and the saints, not allowing it to spill out untidily into other areas where humanity was perfectly well in control." On the other hand, "To the Iconodules . . . the divine was very much present in the world, and was not subject to neat barriers. They are in fact heirs of that tradition of spirituality that saw the world as a sacrament, and that allows for the transformation and transfiguration of matter by means of the spirit."[83] Thus to struggle against the iconoclast emperors was to struggle not only against a kind of political centralization and control but also against a kind of spiritual centralization and control. Again the participation of most secular clergy in the initiatives of the iconoclast emperors is explicable: like the emperors, they were suspicious of individualist spirituality practiced by monks or laypeople (women?).[84] And that individualism was intimately connected to icons.

The struggle over the emperor's role in the church was certainly not resolved once and for all in 843, and imperial power over the church would wax and wane for a variety of reasons in the next few centuries. So, too, the tension between the imperial and episcopal desire for order and control, on the one hand, and lay/monastic spirituality that refused to be controlled, on the other, did not end. But the rhetoric about illicit imperial interference allowed the church to adapt to the relative weakness of the empire and, probably more importantly, to blame that weakness not on some error of their own but rather on imperial error. It is all the fault of the iconoclasts—as Paul Speck so memorably put it, "Constantine V did it!"

Having dealt with the disasters of the seventh and eighth centuries in this way—having, as it were, made sense of them in familiar terms of heresy and orthodoxy, God's punishment and God's rewards—the Byzantines of the ninth century could then turn to the results of those disasters. They could begin to explain not just their own society, polity, and church, but also the world as it had changed around them and their own place in it. After the Restoration of Orthodoxy in 843, the backward-looking rationalization that made sense of a smaller empire and its struggle with iconoclasm gave way to three ninth-century initiatives to deal with the three powers who had changed the world so radically in the seventh and eighth centuries: Islam, the western Christians north of the Alps, and the Slavs. From the accusations of Saracen-mindedness in iconoclasm, Byzantine scholars moved on to write the first systematic anti-Muslim polemic. Meanwhile, political fragmentation in the west and growing papal autonomy characterized the so-called Photian Schism and the concern about the Franks' addition of the Filioque to the creed. Finally, the settlement of Slavic groups throughout the Balkans and parts of central Europe required an imperial response. These issues are not separable, especially when we are speaking of religious polemic, and they form the necessary background for an understanding of the earliest anti-Filioque treatises. Thus, although they are not the subject of this book, the earliest anti-Islamic polemicists, the missionaries to the Slavs, and various tensions between Constantinople and Rome will appear repeatedly in its pages. Without them, we limit our comprehension of the treatises against the double procession of the Holy Spirit, for the story of a growing sense in Byzantium of a distinction between them and their Christian brothers in the west parallels a growing understanding and definition of the new and dangerous Muslim enemy and an unprecedented reaching-out to "barbarians" beyond the empire's borders. To see all of this activity together is to understand each piece of it more deeply.

NOTES

1. The sort of method and assumptions I use throughout this work are criticized as reductionist in, for example, John Macquarrie, "Doctrinal Development: Searching for Criteria," in *Making and Remaking*, ed. Coakley and Pailin, 161–76.

2. Macquarrie, "Doctrinal Development," 167.

3. David A. Pailin, "The Supposedly Historical Basis of Theological Understanding," in *Making and Remaking*, ed. Coakley and Pailin, 233.

4. For a more detailed statement of a position essentially the same as mine see Pailin, "Historical Basis."

5. As Macquarrie suggests it should be: "Doctrinal Development," 165–66.

6. Pailin, "Historical Basis," 220, cites Lessing, who called this gulf an "ugly, broad ditch."

7. Jack T. Sanders, *Schismatics, Sectarians, Dissidents, Deviants: The First One Hundred Years of Jewish-Christian Relations* (Valley Forge: Trinity Press International, 1993), 82.

8. Citing a selection of works that have influenced my thinking here is necessarily arbitrary rather than comprehensive: Alain Le Boulluec, *La notion d'hérésie dans la littérature grecque IIe–IIIe siècles*, 2 vols. (Paris: Études augustiniennes, 1985); Daniel Boyarin, *Border Lines: The Partition of Judaeo-Christianity* (Philadelphia: University of Pennsylvania Press, 2004); Aline Pourkier, *L'hérésiologie chez Epiphane de Salamine*, Christianisme antique 4 (Paris: Beauchesne, 1992). More works on early Christianity appear in the bibliography and notes below.

9. Averil Cameron, "How to Read Heresiology," *Journal of Medieval and Early Modern Studies* 33 (2003): 471–92, with extensive bibliography. For early Christianity and late antiquity, the *locus classicus* is Walter Bauer, *Rechtgläubigkeit und Ketzerei im ältesten Christentum*, 1st ed. (Tübingen: Mohr, 1934); 2nd German ed. (Tübingen: Mohr, 1964); 2nd German ed. trans. by Philadelphia Seminar on Christian Origins,

ed. Robert A. Kraft and Gerhard Krodel, in *Orthodoxy and Heresy in Earliest Christianity* (Philadelphia: Fortress Press, 1971); electronic version of the English translation periodically updated (since 1993) by Kraft, http://ccat.sas.upenn.edu/rs/rak/publics/new/ BAUER00.htm). See also Le Boulluec, *La notion;* Elm et al., *Orthodoxie, Christianisme, Histoire.* For the Latin west, see: R. I. Moore, *The Formation of a Persecuting Society: Power and Deviance in Western Europe 950–1250* (Oxford: Blackwell, 1987); Mark Pegg, *The Corruption of Angels: The Great Inquisition of 1245–1246* (Princeton: Princeton University Press, 2001).

10. Margaret Mullett, "The 'Other' in Byzantium," in *Strangers to Themselves: The Byzantine Outsider*, ed. Dion C. Smythe, Society for the Promotion of Byzantine Studies Publications 8 (Aldershot: Ashgate/Variorum, 1998), 1–22. Dion C. Smythe, "Alexios I and the Heretics: The Account of Anna Komnene's *Alexiad*," in *Alexios I Komnenos, I, Papers*, ed. Margaret Mullett and Dion C. Smythe, Belfast Byzantine Texts and Translations 4.1 (Belfast: Belfast Byzantine Enterprises, 1996), 232–59. Tia Kolbaba, *The Byzantine Lists: Errors of the Latins* (Urbana: University of Illinois Press, 2000), 133–36.

11. Cameron, "How to Read," 472–73.

12. Cameron, "How to Read": "Finally, like writing against Judaism, arguments against and condemnation of heresy can be found as an integral part of almost every type of Byzantine religious literature. Our challenge is to understand why this was so, and what form it took" (479); "Whether we like it or not as historians, writing heresy, in all its various forms, did occupy a major place in Byzantium—so much so indeed that a full treatment would in its way constitute a new history of Byzantium. This is far from having been written. But meanwhile, at the very least, I suggest that one ought to read these compositions, so strange to our minds, as part of Byzantine pedagogy and the Byzantine sociology of knowledge, self-perpetuating constructions that helped to formulate thought and underpin social norms" (484).

13. Cameron, "How to Read," 474.

14. For an introduction to the historiography, the debates, and the bibliography of the issue of Christians and Jews see Annette Yoshiko Reed and Adam H. Becker, "Introduction: Traditional Models and New Directions," in *The Ways That Never Parted: Jews and Christians in Late Antiquity and the Early Middle Ages*, ed. Reed and Becker (Tübingen: Mohr Siebeck, 2003), 1–33. *Locus classicus:* Marcel Simon, *Verus Israel: A Study of the Relations between Christians and Jews in the Roman Empire 135–425*, trans. H. McKeating (New York: The Littman Library of Oxford University Press, 1986). Sanders, *Schismatics, Sectarians, Dissidents.* Various other works by Daniel Boyarin, Averil Cameron, Shaye Cohen, John G. Gager, and E. Leigh Gibson, listed in the bibliography below, have also helped me think through these issues.

15. Reed and Becker, "Introduction," 23. Sanders, *Schismatics, Sectarians, Dissidents*, 61–67, 78–81, sees more hostility between "mainstream" Jews and Jewish

Christians than I present here, but he also notes that the rabbis protest too much—that is, their emphasis on utter separation from the "Nazarenes" reveals that others in their communities associated with Christians rather more than the rabbis would have liked.

16. Daniel Boyarin, "Semantic Difference; or, 'Judaism'/'Christianity,'" in *The Ways That Never Parted*, 77; see also Boyarin, *Border Lines*.

17. Boyarin, *Border Lines;* Sanders, *Schismatics, Sectarians, Dissidents:* "From the sociological point of view that is what the rabbinic enterprise was about—group definition; the rabbis were redefining Judaism" (140).

18. Averil Cameron, "Jews and Heretics—A Category Error?" in *The Ways That Never Parted*, 345–60; Cameron, "Blaming the Jews: The Seventh-Century Invasions of Palestine in Context," *Travaux et mémoires* 14 (2002): 57–78.

19. A dualism often noted with regard to both Jews and heretics. See, for example, Sanders, *Schismatics, Sectarians, Dissidents*, 127–28.

20. Roughly, in English, "plan," "dispensation," and "providence" all rolled into one.

21. Le Boulluec, *La notion*, is a full account of the development of these stereotypes; a brief sketch is also provided by Pourkier, *L'hérésiologie*, 486–92.

22. Bauer, *Rechtgläubigkeit* (Orthodoxy and Heresy).

23. But see Bart Ehrman, *The Orthodox Corruption of Scripture: The Effect of Early Christological Controversies on the Text of the New Testament* (Oxford: Oxford University Press, 1993).

24. Boyarin, "Semantic Difference," 77.

25. Richard A. Norris, Jr., "Articulating Identity," in *The Cambridge History of Early Christian Literature* (Cambridge: Cambridge University Press 2004), 78.

26. J. Rebecca Lyman, "The Making of a Heretic: The Life of Origen in Epiphanius' Panarion 64," *Studia Patristica* 31 (1997): 445–51.

27. Richard Lim, *Public Disputation, Power, and Social Order in Late Antiquity* (Berkeley and Los Angeles: University of California Press, 1995).

28. Le Boulluec, *La notion*, is the model study here.

29. A lucid summary account, with bibliography, of both the theological principles at stake in the "Arian" controversy and the general alignment of key figures is Ayres, "Articulating Identity," 414–63. For a fuller account of Ayres's arguments, see Ayres, *Nicaea and Its Legacy: An Approach to Fourth-Century Trinitarian Theology* (Oxford: Clarendon Press, 2004). For bibliography and interesting discussion see also Michael R. Barnes and Daniel H. Williams, eds., *Arianism after Arius: Essays on the Development of the Fourth Century Trinitarian Conflicts* (Edinburg: T&T Clark, 1993). Useful for those just beginning to study this period is Richard R. Rubenstein, *When Jesus Became God: The Struggle to Define Christianity during the Last Days of Rome* (New York: Harcourt Brace, 1999).

30. For a summary of the sources for this story, see G. W. Trompf, "Church History as Non-Conformism: Retributive and Eschatological Elements in Athanasius and Philostorgius," *Byzantinische Forschungen* 24 (1997): 16–17.

31. Ayres, "Articulating Identity," *passim*.

32. E.g., Peter Brown, *The World of Late Antiquity from Marcus Aurelius to Muhammed* (London: Thames and Hudson, 1971), 145.

33. Lim, *Public Disputation*.

34. This is summarized by R. A. Markus, "Social and Historical Setting," in *Cambridge History of Early Christian Literature*, ed. Young et al., 399–413.

35. The interweaving of substantive theological differences with other factors is exemplified in Ayres, "Articulating Identity." Ayres emphasizes the theological principles at stake more than I do, and rightly so. In an account of Christian literature in the fourth century, positive statements of Christian doctrine are crucial. I stress them less than Ayres because I am following the heresiologists, who can seldom be believed when they describe the theology of heretics and whose purposes go beyond clarification of doctrine.

36. See, for example, Charles Pazdernik's discussion of Ammianus Marcellinus's work: "Justinianic Ideology and the Power of the Past," in *The Cambridge Companion to the Age of Justinian*, ed. Michael Maas (Cambridge: Cambridge University Press, 2005), 192–93.

37. Pourkier, *L'hérésiologie*, 487–88.

38. Lyman, "Making of a Heretic," 446; Pourkier, *L'hérésiologie*, 23.

39. Lyman, "Making of a Heretic," 447.

40. This is a central theme of Lim, *Public Disputation*.

41. Lim, *Public Disputation*, 182–216. An example of how this sort of glossing-over of conflict could be expressed in sources the historian must use: Averil Cameron, "Eustratius' *Life* of the Patriarch Eutychius and the Fifth Ecumenical Council," in *Kathegetria: Essays Presented to Joan Hussey*, ed. Julian Chrysostomides (Camberley: Porphyrogenitus, 1988), 225–47 (repr. in Cameron, *Changing Cultures in Byzantium* [Aldershot: Variorum, 1996], art. 1).

42. Helen Marie Sillett, "Culture of Controversy: The Christological Disputes of the Early Fifth Century" (PhD diss., University of California, Berkeley, 1999), 9.

43. Sillett, "Culture of Controversy," 27; for additional examples of competing propaganda, see ibid., 28–29. See Cameron, "Eustratius' *Life*," 233–36, for examples from another era.

44. Patrick T. R. Gray, "'The Select Fathers': Canonizing the Patristic Past," *Studia Patristica* 23 (1989): 21.

45. Evangelos Chrysos, "The Synodal Acts as Literary Products," in *L'Icone dans la théologie et l'art* (Chambesy: Éditions du centre orthodox du patriarcat oecuménique,

1990), 92–93. John Haldon and Leslie Brubaker, *Byzantium in the Iconoclast Era (ca. 680–850): The Sources; An Annotated Survey* (Aldershot: Ashgate, 2001), chap. 14, 233–42.

   46. Sillett, "Culture of Controversy," 18. A new translation of the Acta of Chalcedon has just appeared, which will accelerate the progress of scholarship on the fifth-century councils; see *The Acts of the Council of Chalcedon*, trans. Richard Price and Michael Gaddis (Liverpool: Liverpool University Press, 2006).

   47. Chrysos, "Synodal Acts," 88–89.

   48. Patrick T. R. Gray, "Forged Forgeries: Constantinople III and the Acts of Constantinople II," in *Abstracts of Papers, Byzantine Studies Conference, 31st, 2005* (Atlanta: Byzantine Studies Conference, 2005), 90.

   49. My comments here only a generalized and pale shadow of much recent work on the fifth through seventh centuries and theological discourse therein. Important influences on my analysis include Haldon, *Byzantium in the Seventh Century;* Judith Herrin, *The Formation of Christendom* (Princeton: Princeton University Press, 1987); Haldon and Brubaker, *Byzantium in the Iconoclast Era;* Averil Cameron, "Models of the Past in the Late Sixth Century: The Life of the Patriarch Eutychius," in *Reading the Past in Late Antiquity*, ed. G. Clarke (Canberra: Australian National University Press, 1990), 205–23 (repr. in Cameron, *Changing Cultures*, art. 2); Cameron, "Byzantium and the Past in the Seventh Century: The Search for Redefinition," in *The Seventh Century: Change and Continuity*, ed. J. Fontaine and J. N. Hillgarth (London: Warburg Institute, 1992), 250–76 (repr. in *Changing Cultures*, art. 5); Cameron, "The Language of Images: The Rise of Icons and Christian Representation," in *The Church and the Arts*, ed. Diana Wood, Studies in Church History 28 (Oxford: Blackwell, 1992), 1–42 (repr. in Cameron, *Changing Cultures*, art. 12); Marie-France Auzépy, "Manifestations de la propagande en faveur de l'orthodoxie," in *Byzantium in the Ninth Century: Dead or Alive? Papers from the Thirteenth Spring Symposium of Byzantine Studies, Birmingham, March 1996*, ed. Leslie Brubaker (Aldershot: Ashgate, 1998), 85–99; Peter Brown, "A Dark-Age Crisis: Aspects of the Iconoclastic Controversy," *English Historical Review* 88 (1973): 1–34 (repr. in Brown, *Society and the Holy in Late Antiquity* [Berkeley and Los Angeles: University of California Press, 1982], 251–301). Certain arguments of Paul Speck have been particularly fruitful: see "The Origins of the Byzantine Renaissance," in Speck, *Understanding Byzantium: Studies in Byzantine Historical Sources*, ed. and trans. Sarolta Takács (Aldershot: Ashgate 2003), 143–62 (trans. of "Die Ursprünge der byzantinischen Renaissance," in *The 17th International Byzantine Congress, Major Papers* [Aristide D. Caratzas: New Rochelle, N.Y., 1986], 555–76); "Further Reflections and Inquiries on the Origins of the Byzantine Renaissance, with a Supplement: The Trier Ivory and Other Uncertainties," in *Understanding Byzantium*, 179–204 (originally published as "Weitere Überlegungen und Untersuchungen über die Ursprünge der byzantinischen Renaissance, mit einem Nachtrag: Das Trierer Elfenbein und andere

Heresiology and the Invention of Heretics

Unklarheiten," in *Varia II*, Poikila byzantina 6 [Bonn: Habelt, 1987], 252–83); *Ich bin's nicht, Kaiser Konstantin ist es gewesen. Die Legenden von Einfluss des Teufels, des Juden und des Moslem auf den Ikonoklasmus*, Poikila byzantina 10 (Bonn: Habelt, 1990). Finally, numerous articles by Patrick T. R. Gray have detailed the theological discourse of the period while arguing for substantial revision of our understanding of the transition from late antique to Byzantine theology. Gray's influence is evident throughout my account; the articles in question are listed in the bibliography, below.

50. Gray, "Select Fathers," 21–22.

51. Gray "Select Fathers"; Averil Cameron, "Disputations, Polemical Literature and the Formation of Opinion in the Early Byzantine Period," in *Dispute Poems and Dialogues in the Ancient and Mediaeval Near East*, ed. G. J. Reinink and H. L. J. Vanstiphout, Orientalia Lovaniensia Analecta 42 (Louvain: Uitgeverij Peeters, 1991), 101 (repr. in *Changing Cultures*, art. 3). See also Alexander Alexakis, *Codex Parisinus Graecus 1115 and Its Archetype* (Washington, D.C.: Dumbarton Oaks, 1996). Alexakis's discussion of the use of florilegia at various councils should be read in the context of more skeptical accounts: see Patrick T. R. Gray, "The Legacy of Chalcedon: Christological Problems and their Significance," in *Cambridge Companion to the Age of Justinian*, ed. Maas, 215–38; Gray, "Select Fathers"; and Gray, "Covering the Nakedness of Noah: Reconstruction and Denial in the Age of Justinian," *Byzantinische Forschungen* 24 (1997): 193–206.

52. Sillett, *Culture of Controversy*, 44, 53–54.

53. Gray, "Select Fathers," 24.

54. Gray, "Select Fathers," 27–28, 34; Gray, "Covering the Nakedness," 197–205.

55. See Averil Cameron's discussion and the other works she cites in "Ascetic Closure and the End of Antiquity," in *Asceticism*, ed. Vincent L. Wimbush and Richard Valantasis (New York: Oxford University Press, 1995), 147–51; but note that Cameron, "How to Read," 484, now finds "ascetic closure" as an explanation "too ready to take Byzantium on its own terms." Other important works include Robert Markus, *The End of Ancient Christianity* (Cambridge: Cambridge University Press, 1990); Gray, "Legacy of Chalcedon," and other publications; Lim, *Public Disputation*.

56. What Lim aptly calls "apophatic obfuscation," *Public Disputation*, 154.

57. Gray, "Legacy of Chalcedon," 236. The Byzantines are not alone in this tendency: Giles Constable, "Forgery and Plagiarism in the Middle Ages," *Archiv für Diplomatik* 29 (1983): 20–21, including the bibliography cited on p. 21 n. 101.

58. Cameron, "Models of the Past," 207.

59. Cameron, "Disputations," 108.

60. Cameron, "Byzantium and the Past," 254–58, 267–68 (254).

61. Cameron, "Byzantium and the Past," 267–70.

62. Cameron, "Language of Images," 41.

63. Cameron, "Byzantium and the Past," 266–67; Cameron develops these themes here and in "Language of Images."

64. Cameron, "Language of Images"; Leslie Brubaker, *Vision and Meaning in Ninth-Century Byzantium: Image as Exegesis in the Homilies of Gregory of Nazianzus*, Cambridge Studies in Palaeography and Codicology 6 (Cambridge: Cambridge University Press, 1999); Leslie Brubaker, "Icons before Iconoclasm?" in *Morfologie sociali e culturali in Europea fra tarda antichità e alto medioevo*, 2 vols., Settimane di studi del Centro italiano di studi sull'alto medioevo 45 (Spoleto: Centro italiano di studi sull'alto medioevo, 1998), 2:1215–54; J.-M. Sansterre, "La parole, le texte et l'image selon les auteurs byzantins des époques iconoclaste et posticonoclaste," in *Testo e imagine nell'alto medioevo*, Settimane di studi del Centro italiano di studi sull'alto medioevo 41 (Spoleto: Centro italiano di studi sull'alto medioevo, 1994), 197–240; Charles Barber, "The Koimesis Church, Nicaea: The Limits of Representation on the Eve of Iconoclasm," *Jahrbuch der österreichischen Byantinistik* 41 (1991): 43–60; Barber, *Figure and Likeness: On the Limits of Representation in Byzantine Iconoclasm* (Princeton: Princeton University Press, 2002).

65. Speck, *Ich bin's nicht;* Kathleen Corrigan, *Visual Polemics in Ninth-Century Byzantine Psalters* (Cambridge: Cambridge University Press,1992); Haldon and Brubaker, *Byzantium in the Iconoclast Era*, 268–71; Cameron, "Language of Images," 35–37.

66. Cameron, "Language of Images," 35–37; Cameron, "Byzantium and the Past," 263–64; see chapter 7, below.

67. The quotation marks here indicate skepticism both about the label "heretic," for reasons which should be obvious by this point, and skepticism about the label of "iconoclast," at least as far as Leo III was concerned. The evidence that Leo actually destroyed icons has mostly been discredited.

68. See, for example, Cyril Mango's discussion of the patriarchs Photios and Ignatios: "The Liquidation of Iconoclasm and the Patriarch Photios," in *Iconoclasm: Papers Given at the Ninth Spring Symposium of Byzantine Studies*, ed. Anthony Bryer and Judith Herrin (Birmingham: Centre for Byzantine Studies, University of Birmingham, 1977), 133–40, and Patricia Karlin-Hayter, "Gregory of Syracuse, Ignatios and Photios," in ibid., 141–45.

69. Relations between the first few patriarchs after 843, the cenobitic monks of the capital, the peripatetic holy men from elsewhere, the secular clergy, and the hierarchy are more complex than the picture Francis Dvornik paints in *The Photian Schism: History and Legend* (Cambridge: Cambridge University Press, 1948; repr. 1970). Karlin-Hayter, "Gregory of Syracuse"; Karlin-Hayter, "Methodios and his Synod," in *Byzantine Orthodoxies: Papers from the Thirty-sixth Spring Symposium of Byzantine Studies, Durham*, ed. Andrew Louth and Augustine Casaday (Aldershot: Ashgate, 2006), 55–74; Dmitry E. Afinogenov, "The Great Purge of 843: A Re-examination," in *Leimôn: Studies Presented to Lennart Rydén on His Sixty-fifth Birthday* (Uppsala: Uppsala University, 1996), 76–91.

70. Leslie Barnard, "The Theology of Images," in *Iconoclasm*, ed. Bryer and Herrin, 12–13.

71. For a concise refutation of a connection between Monophysitism and iconoclasm, see Sebastian Brock, "Iconoclasm and the Monophysites,"in *Iconoclasm*, 53–57.

72. Brock, "Iconoclasm and the Monophysites," 55.

73. Speck, *Ich bin's nicht;* Haldon and Brubaker, *Byzantium in the Iconoclast Era*, 169 n. 8, and 170 nn. 9–12, for more bibliography.

74. Simony was one of the most frequent charges against iconoclast patriarchs and bishops. Haldon and Brubaker, *Byzantium in the Iconoclast Era*, 43–47, with plates and bibliography; Corrigan, *Visual Polemics*.

75. Brubaker, "Icons before Iconoclasm?"; Haldon and Brubaker, *Byzantium in the Iconoclast Era*, 55; Barnard, "Theology of Images," 3.

76. Brubaker, "Icons before Iconoclasm?"; Herrin, *Formation*, 307–15, 330–43; Cameron, "Byzantium and the Past," 252–53; Cameron, "Language of Images," 4–15; Brubaker, *"In the Beginning Was the Word:* Art and Orthodoxy at the Councils of Trullo (692) and Nicaea II (787)," in *Byzantine Orthodoxies*, ed. Louth and Casaday, 95–98; Barber, "The Koimesis Church."

77. Theodore of Stoudios, Joanni Spathario, Ep. 1, 17, PG 99, 961; trans. by Cyril Mango, *The Art of the Byzantine Empire 312–1453: Sources and Documents* (Toronto: University of Toronto Press, 1986) 174–75.

78. Brubaker, *"In the beginning,"* 97.

79. Gilbert Dagron, *Empereur et prêtre. Étude sur le 'césaropapisme' byzantin* (Paris: Éditions Gallimard, 1996), 51–52; trans. Jean Birrell, *Emperor and Priest: The Imperial Office in Byzantium* (Cambridge: Cambridge University Press, 2003), 31–32.

80. Judith Herrin, "The Context of Iconoclast Reform," in *Iconoclasm*, ed. Bryer and Herrin, 15–20.

81. Dagron, *Empereur et Prêtre*, 118; trans. 103–4.

82. Cameron, "Language of Images," 41.

83. Brock, "Iconoclasm and the Monophysites," 57.

84. Judith Herrin has posited a particular affinity for icons among women: "Women and the Faith in Icons in Early Christianity," in *Culture, Ideology and Politics: Essays for Eric Hobsbawm*, ed. Raphael Samuel and Gareth Stedman Jones (London: Routledge and Kegan Paul, 1982), 56–83; also Herrin, *Formation*, 308–9, 331–32. Robin Cormack critiques Herrin's thesis in "Women and Icons and Women in Icons," in *Women, Men and Eunuchs: Gender in Byzantium*, ed. Liz James (London: Routledge, 1997), 24–51. But if Cormack's arguments undermine Herrin's claim that women really were more devoted to icons, they reinforce my point about the heresiology: to associate women with icons was to weaken the iconophile case (because we all know that women are naturally superstitious).

CHAPTER 2

Latins and Greeks before the Age of Photios

Interactions between Greek-speaking and Latin-speaking Christians in the second half of the ninth century were the products of a complex world with many features unfamiliar to most modern students. We are particularly prone to two kinds of misunderstandings of what we might call the age of Photios—after an eminent figure in the literary world of his time, ambassador to Abbasid lands, patriarch of Constantinople, tutor of princes, opponent and friend of popes, imperial favorite and exile, sponsor of missions to the Slavs, and much more. First, centuries of hindsight have foreshortened our perspective, and we are easily misled into attributing the ideas of one generation—even of a much later generation—to earlier ones. As noted in the introduction above, Byzantine authors were willing to encourage such misapprehensions. Second, we fall easily into a view of ninth-century Europe divided into "east" and "west." The cold war was no help to our historiography here, and more recent assertions about clashing civilizations have exacerbated the problem.[1] Photios's world certainly had distinctions between eastern and western Europe—language, history, social structures, and more.[2] But these were neither the only nor the most important distinctions for him and his contemporaries. In the ninth century, relations between what had been the western Roman Empire, on the one hand, and the continuation of the Roman Empire in the east, on the other, were nuanced, ambiguous, and varied. Much that would ossify that relationship and form two distinct cultures had not yet happened. The ninth century preceded the papal reform movement, the twelfth-century renaissance, the rise of universities and Scholasticism, the Reformation, the

Enlightenment, and a multitude of other events that changed both eastern and western Europe. Photios lived before imperial military expeditions in the tenth and eleventh centuries reshaped Byzantine society in favor of a militarized aristocracy; long before the crusades, centuries of Ottoman rule, nineteenth-century nationalism, and twentieth-century geopolitics shaped the east as it is today. Although much that would contribute to the eventual—never total—separation of Greek from Latin, Orthodox from Roman Catholic, had already happened, remnants of an ancient Mediterranean culture that defined itself not in terms of east and west, Greek and Latin, as much as in opposition to northern barbarians remained intact.[3] Moreover, western Europe was still becoming western Christendom, and that process of becoming was fraught with conflict, ambiguity, and ambivalence. The rules were not yet chiseled in stone; renegotiation and redefinition of boundaries were the rule. What were the boundaries between ethnic groups, if such things even existed? Romans and Greeks? Barbarians and Romans? What were the boundaries that separated the saved from the damned? The sacred from the profane? The heretics from the orthodox? Different categories generated different boundaries and definitions. It is this embryonic, amorphous west that Photios and his contemporaries faced—not the more coherent entity we call western Christendom in, say, the twelfth century.[4]

What were those shared remnants of antiquity? Until the seventh century, intellectuals throughout the Mediterranean still shared elements of a common culture of classical *paideia* and Christian religion. Although differences existed between the Roman, Latin world of the western empire and the Constantinopolitan, Greek one of the eastern empire, some of these differences were older than history itself.[5] In themselves, they did not so much rupture Mediterranean unity as keep it interesting. In the second and third centuries of the Common Era, the linguistic divide between Latin and Greek was less one of geography than one of function:[6] Latin was certainly the language of people in the heart of the western empire, but it was also the language of northwestern Africa and parts of Illyricum.[7] Greek was certainly the language of the upper classes throughout much of the urban east, but it was also a language of high culture used by the upper classes in the urban west. As Gilbert Dagron put it, "The ideal citizen of the Empire had to know Greek to participate in culture and speak Latin to participate in power."[8] Well into the sixth century some rhetoricians and philosophers argued that there was no truly high culture that was not Greek, despairing when their gifted pupils took up government service.

Meanwhile the imperial government and the army still used Latin at least some of the time, but defenders of Latin decried the diminished use of that language of power, the truly imperial language, in imperial business.[9] Other groups in Constantinople still spoke Latin, as well.[10]

This situation began to change when imperial power shifted east under Diocletian and then Constantine. It had changed beyond recognition by the end of the sixth century. The change was gradual, so that it is only by looking at this relatively long stretch of time that we can see what happens. The shift begins "at the height of the latinization of the Hellenic East" and ends "towards the end of the reign of Justinian, at the moment where eastern *romanité* definitively adopts Greek as the language of state as well as the language of culture."[11] The boundary between the two languages had become a geographical one—Latin in the west for both culture and power; Greek in the east for both power and culture. It would take the invasions and migrations of the seventh century to complete this geographical division—to remove the anomalous Latin-speaking communities from Illyricum, for example—but the process was well underway by the end of the sixth.

If we narrow our focus to the churches, we see at least an illusion of harmony between Rome and Constantinople in the ninth decade of the seventh century. At the Sixth Ecumenical Council (Constantinople 680–81), the last of the attempts to compromise with the non-Chalcedonians of what we now call the oriental churches was anathematized, and the pope's orthodoxy was praised.[12]

Yet in many ways western Latinophone and eastern Hellenophone Christians already inhabited different worlds. The touchstone decisions of Chalcedon 451 came from a meeting dominated by eastern bishops, eastern politics, and the ideas of eastern theologians. The Chalcedonian acceptance of Pope Leo's Tome, so crucial for the western church, was probably made possible only because it was not translated into Greek and read aloud.[13] Certainly Nestorius, condemned by the bishops at Chalcedon, thought that Leo's Tome exonerated his theology; many modern scholars agree. At Constantinople in 553 (the Fifth Ecumenical Council) Pope Vigilius actively opposed the work of the bishops and considered their condemnation of the "Three Chapters" "a betrayal of Chalcedon." In the end, Rome accepted the decisions of Constantinople 553, but "only by means of chicanery."[14] Nevertheless, Rome and Constantinople remained united at Constantinople 680–81 and beyond because it was still integral to the self-definition of those churches to believe that they were in harmony with one another. The agreements of Chalcedon 451 or Constantinople 680–81 may seem illusory to modern scholars, but to the leaders of both churches, these ecumenical councils were real and substantive, their decisions and the unity of the church were important parts of Christian identity. Similarly, modern scholars may see eastern and western theologies at this point (or indeed earlier), but it was still in the interests of most people involved to emphasize similarity over difference.

The differences continued to grow. In the middle of the seventh century peoples from the Arabian peninsula began that series of conquests that would rupture Mediterranean unity and change the shape of the world. By the early eighth century these conquerors had removed most of the territory inhabited by non-Chalcedonian populations from the empire, making the doctrinal agreement between Rome and Constantinople at Constantinople 680–81 much easier. But if it was ironic that the Islamic conquests of the most ancient Christian regions should lead to a consensus between Rome and Constantinople regarding doctrine, a still greater irony was to follow. In general, relations between the great sees of Rome and Constantinople became more contentious. After the conquests, Constantinople was the only eastern patriarchate remaining in the empire; its patriarch's claims to be preeminent in the east gained credibility. Whereas in earlier times the patriarchs of Alexandria and Antioch had competed for primacy, now Rome and Constantinople were the only serious contenders. In the centuries to come, a series of struggles between Rome and Constantinople ensued—many of them famous instances of schism. So, in addition to the Photian Schism that plays an important role in this book, there were disagreements about which patriarch had jurisdiction over Illyricum, Sicily, and Calabria.[15] There were instances in which clergy who thought they had been mistreated by one patriarch appealed to the other. Accusations of arrogance, ambition, duplicity, and interference abounded at such times. Throughout, the fault line that divided the Christian world into Greeks and Latins, east and west, continued to widen—sometimes slowly and imperceptibly, sometimes with the sudden jolt of an earthquake.

In addition to their role in ecclesiastical separation, the Arab invasions also contributed to the political separation of the western empire from the eastern. There had been an emperor only in Constantinople, not in the west, since the fifth century, and the imperial exarch in Ravenna until 751 had little power. As the Arabs forced the eastern empire to fight for its very existence, the empire sent ever-fewer resources to the exarch until he became less capable of military defense or public services than the pope in Rome. From the late sixth century on, both Rome and the exarchate were constantly threatened by the Lombards and both pled desperately for help that Constantinople could not afford. The popes filled the vacuum of power and authority in Rome, organizing the defense of the city, negotiating with the leaders of the barbarian armies, and generally acting like powerful consuls. Increases in papal authority, autonomy, and prestige resulted, as the loyalty of Italians to Rome grew apace with their disillusionment with Constantinople. Much of the political power in Italy that was not in the hands of the pope was held by what Thomas F. X. Noble has called "a new military aristocracy . . . , and alongside it a complex social structure that did not necessarily identify with its imperial masters in Constantinople, or with the emperor's representative in Ravenna."[16]

Then there was yet another force separating Rome from Constantinople, Greek Christians from Latin ones. From the middle of the sixth century Slavic groups began to migrate into the Balkans and the Peloponnese. The Balkans escaped imperial control altogether except for the isolated Greek and Christian city of Thessaloniki. The imperial land routes across the Balkans, connecting Constantinople to Thessaloniki and then to the ports of the eastern Adriatic, were severed.[17] When Emperor Justinian II traveled by land from Constantinople to Thessaloniki in 688–89 his was not a leisurely journey but a hard-fought military campaign. He was welcomed in Thessaloniki as a savior and revered there long after the rest of the empire had come to consider him a monster. Because land routes had often been the least expensive mode of travel for ordinary people—pilgrims, men seeking work, the imperial post—this severing of the Roman roads across the Balkans led to a significant reduction in the everyday flow of information, artifacts, artisans, theological ideas, literary trends, and more from east to west and back again. A kind of unity of Mediterranean culture that had characterized an earlier age perished.

Moreover, the Islamic, Lombard, and Slavic incursions, each in its own way, removed some of those populations that had, by virtue of geography and historical accident, served as intermediaries between Greeks and Latins: the people of Illyricum and the people of North Africa.[18] Latin-speakers, Latin towns, and Latin churches in the Balkans disappeared as the Slavs moved in.

In these ways, the empire slowly became irrelevant to the Latin and Lombard inhabitants of Italy. Different kinds of changes began at different times and progressed at different speeds in different places, but all changed markedly, especially over the course of the seventh and eighth centuries.

The eastern, Hellenistic culture that had united elites throughout the empire faced extinction in the west and radical transformation in the east. Even as the imperial language of Rome came to dominate western culture, knowledge of Latin in Constantinople was confined to a small corps of translators. Even as the Greek elite came to speak, read, and write only Greek, the Latin elite stopped learning Greek. In the fifth century, Augustine was a bit ashamed of his inadequate Greek; by the end of the sixth century, Pope Gregory I was not ashamed to know no Greek and complained bitterly of the lack of translators in Constantinople who could render Latin into Greek.[19] The same emperor who planned to move the imperial capital back to the western Mediterranean—to Syracuse—was also the first emperor to use Greek inscriptions on his coins.[20] It was as if the people on the northeastern and northwestern shores of the Mediterranean basin, once the same species, were now separate populations left to evolve differently under different environmental conditions. One cannot stress enough that this process was gradual, intermittent, and geographically diverse: southern Italy and the British Isles, for example, probably had less in common with one another than Rome and Constantinople did. Yet by the early eighth century some things had changed noticeably.

In the east, the people had become less ecumenical in thought and culture. The old Mediterranean-wide empire and church had ruled in part by accepting subjects of different *ethnoi*, cultures, and rituals.[21] Its elite seems to have possessed a kind of confidence in the ability of their Roman, civilized, and Christian culture to assimilate, civilize, and convert outsiders. It was a confidence founded on centuries of being the civilization that others emulated. In contrast, the empire that emerged from the dark days of the seventh century, when first Persians and Avars, then Arabs and Slavs, had threatened Constantinople itself, was more homogeneous in fact and in ideology. Nearly all of its inhabitants were Chalcedonian Christians in belief, Greek in rite and speech. The empire encompassed fewer regions and therefore fewer regional varieties of thought and worship. Its intellectuals, writing history, hagiography, and encomia for emperors, portrayed a civilization that had survived by purifying itself of all deviance, by returning to a state of purity which returned its people, the Chosen People, to their proper relationship with God. This people tended to see variety and innovation as heresy and deviance; and heretics and deviants, unlike barbarians, could not be converted and civilized. They were to be resisted and fought off, destroyed and excluded, not integrated and assimilated.[22]

All was not separation and isolation, however. In southern Italy, in fact, a transformation occurred in these centuries that was going to have an enormous impact on the future of relations between Greeks and Latins. While there may have been very few Greek-speakers in southern Italy before the Islamic invasions, many Greek-speaking, Greek-rite Chalcedonian clergy from Syria, the Balkans, the Peloponnese, and the Mediterranean islands fled west in the seventh and eighth centuries when Muslim raiders made life unsafe in their homelands.[23] In the iconoclast period (probably in 732–33), the emperor transferred the ecclesiastical jurisdiction of the theme of Calabria in southern Italy and the island of Sicily to the patriarchate of Constantinople.[24] From this time, these territories would be places where Greek rite and Latin rite, Greek hierarchs and Latin hierarchs, patriarchal institutions and papal ones, defy generalization. There are, for examples, Greek bishops and abbots who accept papal jurisdiction, Greek monks and monasteries patronized by Norman rulers, and Latin monks living on Mt. Athos.

In other words, to return to the analogy of a fault line between the two Christian churches, people in the Byzantine areas of southern Italy lived on a wide and roomy bridge across the fault. As a result of shifting relations among ethnic groups and religious ones, no single factor separated or united groups. Although elites of various kinds occasionally tried to manufacture boundaries between imperial Byzantine and Latin, between Lombard and Latin, or between Greek-rite Christians and Latin ones, southern Italy and Sicily remained places of shifting and multiple identities, and people deployed (or did not deploy) their various identities as it suited their needs.[25] The Greek-speaking, Greek-rite clergy and hierarchy of this area often served as natural ambassadors between Rome and Constantinople—translators not only of language but of customs. As Francis Dvornik put it, "As long as there existed in South Italy this bridge between Byzantium and the West, it was still possible that contacts between Constantinople and Rome could become more frequent and more cordial."[26]

In addition to benefiting from this bridge in southern Italy, the Byzantines still afforded a kind of special status to their brothers in Rome. Even if the rest of the western empire had fallen to the barbarians, it was hardly conceivable for the *Rhomaioi* of the east to call the *Romani* of Old Rome uncivilized. St. Peter's successors on the papal throne in Rome were recognized as defenders of orthodoxy. Many Chalcedonian monks, clergy, and bishops fled from Asia and North Africa during the Islamic invasions to Rome, Sicily, and southern Italy. Some of them were of Greek language and rite. Some of their sons became popes.[27] Later, monks and churchmen opposed to imperial iconoclasm also fled to Rome in numbers large enough to make an impact, at least temporarily.[28] In fact, the papacy came out of the period of iconoclasm with extraordinary prestige in the eastern church. Rome's distance from Constantinople and the popes' autonomy had made them defenders of orthodoxy when emperors had been, first, monophysites, monenergists, or monotheletes, then iconoclasts.[29] Among the leaders of the Constantinopolitan church after 843 were those, such as Patriarch Methodios I (843–47), who had spent time in exile in Rome. Greek monasteries in Rome were thriving.[30]

On the other hand, during the period of iconoclasm a thundercloud had appeared on the horizon, and the first rumblings of thunder had begun. Neither Rome nor Constantinople saw the storm coming or could have predicted its force, but it was to change the world. A supernaturally prescient forecaster might have seen the first clouds gathering when Pope Gregory I (590–604) and his successors supported and inspired missions to the northern barbarians. These missions were to provide the popes with a new, larger flock, entirely separate from and largely ignorant of the Mediterranean culture of antiquity. To these peoples, the pope, the source of their conversion, was not "simply the highest dignitary in the ecclesiastical hierarchy," but "a quasi-transcendental figure in whom Peter lived again." This was an altogether different perspective on Rome from that of the older churches, be they eastern sees, cisalpine western sees such as Ravenna and Milan, or southern Italian sees such as Salerno.[31] Eventually, it was from these northern peoples that the papal "reformers" would come, and the role that their reform and its exaltation of the papacy played in the separation of Rome from Constantinople can hardly be overstated.[32]

A shorter-range forecast might have noted the rumbling thunder when Pope Stephen II (752–57), seeking help against the Lombards and finding none from Constantinople, which was at this time caught up in the iconoclast controversy, crossed the Alps and allied his see with the king of the Franks. The long-term consequences of this move were enormous and can be found in any survey of western European history.[33] What matters for the ninth century, however, is that much we attribute to the alliance of pope and Frankish king did not happen immediately. For example, although Byzantines and Romans alike recognized that the Franks were a military power to be reckoned with, neither was prepared for the erudite and ambitious dreams of Charlemagne's intellectuals, those men who imagined a new Constantine, a new Roman Empire, and a new Vicar of Christ on earth. From the Mediterranean point of view, these Franks were still barbarians, even if they had also become the pope's devoted servants.[34] It was a dangerous illusion, and when these "barbarians," who had been neither consulted about nor represented at the Seventh Ecumenical Council, formulated a sophisticated theological rejection of that council, they "gave notice to the older centres of Christianity of significant changes in the medieval world order."[35] Hampered by a bad Latin translation of the Acta of the council and lacking sympathy for eastern ecclesiastical customs, the Carolingian theologians were nonetheless erudite and confident. Indeed, they were confident enough to suggest, diplomatically, to the pope that he may have erred in his acceptance of eastern reverence for icons (which smacked of idolatry) and in not reprimanding Patriarch Tarasios of Constantinople (784–806) for confessing a creed that lacked the Filioque.[36] The pope told them that they were wrong, but the thunder had now been heard in Rome. There were two centers of theological inquiry in the west, and they did not always agree with one another, especially in the eighth and ninth centuries and especially about the Greeks. The great sees of Rome and Constantinople still shared as much with one another as either did with the peoples further north, but the balance was shifting. The conflicts of the later ninth century would alter the weight further.

NOTES

1. See Ian Wood, "Conclusion: Strategies of Distinction," in *Strategies of Distinction: The Construction of Ethnic Communities, 300–800*, ed. Walter Pohl, with Helmut Reimitz (Leiden: Brill, 1998): "Like all binary opposites the distinction between Romans and barbarians has a function, or rather a series of functions depending on the intention of the author who employs it. When the distinction and the contexts in which it is used are placed under the microscope inevitably something very much more complicated than the initial polarity appears" (297). The same could be said of the binary opposites east and west.

2. See, for example, Markus, *The End of Ancient Christianity*, xiii, 30–32.

3. Peter Brown, "Eastern and Western Christendom in Late Antiquity: A Parting of the Ways," in *The Orthodox Churches and the West*, ed. D. Baker (Oxford: Blackwell, 1976), 1–24 (repr. in Brown, *Society and the Holy*, 166–95).

4. For a concise introduction to and bibliography of this amorphous early medieval state see Valerie Ramseyer, *The Transformation of a Religious Landscape: Medieval Southern Italy, 850–1150* (Ithaca: Cornell University Press, 2006), 6–11. No doubt it

is also easy to overestimate the coherence of western Christendom in the twelfth century. But the Byzantines of the twelfth century tended, as their ancestors of the ninth century had not, to see the Latin world as a single, coherent unit; I do not think they were entirely wrong.

5. Herbert Hunger, *Graeculus Perfidus. Italos Itamos. Il senso dell'alterità nei rapporti greco-romani ed italo-bizantini* (Rome: Unione internazionale degli istituti di archeologia storia e storia dell'arte in Roma,1987).

6. The following argument about the meaning of linguistic difference depends on the seminal article by Gilbert Dagron: "Aux origines de la civilisation byzantine: Langue de culture et langue d'état," *Revue historique* 489 (1969): 29–76.

7. This includes the family of the Emperor Justinian I; Brian Croke, "Justinian's Constantinople," in *Cambridge Companion to the Age of Justinian*, ed. Maas, 75–76.

8. Dagron, "Aux origines de la civilisation byzantine," 25–26.

9. The most famous of these is John Lydus: see Croke, "Justinian's Constantinople," 74; Dagron, "Aux origines de la civilisation byzantine," 27–28.

10. Claudia Rapp, "A Medieval Cosmopolis: Constantinople and Its Foreign Inhabitants," in *Alexander's Revenge: Hellenistic Culture through the Centuries*, ed. J. Ma and N. Van Deusen (Reykjavik: University of Iceland Press, 2002), 153–72. Croke, "Justinian's Constantinople," 75–76.

11. Dagron, "Aux origines de la civilisation byzantine," 23.

12. F. X. Murphy, and P. Sherwood, *Constantinople II et Constantinople III* (Paris: Orante, 1974); Herrin, *Formation*, 275–80.

13. Letter 28 to Flavian of Constantinople: PL 54:756–82; also ed. E. Schwartz, *Concilium Chalcedonense*, vol. 1 (Berlin: de Gruyter, 1933), 10–20; Eng trans. C. L. Feltoe, *Select Letters and Sermons of Leo I* (Oxford 1895), 38–43. On the process by which the letter, known as the Tome of Leo, was accepted at Chalcedon see Richard Price and Michael Gaddis, trans. and comm., *The Acts of the Council of Chalcedon*, 3 vols. (Liverpool: Liverpool University Press, 2005, 2: 115–63. Herrin, *Formation*, 103.

14. Gray, "Legacy of Chalcedon," 234; for a succinct survey of the relations between Rome and Constantinople see Claire Sotinel, "Emperors and Popes in the Sixth Century: The Western View," in *Cambridge Companion to the Age of Justinian*, ed. Maas, 267–90.

15. Milton V. Anastos, "The Transfer of Illyricum, Calabria and Sicily to the Jurisdiction of the Patriarchate of Constantinople in 732–33," *Studi bizantini e neoellenici* 9 (1957): 14–31.

16. Thomas F. X. Noble, *The Republic of St. Peter: The Birth of the Papal State, 680–825* (Philadelphia: University of Pennsylvania Press, 1984), 9; see also T. S. Brown, *Gentlemen and Officers: Imperial Administration and Aristocratic Power in Byzantine Italy, A.D. 554–800* (London: British School at Rome, 1984).

17. John V. A. Fine, Jr., *The Early Medieval Balkans: A Critical Survey from the Sixth to the Late Twelfth Century* (Ann Arbor: University of Michigan Press, 1983), 24–26; Herrin, *Formation*, 133–35.

18. Herrin, *Formation*, 107.

19. "Hodie in Constantinopolitana civitate, qui de latino in graeco dictate bene transferant non sunt"; *Gregorii I Papae Registrum Epistolarum*, ed. P. Ewald and L. M. Hartmann, in MGH Epp. 1, VII, 27, 2nd ed. (Berlin: MGH, 1957), 474. NB: Gregory is not claiming that nobody in Constantinople spoke Latin; in fact, he had friends among the senatorial class there who did speak and write Latin. What he is saying is that it is hard to find competent bilingual people who could take what was said in Latin and translate it into Greek. Analysis and bibliography of the language issues: Herrin, *Formation*, 10–12, 75–76, 85–87, 99–100.

20. *The Oxford Dictionary of Byzantium*, ed. Alexander Kazhdan et al. (Oxford: Oxford University Press, 1991), s.v. "Constans II."

21. See, for example, the descriptions in Croke, "Justinian's Constantinople."

22. This is not the place to give the details upon which this generalization is based. See Haldon, *Byzantium in the Seventh Century*, especially chaps. 8–10; Gilbert Dagron, "L'Église et la chrétienté Byzantines entre les invasions et l'iconoclasme (VIIe–début VIIIe siècle)," in *Histoire du christianisme*, ed. Mayeur et al., 61–66; Herrin, *Formation*, 137–42, 285–86, 305–6; David Olster, *Roman Defeat, Christian Response, and the Literary Construction of the Jew* (Philadelphia: University of Pennsylvania Press, 1994).

23. For a discussion and fundamental bibliography on this, see Jean-Marie Sansterre, *Les moines grecs et orientaux à Rome aux époques byzantine et carolingienne (milieu du VIe s.–fin du IXe s.)* (Brussels: Palais des academies, 1983), 17–18.

24. Anastos, "Transfer." On what this transfer meant for the Hellenization of the church hierarchy in these regions, see Vitalien Laurent, "L'Eglise de l'Italie méridionale entre Rome et Byzance à la veille de la conquête normande," in *La chiesa greca in Italia dall'VIII al XVI secolo. Atti del convegno storico interecclesiale (Bari, 30 Apr.–4. Magg. 1969)*, 3 vols., Italia sacra 20–22 (Padua: Editrice Antenore, 1973), 1:14–20.

25. "Ethnicity . . . is not a primordial category, but a negotiated system of social classification. Difference only matters . . . as long as there is somebody capable of 'making the difference'; it is a relational category. . . . To make ethnicity happen, it is not enough just to be different. Strategies of distinction have to convince both insiders and outsiders that it is significant to be different, that it is the key to an identity that should be cherished and defended" (Walter Pohl, "Telling the Difference: Signs of Ethnic Identity," in *Strategies of Distinction*, ed. Pohl and Reimitz, 21–22).

26. Francis Dvornik, *Byzantium and the Roman Primacy* (New York: Fordham University Press, 1966), 127–28. The status of southern Italy's Greek population from the ninth century to the end of the Middle Ages is an immense subject, with much admirable research done and, unfortunately, much nonsense that assumes essential, universally recognized, unchanging ethnic and/or religious boundaries and markers. Ramseyer, *Transformation*, contains an exhaustive bibliography. She also shows how few of the conventional dichotomies of Greek/Latin or east/west apply to the territory of Salerno or other regions in southern Italy before the Normans. See, for example, her description of the Church of San Nicola of Gallocanta (79–84) and her discussion of "Greek Foundations" (85–92). Some of the best discussions of church and religious matters are in a collection of papers by various scholars: *La chiesa greca in Italia dall'VIII al XVI secolo* (see n. 24, above). Other excellent studies include Ghislaine Noyé's work in many publications; for Photios's period, see Noyé, "Byzance et Italie méridionale," in *Byzantium in the Ninth Century*, ed. Brubaker, 229–43; Ramseyer, *Transformation*. The two comprehensive studies, fundamental still for scholarship on southern Italy are Jules Gay, *L'Italie méridionale et l'empire byzantin depuis l'avènement de Basil Ier jusqu'a la prise de Bari par les Normands*, Bibliothèque des Écoles françaises d'Athénes et de Rome 90 (Paris: A. Fontemoing, 1904); and Vera von Falkenhausen, *La dominazione bizantina nell'Italia meridionale dall IX all'XI secolo* (Bari: Ecumenica Editrice, 1978), as well as a multitude of other articles. See also André Guillou, "Grecs d'Italie du Sud et de Sicile au moyen âge: Les moines," *Mélanges d'archéologie et d'histoire* 75 (1963): 79–110 (repr. in Guillou, *Studies on Byzantine Italy* [London: Variorum, 1970], art. 12); Guillou, "Italie méridionale byzantine ou Byzantins en Italie méridionale?" *Byzantion* 44 (1974): 152–90 (repr. in Guillou, *Culture et Société en Italie Byzantine (VIe–XIe s.)* [London: Variorum, 1978], art. 15); Guillou, "Cultura, insegnamento e ricerca in istoria. Un esempio: l'Italia bizantina," *Quaderni medievali* 2 (1976): 154–61 (repr. in *Culture et Société*, art. 16). For a later period, see G. A. Loud, "Byzantine Italy and the Normans," *Byzantinische Forschungen* 13 (1988): 215–33.

27. Eleven of thirteen popes between 678 and 752 were men of Greek descent from Sicily, Syria, and the empire; see Andrew J. Ekonomou, *Byzantine Rome and the Greek Popes: Eastern Influences on Rome and the Papacy from Gregory the Great to Zacharias, A.D. 590–752* (Lanham, Md.: Lexington/Rowman & Littlefield, 2007); Noble, *Republic*, 185–88; Sansterre, *Moines*, 19–21; Bernard Hamilton, "The City of Rome and the Eastern Churches in the Tenth Century," *Orientalia Christiana Periodica* 27 (1961): 5–26.

28. Sansterre, *Moines grecs et orientaux*, 50; Lynn Townsend White, Jr., *Latin Monasticism in Norman Sicily* (Cambridge, Mass.: Mediaeval Academy of America, 1938), 28.

29. Dagron, *Empereur et prêtre*, 170–79, trans. 159–68; Dvornik, *Byzantium and the Roman Primacy*, 19; Herrin, *Formation*, 250–59; Jane Carol Bishop, "Pope

Nicholas I and the First Age of Papal Independence" (PhD diss., Columbia University, 1980), 372–82.

30. Sansterre, *Moines grecs et orientaux*, 49–51.

31. Aidan Nichols, *Rome and the Eastern Churches: A Study in Schism* (Edinburgh: T&T Clark, 1992), 182–83; Herrin, *Formation*, 105–6, 267–72, 289–90, 358–59, 375–77; Ramseyer, *Transformation*, 40–42.

32. This is a central theme of Aristeides Papadakis and John Meyendorff, *The Christian East and the Rise of the Papacy: The Church 1071–1453 A.D.* (Crestwood, N.Y.: St. Vladimir's Seminary Press, 1994). See also Nichols, *Rome and the Eastern Churches*, 183, 210; Dvornik, *Byzantium and the Roman Primacy*, 126–28.

33. Noble, *Republic*, 94–97; Herrin, *Formation*, 387–95.

34. For a discussion of Roman patriotism and anti-Frankish attitudes, see Bishop, *Nicholas I*, 366–68.

35. Herrin, *Formation*, 426–44 (435); Ann Freeman, "Carolingian Orthodoxy and the Fate of the Libri Carolini," *Viator* 16 (1985): 105–6; Haldon and Brubaker, *Byzantium in the Iconoclast Era*, 241–42.

36. The claim of Latins, from these Carolingians to Humbert of Silva Candida (mid-eleventh century) that the Greeks had removed the Filioque from the creed may seem risible and has evoked scorn from many historians, especially Orthodox ones. It was none the less sincere, stemming from a genuine belief that the so-called Athanasian Creed, which professes double procession of the Holy Spirit, was written by St. Athanasius the Great, who was also believed to be the author of the Nicene Creed. Westerners in Spain and the kingdom of the Franks assumed that the Greeks had tried to "suppress" that part of the creed. Nichols, *Rome and the Eastern Churches*, 195–98.

CHAPTER 3

The Patriarch, the Pope, and the Barbarians

Photios (patriarch of Constantinople 858–67, 877–86) is best known among historians of the western Middle Ages for the schism between Rome and Constantinople that is usually given his name. The "Photian Schism," which continued and escalated the rivalry between the sees of Rome and Constantinople, began with Photios's contested election and Pope Nicholas I's (858–67) ambitions for the papal office.[1] When Photios became patriarch in 858 his election was canonically irregular in two ways. First, his predecessor Ignatios was not dead, but had resigned. If Frances Dvornik is correct, this resignation was not, in a strictly legal sense, coerced. Still, Ignatios resigned while in captivity and under considerable imperial pressure—de facto coercion despite Dvornik's *apologia*.[2] Second, Photios was a layman when elected and Christmas was fast approaching, with much ceremonial that required a patriarch, so he was rushed through the clerical grades and ordained patriarch in only a week. This process was irregular, but not unprecedented.[3] Meanwhile, some of Ignatios's most loyal and vociferous supporters did not accept their leader's abdication and considered Photios a usurper. Since the emperor had been the force behind Ignatios's resignation, they could not seek support in the Great Palace. So they appealed to the only authority available to them: the pope. Pope Nicholas I, given an opportunity to intervene in the Constantinopolitan church, obliged them, supported Ignatios, and opposed and excommunicated Photios. Thus started a long conflict that would cast a shadow over both of Photios's patriarchates and play a role in one of his abdications. It has played an even larger role in western historiography, for the schism between Constantinople under Photios and Rome under Nicholas I and John VIII (872–82) became a central part of the narrative of schism. Later historians in the west saw in Photios the proud and ambitious instigator of schism, a liar, a hypocrite, a cheat.

This image of Photios was demolished (mostly) for all time in 1948 when Francis Dvornik published *The Photian Schism*—a work of exemplary erudition and nearly flawless logic. Dvornik not only redeemed Photios's reputation by careful reassessment of the sources, but also overturned the idea that the later schism between Rome and Constantinople dated in any way to Photios's time and was Photios's fault. *The Photian Schism* is an unparalleled piece of scholarship, transcending confessional boundaries and eschewing the anachronism that had characterized much previous work regarding Photios. It is not my aim to repeat or update that work, for more than fifty years later it still needs little amendment. Instead, where Dvornik was concerned to show that Photios was not a power-hungry politique who set out to deny and destroy papal authority, I am interested in his role in the centuries-long controversy about various differences between Greek and Latin practices, and specifically about the single most important theological issue to divide Constantinople from Rome. This was the so-called Filioque controversy: a difference between western theology and creed, which professed that the Holy Spirit proceeds from the Father *and the Son* (in Latin, *Filioque*), and the Greek Church, which insisted that both the theology of double procession and the addition of Filioque to the creed were wrong.

First, however, it is important to re-emphasize that eastern and western Europe during the early Middle Ages, although more isolated from one another than they had been in late antiquity, still maintained certain important contacts. Such postal systems as remained were unreliable, and travel overland from Constantinople to Rome was often impossible, but at some levels an infrastructure existed that kept lines of communication open. One need only look at various events in the schism between Photios and the popes to see how news could travel from one capital to the other, and how quickly. There was not only much sending and receiving of formal legations from pope to patriarch, from pope to emperor, and vice versa. There were also rumors and accusations carried by supporters of Ignatios who could travel to Rome to plead their case even when the imperial government was trying to stop them.[4] In the second half of the ninth century several Greek monasteries still flourished in Rome, and news flowed from them to Constantinople and vice versa.[5] Photios had his partisans in Rome; Ignatios had his also, probably in greater numbers.[6]

More important for the Filioque controversy, however, was another region of contact and mutual awareness that had opened up in ninth-century central Europe. The Franks had converted the Moravians, only to be supplanted by Byzantines, who were then supplanted again by Franks. In Bulgaria, too, the competition for souls was intense: Franks, Byzantines, and representatives of the pope struggled to convert the Khan and his people. The steps to their conversion are so distorted in the tendentious sources, each of which claims victory for its side, that the chronology of Bulgarian conversion may never be clear.[7] In both Moravia and Bulgaria, Franks and Greeks battled for control of the church and each side became aware of how the other worshipped and observed (or failed to observe) the rules of the church. This was a less positive experience than the contacts with Romans and Venetians that had been common in earlier decades and centuries. As Jonathan Shepard has pointed out, in the early Middle Ages "the Byzantines' notion of a special relationship with the Western Christians partly reflects their ignorance of the actual cultural and political conditions of the West."[8] They knew papal legates; Greek-speaking westerners on high-level missions, such as Liutprand of Cremona; Italian merchants from Amalfi and Venice; monks from Italian monasteries, both Greek and Latin. The eastern Frankish missionaries in Bulgaria turned out to be less friendly, admiring, and diplomatic than these groups.[9] All of this forms the context in which we must analyze and understand ninth-century Byzantine criticism of the Latin use of Filioque.

There may have been differences in the precise language used by Greek and Latin theologians to describe the relations and distinctions among the three persons in the Godhead as early as the fourth century.[10] Some of these early differences, and the discussion of them by such illustrious theologians as Maximos the Confessor, were to have repercussions later in the Middle Ages, but they seem largely to have been forgotten from the seventh through the middle of the ninth centuries. It was only after the Latins changed the creed that the controversy began to grow. Where the most comprehensive creed used consistently by both churches, the Nicene-Constantinopolitan Creed, stated that the Holy Spirit "proceeds from the Father," some Latin churches had added "and from the Son" as early as the sixth century.[11] By the seventh century the addition had spread to Anglo-Saxon England, to areas of northern Italy, and to the Frankish realm.[12] In the early eleventh century the creed with the Filioque was accepted by the pope in Rome.[13] When they learned of this development, probably only in the late ninth century when Greek missionaries met Latin ones in the Slavic lands, Greek ecclesiastics objected—in fact, their awareness of this addition to a conciliar creed probably came at the worst possible time. With the Seven Ecumenical Councils complete, a consensus of sorts about conciliar infallibility had become the cornerstone of Byzantine orthodoxy. Consciously or not, the churchmen of the ninth century elevated the ecumenical councils in this way because only thus could previous conflicts be ended once and for all. The so-called creed of Nicea 325 (which is only recorded in full for the first time at Chalcedon 451) was not seen as the product of a half-century or more of doctrinal debate, imperial politics, and street fighting; it was now sacrosanct, the divinely inspired product of the divinely inspired Fathers, who could not and did not differ with one another. Those who had added the Filioque to the creed had meddled with a sacred and unchanging text. In doing so, they had hit the post-iconoclast Byzantines where it hurt.

The ninth-century Byzantines, however, were not the first to raise the issue. Frankish theologians decried the difference when, around 790, they received their first account of the Second Council of Nicea, the Seventh Ecumenical Council (Nicea 787). They objected immediately to that council's definition and encouragement of icon veneration—in part because they did not understand the definition, in part because Byzantine developments in icon veneration were alien to them. These Frankish objections, which led to some infamous exchanges between the pope and the Franks and to the composition of the renowned *Libri Carolini* (793), are well known.[14] Less often stressed is that the same men who objected to the Greek definitions of icon veneration objected also to something they had noticed in the fine print of the conciliar Acta. Tarasios, patriarch of Constantinople, in his confession of faith before the council, had said that the Spirit proceeded from the Father. It was the only version of the creed that the Greeks knew. In contrast, by this time the Franks sincerely believed that the creed as they chanted it, with the Filioque, was the original and unchanged creed.[15] Frankish church leaders immediately condemned what they thought was a Greek truncation of the creed. One chapter of the *Libri Carolini* is devoted to the question of "whether Tarasios thinks correctly when he professes that the Holy Spirit proceeds not from the Father and the Son, according to the truest rule of the holy faith, but that he proceeds from the Father through the Son."[16] Throughout the 790s and into the early decades of the ninth century, Franks regularly took up this issue, determined to defend their creed in various ways and various venues.[17]

But were these defenses of the Filioque attacks on the Greeks? Certainly the response in the *Libri Carolini* attacked Greek teachings promulgated at Nicea 787. In contrast, however, the later (790s–800s) treatises on the subject were directed not at the east, but at the popes, who had not yet adopted the Filioque, and at Adoptionist heretics. In other words, the conflict was between Franks, who added the Filioque to the creed, and the Roman Church, which did not. Pope Leo III (795–816) was firm in his condemnation of the Frankish practice. He flatly told a Frankish delegation in 810 that, although correct in believing and teaching that the Holy Spirit proceeded from both the Father and the Son, they were wrong to add a phrase to the creed.[18] Anastasius Bibliothecarius reports that Leo went further: he ordered that the Nicene Creed without the Filioque be engraved on two shields, one Greek and one Latin, and the shields erected in St. Peter's.[19] The Greeks learned of this action, too, for the story of Leo's shields appears already in Photios's Ep. 291 (AD 883 or 884) and becomes a common element in both Greek treatises against the Latins and Greek histories of the schism.[20] Byzantine contact with Rome in this period was often interrupted, but some channels remained open—formal missions and informal contact between Greek monks in Rome and their compatriots. Roman popes continued to send their enthronement letters eastward with the creed recognized by the Byzantines.

If Byzantine contact with the Frankish Church was limited, and the Byzantines were unaware of, or at least unconcerned about, the Franks' use of the Filioque in the early ninth century, that changed in the 860s when Latin and Greek missionaries were competing in central Europe. Each side criticized the other openly and then refuted the criticisms offered by the other side. A cycle of polemic began that has not yet ended. We have four extant texts, and indirect evidence for a fifth, from this period when Byzantines were just becoming aware of Latin differences. Two of these—Photios's second letter and the document summarized in a letter of Pope Nicholas I (see chapter 8, below)—accuse the Latins of multiple errors. The other three deal only with the Filioque. Three of the extant texts are attributed to Photios, as part of the tradition that has made him the leading man in the conflict between east and west: an encyclical to the eastern patriarchs;[21] a treatise gathering many arguments against the Filioque in one place, known as the *Mystagogia*; and a letter to the metropolitan of Aquileia.[22] The fourth is attributed to a figure little known beyond his writings, Niketas Byzantios, also known as Niketas Didaskalos and Niketas Philosophos. More famous for writing a sura-by-sura refutation of the Qur'an, Niketas also wrote some "syllogistic chapters" against those who taught that the Spirit proceeds from the Son.[23]

But before we can allow these texts to enlighten us about the earliest Greek arguments regarding the double procession of the Holy Spirit, we must do a close, detailed, and necessarily technical study of the textual tradition, for they are far from simple treatises with secure attribution. Especially in the case of the *Mystagogia*, attribution to Photios is problematic—a point worth making for its impact on the biography of this remarkable patriarch, as well as for the history of Filioque arguments.

Regardless of Photian authorship, all of these texts are extremely important for understanding Byzantine antiheretical literature directed at Latins. Extant in late ninth- or early tenth-century manuscripts, they are the earliest dated refutations of the western belief that the Spirit proceeds from the Father and the Son and thus reveal how much the Greeks knew about that doctrine and when. As the first in a tradition that continues today, these arguments are used and reused. For theologians, historians of theology, and historians of Latin-Greek relations in the Middle Ages, they are indispensable evidence.

The next three chapters comprise a close study of the manuscript tradition and attribution of the three Photian texts. While all three are extant in manuscripts that seem to date to the late ninth and early tenth centuries, only Ep. 291 is a relatively straightforward text—clearly a single letter by Photios himself, with little or no later revision and/or augmentation. Some of my conclusions here may seem less than earth-shattering, but in the end and as a whole they are important. There is something salutary about recognizing just how shaky the evidence for the history of Byzantine theology can be. Note again that this first part of the book is the part a nonexpert reader can skip if she is willing to accept my conclusions without slogging through the details. The experts will want to know, but such reading is not for everyone. An "Intermission" after chapter 6, below, summarizes the conclusions of this textual analysis.

NOTES

1. On Nicholas I, see chapter 8, below.

2. Dvornik, *Photian Schism*, 39–48.

3. Dvornik, *Photian Schism*, 50–51.

4. Dvornik, *Photian Schism*, 96.

5. Sansterre, *Moines grecs et orientaux*, 145–46.

6. Sansterre, *Moines grecs et orientaux*, 44–45.

7. Paul Speck, "Die griechischen Quellen zur Bekehrung der Bulgaren und die zwei ersten Briefe des Photios," in *Polupleuros Nous. Miscellanea für Peter Schreiner zu Seinem 60. Geburtstag* (Munich: Saur, 2000), 342–59.

8. Jonathan Shepard, "Aspects of Byzantine Attitudes and Policy towards the West in the Tenth and Eleventh Centuries," *Byzantische Forschungen* 13 (1988): 93.

9. Shepard, "Aspects of Byzantine Attitudes," 93–94.

10. Agreement on the precise nature and importance of the differences is not one of the characteristics of modern theological scholarship, however, in part because of the continued importance of the issue and in part because of the desire to prove that one side is right and the other wrong—a desire that often distorts historical accounts. See further discussion of this issue in the "Conclusion," below.

11. The first use of the Filioque in a conciliar creed was probably the creed of the Council of Toledo in 589; Giovan Domenico Mansi, *Sacrorum conciliorum nova et amplissima collectio*, 53 vols. (Paris: H. Welter, 1801–27), 9:985.

12. The evidence is outlined by Richard Haugh, *Photius and the Carolingians: The Trinitarian Controversy* (Belmont, Mass.: Nordland, 1975), 27–33.

13. According to Berno of Reichenau, PL 142:1060–61, the creed with the Filioque was recited at the coronation of King Henry II as Holy Roman Emperor. See also Papadakis and Meyendorff, *Christian East*, 14; Steven Runciman, *The Eastern Schism: A Study of the Papacy and the Eastern Churches during the Eleventh and Twelfth Centuries* (Oxford: Clarendon Press, 1955), 30; Tia M. Kolbaba, "Latin and Greek Christianity," in *The Cambridge History of Christianity*, vol. 3, *c. 600–c. 1100*, ed. Thomas F. X. Noble and Julia M. H. Smith (Cambridge: Cambridge University Press, 2008), 222.

14. See the editor's introduction to *Opus Caroli Regis adversus synodum (Libri Carolini)*, ed. Ann Freeman, MGH Leg. 3, Conc. 2, supp. 1, and Freeman, "Carolingian Orthodoxy."

15. Haugh, *Photius and the Carolingians*, 45–53.

16. *Opus Caroli Regis (Libri Carolini)*, lib. 3, cap. 3.

17. Haugh, *Photius and the Carolingians*, 55–90; Haugh's survey outlines the various treatises in some detail and provides summaries, along with translations of passages (sometimes lengthy). All of this is useful, but Haugh's study must still be used with caution. He was not sufficiently skeptical about the transmission of these texts, for questions have been raised about the dating and authority of many of them.

18. Haugh, *Photius and the Carolingians*, 81–90, which includes an English translation of an account of this encounter.

19. PL 128:1238. Vittorio Peri, "Il simbolo epigrafico di S. Leone III nelle basiliche romane dei SS. Pietro e Paolo," *Rivista de Archeologia Christiana* 45 (1969): 191–221. See further discussion of this story in the "Conclusion," below.

20. For example, it is included in an epitome of Photios's arguments that circulates in various guises throughout the Middle Ages; one version of this was published in PG 102:391–400. It is also included in all three of the tracts regarding the origins of the schism published by Hergenroether, *Monumenta*, 158–59, 166, 176.

21. Photios, Patriarch of Constantinople, "Encyclica ad sedes orientales," in *Epistulae et Amphilochia*, ed. B. Laourdas and L. B. Westerink, 7 vols. (Leipzig: Teubner, 1983–88), vol. 1, Ep. 2. Hereafter cited as Ep. 2.

22. Photios, Patriarch of Constantinople, "Archiepiscopo Aquileiae," in *Epistulae*, vol. 3, Ep. 291. Hereafter cited as Ep. 291.

23. "Syllogistic chapters put together from the common notions concerning God and from the demonstrative [*apodeiktikos*] and disjunctive [*diairetikos*] method . . . against those who impiously and atheistically add and say and teach in the holy symbol of the orthodox faith of the Christians . . . 'and in the Holy Spirit, the Lord, the Giver of Life, who proceeds from the Father and the Son'—instead of 'from the Father alone'" (Hergenroether, *Monumenta*, 84–138).

CHAPTER 4

Photios's Ep. 2
"Encyclical to the Eastern Patriarchs"

Ep. 2, which purports to be an encyclical from Photios to the patriarchs of Alexandria, Antioch, and Jerusalem, is extant in a late ninth-century manuscript and has been dated by its modern editors to 867. Few have doubted its authenticity, including its editors.[1] Nevertheless, the text as it has come down to us bears troubling signs of cutting and pasting. A summary of the letter—difficult to write and difficult to follow precisely because it is so disjointed—may be enough to make this point.[2] It begins abruptly and emotionally:

> It seems that there are never enough evil deeds for the evil one, nor any end of the inventions and machinations which he has been accustomed, from the beginning, to move against the human race. Rather, before the incarnation of our Lord he led man astray into alien and illicit deeds by many myriads of deceptions and by these also bound mankind securely under his tyranny. After the incarnation, too, he has not ceased to trip up and carry away those persuaded by him with a myriad of errors and baits.[3]

For all his wiles, though, the evil one has not triumphed. He was soundly defeated by the Fathers when they gathered in synods. After the Seventh Ecumenical Council, in fact, there came a time when pious men could hope that all would be well. Indeed, Christianity was no longer beleaguered, but rather growing. There was great joy recently, when the Bulgars were baptized as Christians and the Armenians foreswore their Monophysitism.[4]

And yet—Oh evil and lying and godless intention and deed! For such a narrative, which is the subject of the Gospels, changes to dejection, merriment and joy turn into pain and tears. For when this race [the Bulgars] had honored the right religion of the Christians for not even two years, impious and ill-omened men (For why would any pious person not name them thus?), men rising up from the darkness (For they are offspring of the western region.)—Oi moi, how can I even narrate the rest?—These men came with their audacity to the race newly born and newly established in piety like a thunderbolt or an earthquake or a great hailstorm—no, rather, it is more accurate to say that they, charging like a solitary wild boar, destroyed the beloved, newly planted vineyard of the Lord by overrunning it with claws and teeth or with the paths of disgraceful conduct and the destruction of dogma.[5]

These evil men taught the Bulgars several illicit practices and beliefs: to fast on Saturdays, not to fast properly in the first week of Lent, to insist that priests be men without wives, and to recognize confirmation only if a bishop performed the ceremony. But the worst of their faults, "the crown of all evils, if there is such a thing," was their addition to the creed, "which has its impregnable strength from all the synodical and ecclesiastical decrees."[6]

For this author, then, as for most of his heirs in Byzantine theology, the addition of a phrase to an ecumenically formulated creed would have been wrong even if the doctrine of double procession were correct or permissible. Nevertheless, this letter goes beyond the creed to a refutation of the doctrine of double procession in several paragraphs, comprising almost one-quarter of the letter's length.[7] The author then claims that he could adduce yet more arguments, denigrates the Latin bishops in Bulgaria as "men of darkness" (*episkotoi*), rather than true bishops (*episkopoi*), and tells of the pain that news of these men in Bulgaria has caused him. He then returns to the other issues mentioned in the opening: Sabbath and Lenten fasting, clerical marriage, and confirmation. Brief criticisms of each Latin practice are followed by another short paragraph attacking the Filioque. The author refutes each to his own satisfaction, if not always to the satisfaction of the disinterested reader, by citing canons where he can or by asserting that the errors are self-evidently ridiculous.[8] After exhorting the eastern patriarchs to help him destroy the errors of these wicked men from the land of darkness, the author notes that "the race that surpasses all others in crudeness and bloodthirstiness, that is the one called the Rus," has also been converted and has accepted a bishop to lead them into the fullness of Christian faith.[9] It is all the more necessary, with all of these tender new Christians, that we join together in stopping these errors from spreading.[10] Moreover, he reports that he has received a letter from Italy denouncing the pope for tyrannical behavior toward the bishops of his own patriarchate.[11] So, please, he entreats the other patriarchs, act immediately, send your envoys to an ecumenical council here in Constantinople; if errors spread because of your delay, let it be on your heads. Oh, and by the way, this council will also reaffirm the ecumenicity and binding nature of the Seventh Ecumenical Council, with its decisions about images.[12] The letter closes with further salutations and a blessing.[13]

The Textual Tradition

Despite its early manuscript tradition, this letter's miscellaneous content, the length of the section refuting the Filioque, the manuscript tradition of that section, and a series of other traits make it unlikely that it is what it purports to be.[14] Announcements of the conversions of three *ethnoi*; a denunciation and refutation of the errors of westerners in Bulgaria; an announcement that a synod in Constantinople has condemned those errors; a call for a synod to condemn those errors (?); a call for a synod to reprimand the pope for tyrannical treatment of his bishops; a call for a synod to confirm that the Council of 787 was ecumenical. The issues for the synod are raised separately and at different points in the letter, connected only by the summons to Constantinople to resolve them. Speck argued—and I concur—that it makes more sense to see these varied sections as excerpts from four or more separate texts—a text (maybe a letter) complaining about Latin practices in Bulgaria; a refutation, about one hundred lines in length, of the doctrine of double procession of the Holy Spirit; a call to the council that condemned Pope Nicholas I in the summer of 867; a call to reaffirm the decisions of Nicea 787 in the face of some threat of revived iconoclasm.[15]

The treatise on the Filioque is the largest and most anomalous of these pieces of Ep. 2, and several things become clear if we see this section of the letter as a separate treatise, interpolated here into Ep. 2 or combined with other excerpts to form Ep. 2. The strongest point in favor of this argument is what happens if one removes the long section about the Filioque (lines 108–99) from the text.[16] If we perform this operation, the remaining text has a more coherent and concise structure. The author begins with a list of five heinous practices of the western missionaries in Bulgaria. Then, instead of launching into several paragraphs of refutation of only the last of these—the Filioque—he refutes each practice briefly in the order in which he first mentioned them. The Filioque gets no longer or broader treatment than any of the others, and this section of the letter now takes a form familiar to readers of anti-Latin polemic from a later period.[17]

Paul Speck and I are not the only ones to see the longer Filioque refutation as somehow separate from the rest of the text; medieval scribes and anti-Latin polemicists saw it, too. To understand this, it helps to be familiar with the ways in which antiheretical texts circulate. A Byzantine polemicist who wished to put together a collection of arguments might choose excerpts from a number of different texts. Dramatic changes of genre and style, repetition and even contradiction in the content, do not seem to bother such compilers. The only necessary connection between the various pieces is the subject: in these cases, the heresy or the heretics being attacked. For example, Michael Keroularios, patriarch of Constantinople (1043–58), wrote a letter to Peter III, patriarch of Antioch (1052–56) in 1054, in which he listed a number of Latin errors.[18] That letter began with Keroularios's version of relations between the papacy and Constantinople before the visit of papal legates in 1053–54; went on to relate some of the behavior of those legates; asked the patriarch of Antioch to admonish the patriarchs of Jerusalem and Alexandria if, as Keroularios had heard, they were concelebrating with Latins who used unleavened bread in the Eucharist; congratulated the Antiochene on a recent treatise he had written against the use of unleavened bread; and only then launched into his long list of the errors of the Latins. This letter circulated as a whole, but not widely. What did circulate widely and was considered an expandable and adaptable text by later antiheretical writers was the list of Latin errors, extracted from its context in the letter and usually not attributed to Keroularios.[19]

The same thing happens to the Filioque section of Photios's Ep. 2: it circulates, like Keroularios's list of Latin errors, separately from the rest of the letter. Sometimes it appears in a manuscript as a freestanding text, and not always as one attributed to Photios. At other times it appears in the midst of longer texts, as it does in the so-called *Mystagogia* of Photios (more on that in chapter 5). This does not, of course, mean that the text in question was not originally part of a letter by Photios, but it does increase the likelihood that, as a freestanding piece, it was combined with other material to make up this particular "letter," Ep. 2.

Speck outlined further arguments for the composite nature of Ep. 2. As mentioned above, the letter says there has been a synod, then calls for a synod, and is internally inconsistent about the purpose of the synod its author is summoning. It is allegedly an encyclical letter to the eastern patriarchs, but the formulae we expect in such a letter are either missing or very oddly placed.[20] The conversion of the Rus mentioned in the letter is anachronistic (said conversion is given different dates by different people, but none of them is as early as 867), unless it refers to some small group of them for whom we have no further evidence. Speck doubts that Photios would have made the "cheap joke" (der billige Witz) of equating heretical bishops (*episkopoi*) with men of darkness (*episkotoi*); finds the paragraphs about Italy and the Seventh Ecumenical Council out-of-place; and thinks the comment about the Armenians is also a later interpolation.[21]

Additional doubts about Ep. 2 arise from a closer look at its manuscript tradition, for it seldom circulates with the rest of Photios' letters. On the one hand, it does appear in one of the earliest manuscripts, the late ninth-century Oxford, Bodleian Library, MS Baroccianus gr. 217.[22] This manu-script's transmission of Epp. 1–248 is the basis for the modern editorial numbering of the letters. But another, probably more common collection of Photios's letters has them in a different order, transmitting Epp. 1, 9, 3–8, 10, in that order.[23] One could conclude that Ep. 2 is not in the latter collection because it was lost in the exemplar, but evidence for this is lacking. Most collections of Photios's letters simply do not include the "Encyclical to the Eastern Patriarchs." Instead, Ep. 2 circulates independently of the other letters, often with three of Photios's other works: the *Amphilochia*, the *Mystagogia*, and *Contra Manichaeos*. Interestingly, each of these other works is a composite and a re-editing of earlier material, some of it Photios's own (all of it in the *Amphilochia*), but other parts of it borrowed from the work of other authors. A detailed analysis of what these other works, along with Photios's most famous encyclopedic work, the *Bibliotheca*, tell us about the final form of Photios's works provides additional clues regarding the nature of Ep. 2. If Ep. 2 is not a letter, what is it? How was it put together? And who put it together?

The *Bibliotheca* is the earliest of these works. It is, as Photios himself entitled it, "An Inventory and Enumeration of the Books that We Have Read," compiled at the request of his brother Tarasios.[24] Tarasios asked this of his brother because Photios had been appointed by the emperor to an "embassy to the Assyrians"—a journey to meet with representatives of the Arabs in the east. This journey would separate the brothers, at least temporarily—given the hazards of such travel and diplomacy, it might separate them permanently—and Tarasios wanted something to remember his brother by while he was gone. Probably he also did not want Photios's already renowned knowledge to go with him to an early grave. The resulting "inventory" has been invaluable to scholars; if it alone of all Photios works had survived, and even if Photios had never held church office, his reputation with future generations would have been assured. Nevertheless, the *Bibliotheca* does not immediately impress the reader with its consistency and organization. Some works get only what we would call a brief bibliographical reference. Others have summaries nearly as long as the works themselves. Sometimes Photios merely summarizes a work's content; usually he adds his own appraisal, including remarks on the style. Some entries have brief biographies of their authors. Others do not. All in all, it is an odd collection, and there has been much scholarly debate about the nature of this text.

Warren Treadgold has explained a great deal of this oddity by suggesting that we take seriously what Photios himself wrote about it—that it was compiled hastily before he departed for the east.[25] This must have required considerable secretarial help. Even with such help, and perhaps more than a month to work on it, the task was monumental. To accomplish it, Photios sometimes dictated to his secretary—from his memory, from written summaries in his notes, perhaps from reference works such as a biographical dictionary available in his time. At other times he simply handed written notes to the secretary for inclusion. The work may not have been complete before he had to leave Constantinople; this would explain why the second half "is in very rough shape."[26]

All of this is only the briefest summary of Treadgold's reconstruction, and I have obviously not reproduced all of his evidence. For the purposes of this book, the important points are that Photios made extensive use of secretaries, to whom he often dictated, and that he was not averse to handing his notes over to a secretary who was then left to edit them.

Examination of another of Photios's works, written later in his life, expands this picture. The *Amphilochia* purports to be more than three hundred answers to questions posed to Photios by Amphilochios, metropolitan of Kyzikos. Perhaps it did have its roots in a question or questions that Amphilochios asked Photios about a point of scriptural exegesis, but it grew into something larger—329 questions and answers regarding scriptural exegesis (mostly), doctrine (occasionally), and church discipline (rarely). There are obvious differences between the first part of this work (questions 1–75) and the rest. The first part circulates independently in some manuscripts, is generally consistent in its numbering of the questions, and is considerably more polished. For example, each question indicates its subject at the beginning and is complete in itself. Most strikingly, none of these first seventy-five questions draws verbatim on any of Photios's other treatises or letters. Occasionally they repeat ideas found in other works, but they do not insert excerpts from those other works without significant revision. On the other hand, the second section (76–329) does not circulate with consistent numbering, does not always have a clear opening title or question, and relies throughout so closely on Photios's letters that the modern editors often do not republish the text, referring the reader instead to the edition of the letter that is the source.[27]

Photios began this work during his first exile (867–75) and completed it before Amphilochios was transferred from the metropolitanate of Kyzikos to that of Nicea (late 877 or early 878). Because we know this we can speculate about the circumstances of its composition. Perhaps when exiled from Constantinople in 867, Photios decided to pull together his thoughts on exegesis from various earlier notes, letters, and treatises. He had, to this point, published very little in the way of religious writing. He had apparently had little interest in such writing before his elevation from lay status to the patriarchate in 858, although he had never been the impious wretch his enemies sometimes portrayed.[28] After he became patriarch, he apparently grew more interested in religious writing, especially exegesis. Like Thomas à Becket, he took his ordination seriously, which meant that after he became patriarch he had considerably less leisure to read and write. So it was only when he was deposed in 867 and exiled that he could gather his thoughts. The result was the *Amphilochia,* of which he had completed questions 1–75 before he was summoned to return to the capital in 875. The other questions were not finished by him personally, but compiled by someone else. That secretary or disciple had access to the patriarch's papers and composed the rest of the answers from those. Often he took a whole letter on a topic verbatim. Photios did not polish this latter part of the work. Alternatively, we might imagine questions 76–329 in the form we have them as the research done for the project, either by Photios himself or by his amanuensis, to which Photios never had time to return.

For our purpose, then, a few points are crucial: Photios was interested and engaged in revising earlier work during his first exile. It may have been the first time in years that he had time to sit and think, read and write. One of the projects he initiated was a systematic, question-by-question explanation of difficult biblical passages—a way of setting out the principles of exegesis for Amphilochios and others. The *Amphilochia* was never finished by him, although someone thought it worth copying eventually, even in its rough form.

We now return to Ep. 2. It is no more a single letter than the *Amphilochia* is a single answer to a friend's question. Instead, Ep. 2 is a compound, revised work, put together from various earlier materials. If it has a unifying theme, it is the western church—Pope Nicholas I and the Franks. Such a theme can be stretched to include all of the letter, perhaps even the reference to the Armenians[29] and the references to iconoclasm and confirmation of Nicea 787. Photios himself may have put together such a compilation against the Frankish missionaries, as he did with the first part of the *Amphilochia*. Indeed, he may have done so at the same time, during his first exile. The eleventh-century manuscript that is one of our most important sources for Ep. 2 and the *Mystagogia*, places this letter immediately after the *Mystagogia*, with the following title: "another treatise concerning the Holy Spirit," and a marginal inscription: "deposited in the patriarcheion [patriarchal quarters] after the return from exile."[30] Or perhaps the disciple(s) who later edited and arranged his letter collection also edited this work. Regardless, there was some sort of later recognition that this was not a letter, but rather a treatise of sorts—hence the separate history of Ep. 2's transmission.

In light of this reception and transmission, it seems significant that the central paragraphs of Ep. 2, containing a more extended selection of arguments against the Filioque, circulate independently in collections of anti-Latin writings.[31] As such, these paragraphs have a life of their own. Although they are usually attributed to Photios in the manuscripts, this is not invariably the case. As discussed above, this kind of circulation is common for heresiological texts.

Author and Date

Can the Filioque arguments in this "letter" nevertheless be dated and located? Can one say anything about their author? Perhaps not precisely. I would, however, offer the following considerations. First, the text appears in a manuscript dated to the late ninth century. Second, there is no evidence that the author of the Filioque section of Ep. 2 is familiar with any of the Latin arguments defending the double procession, of which there were several circulating in the West in Photios's time. He seems to know merely that the Franks (probably in Bulgaria) are asserting double procession, from which assertion he draws what seem to him the logical—and heretical—conclusions.[32] This may argue for a date more precise than the vaguely late ninth-century manuscript. In a homily that Photios delivered on 2 March 867, he may have addressed the Latin Filioque in similar terms, again with no sign of knowledge of specific Latin arguments.[33] By the time Photios wrote to the archbishop of Aquileia in 883/4—Ep. 291, discussed in chapter 6, below—he knew some of the arguments being used by Latin authors to support the doctrine of double procession. This could mean, if the various parts of Ep. 2 are of Photian authorship, that the Filioque section was written earlier in his career than Ep. 291. Unfortunately, it could also mean merely that the author was not Photios and was ignorant of or uninterested in Latin arguments—in which case the text cannot be dated any more precisely than the manuscript.

Third, the author considers it self-evident that the addition defies the councils and the Fathers—so evident, in fact, that he gathers no specific references. Scriptural citation, too, is rare. One gets a sense of a man confident in his own position, appalled by the innovative position of his adversaries, sure-footed in the kind of theological logic that had characterized the councils. He has no conciliar pronouncements to cite against them because their theology is too new to have been addressed —but, of course, innovation is a characteristic of heresy. This kind of Greek confidence is common to the end of the empire, but especially prominent in the middle Byzantine period. Emperor Michael III (842–67), a contemporary of Photios, had written to Pope Nicholas I that Latin was "a barbarian and Scythic" language.[34] In Ep. 291, Photios says that Latin is too impoverished a language to be adequate for theology.[35] The author of the Filioque portions of Ep. 2 would agree.

If we put all of these considerations together with our knowledge of how the *Bibliotheca* and the *Amphilochia* were composed, it seems probable that Photios wrote the separate parts of Ep. 2 during his first patriarchate. They were separate pieces, perhaps from separate letters, and were combined to make a sort of collection of arguments against westerners in Bulgaria (and Russia?). This was probably done during his exile, between 867 and 885. Nevertheless, doubts about the authenticity of Ep. 2 make it impossible to use it either as evidence that Photios was especially concerned about the Filioque (beyond his concern about other Latin "errors") by 867 or as evidence that certain arguments were made by the Greeks already in 867.

The Arguments

Having listed four erroneous teachings of the Franks in Bulgaria, Ep. 2 addresses the Filioque in lines 101–7:

> Moreover, they have not only been carried to the end of transgression of the law in the aforementioned things, but also have progressed to the crown of all evils, if there is such a thing. For in addition to the aforementioned oddities they have also tried, with spurious reasoning, interpolated arguments, and an excess of impudence, to adulterate the divine and holy creed which has its impregnable strength from all the synodical and ecumenical decrees (Oh, the subtle deceptions of the Evil One!), for they have added new words [to the creed], that the Holy Spirit proceeds not from the Father alone, but also from the Son.

This introduction contains the fundamental argument of the author, so obvious to him that he can mention it only briefly, in a kind of sound-bite with connotations of great importance: the creed "has its impregnable strength from all the synodical and ecumenical decrees." Not only for Photios but for his contemporaries in the Byzantine Church this was a sufficient statement of condemnation.[36] This is yet another reason to suspect that at some point and in some text this was the whole argument against the Filioque, and that the arguments that follow in the manuscripts are from a different text and occasion.

These arguments in the middle section do not, with one exception, invoke authority. Rather, they constitute one of the earliest examples of theological arguments against the notion of double procession. The author begins with an argument that will be fundamental to anti-Filioque texts in the following centuries: to say that the Holy Spirit proceeds from the Father and the Son "introduces two causes into the Holy Trinity—the Father, cause of the Son and the Spirit; and the Son, cause of the Spirit." This constitutes the "dissolving of the monarchy into diarchy."[37] The author does not even try to demonstrate that double procession means two causes; he seems to find that point unquestionable. In his concern with this point he exemplifies the ninth-century Byzantine effort to protect the monarchy of the Father and the unity of the Godhead. This protection of single *ousia* against any theology that would seem to overemphasize the three *hypostases* is a constant theme in this literature in this period. That it shows up from the very beginning does not surprise us, but it is informative.[38] That later writers will be obliged to expand upon it also is not surprising.

Our author continues: "Why would the Spirit proceed from the Son? For if the procession from the Father is perfect (and it is perfect, because the Spirit is perfect God from perfect God), what is the procession from the Son? And why? Obviously this procession would have no purpose."[39] This is another argument that has a long life ahead of it, with much elaboration. Indeed there is some elaboration at a later point in Ep. 2.[40] Here it is stated simply, with confidence that it speaks for itself: if the Spirit is already perfect when it proceeds from the Father, why should the Son be involved?

The next argument shows similar lack of development; it too has a later life, but almost always with elaboration that clarifies its meaning. Here it is merely one of those aporetic statements designed to show that, whether he knows it or not, the opponent's position is logically absurd: "Moreover, if the Spirit proceeds from the Son as from the Father, why would the Son not be begotten of the Spirit as of the Father, so that all things would be impious in their impieties?"[41] This argument and those that follow tend to be based on two premises—one that would be accepted by his opponents and another that would not. The first is that the three persons (ὑπόστασες, *hypostases*; less often πρόσωπα, *prosôpa*) of the Godhead are distinguished from one another only by certain hypostatic properties (ἰδιῶται, *idiôtai*); everyone agrees on that. The further premise of our author, never made explicit, is that the Spirit's hypostatic property (ἰδιώτης, *idiôtês*) consists in his procession from the Father; the Son's in his being begotten of the Father. If we accept this premise, then to say that "the Spirit also proceeds from the Son, as their madness would have it," would mean a number of heretical things: it would confuse the essence or nature (οὐσία, *ousia* or φύσις, *physis*) of the Godhead with the hypostatic properties; it would confuse the hypostatic properties of the Father and the Son with one another; it would make the Spirit inferior to the Father and the Son, and more. The problem, of course, is that the advocates of double procession would *not* accept this premise. But that does not stop our author from using it as a fundamental building-block for his polemic.

He continues: to say that the Spirit proceeds from both the Father and the Son is to distinguish the Spirit

from the Father by more hypostatic properties than the Son. . . . But if the Spirit is distinguished by more differences than the Son is, then the Son would be nearer to the essence of the Father than the Spirit is. And so the audacity of Makedonios against the Spirit peeks in again, showing forth from under their costume and scenery.[42]

In other words, to profess the double procession of the Holy Spirit is to make the Spirit a lesser being than the Son, and that is Pneumatomachianism.

One of the obstacles to mutual understanding here is that the two sides often mean different things when they talk about the procession of the Holy Spirit. By procession, our author means the eternal coming-forth (πρόοδος, *proodos*) or procession (ἐκπόρευσις, *ekporeusis*) of the Spirit within the triune Godhead. The form of that procession must be unique to the Spirit if the persons of the Godhead are unique. We do not have his opponents' arguments here, of course, but if we did we would find that they are thinking of the procession as the way that the Spirit comes to the created world, his descent to this realm. That kind of coming-forth can indeed be from both the Father and the Son without confusing the persons within the Godhead. This fundamental confusion is going to run throughout the literature on the Filioque for the rest of history, although eventually it will be made explicit and dealt with more carefully than happens here.[43]

Regardless of how clearly we see such differences, to understand the logic of this author's position we must continually remind ourselves that he is thinking of that *eternal* coming-forth of the Spirit from the Father within the Godhead. In his next paragraph, he begins with this apodosis: "If all things that are common to the Father and the Son are also completely common to the Spirit—e.g., they are god, king, lord, creator, pantocrator, superessential, single, simple, incorporeal, invisible, and so on." This is a basic point of orthodox theology, shared by Romans, Franks, and Byzantines, as well as many others. There are certain traits that all three persons in the Godhead share; these are characteristics of the essence or nature of God and therefore characteristics equally of all three persons. On the other hand, there are characteristics of one person only, the hypostatic properties: the Father alone is a father, the Son alone is a son, and so on. Unstated here is the further premise: no characteristic can be common to two of the persons but not to the third. To attribute a characteristic to two persons and not to the third is to make the third person inferior to the others. Hence our author's second protasis and his apodosis: "but if the coming-forth of the Spirit is common to the Father and the Son, then the Spirit must also come forth from itself and be the principle (ἀρχή, *archê*) of itself, simultaneously both cause and caused."[44] That is, if the Father and Son are both causes of the Spirit, then the Spirit too must be a cause of the Spirit, which is logically ridiculous. All of this depends on that initial assumption that to say the Spirit proceeds from the Son is equivalent to saying that the Son is a cause of the Spirit.

The argument continues to follow this assumption. For "if being referred back to different principles is [characteristic] of the Spirit alone, how is it not [characteristic] of the Spirit alone to have its origin in more than one principle?"[45] The author is not explicit about several steps in his logic here, and it is initially difficult to do more than guess at his meaning. Fortunately, other anti-Filioque texts and other texts on the Trinity in general elaborate on this point, and we can see the steps in the argument that this author omitted. We are again dealing with the insistence on the essential unity of the Trinity. That unity requires, in the Byzantine view, that only one person of the Trinity is properly the uncaused cause (principle without a principle): the Father. To have two such principles would be to have two gods—a point, as we will see below, that ninth-century Byzantines were confronting in their anti-Islamic polemics.[46] We are also dealing with the assumption, made here and by other anti-Filioque polemicists, that the procession of the Spirit from the Son is equivalent to the Spirit being caused by the Son. Double procession of the Spirit would then mean that the Spirit alone in the Godhead is caused by more than one cause. For this author, the blasphemous nature of that conclusion is obvious, although it may be less so to us. Fortunately, later authors do elaborate, and we can perhaps see where this author's argument is heading: namely, that to have more than one cause is to be a synthesis. Since each person in the Godhead must be simple, unitary, without composition or division, to attribute two causes to the Spirit is blasphemy.

The next paragraph can be similarly opaque, but again is clearer if we detail the assumptions behind it. "Still, if they have excluded the Spirit from their innovation with respect to the Father and the Son, but the Father is joined in communion [κοινωνία, *koinônia*] with the Son according to essence, but not according to a hypostatic property, then they sever the Spirit from relationship according to essence."[47] The unpacking of this argument goes something like this: the Father and the Son are united according to essence and *not* according to hypostasis. Anything that the Father and Son share cannot be a hypostatic property but must be characteristic of the essence of the Godhead. If, according to this innovation of the Franks, the Father and the Son share the sending-forth of the Spirit, then the sending-forth of the Spirit must be characteristic of the essence of the Godhead. But the Spirit cannot share the sending-forth of the Spirit. Therefore the Father and the Son share something in essence that the Spirit does not. As a result, the Spirit is excluded from the essence of the Godhead. And that is clearly blasphemous.

Now our author, to our great but temporary relief, switches tactics, moving from logical arguments to an argument based on authority and ecclesiastical tradition:

> The Spirit proceeds from the Son. Whence have you heard this? From what sort of evangelists do you have this saying? From what sort of synod do you have this blasphemous word? Our Lord and God says, "The Spirit, who proceeds from the Father" [Jn 15:26]; but the fathers of this new blasphemy say, "The Spirit, who proceeds from the Son." Who will not plug his ears against the hyperbole of this blasphemy? This blasphemy sets itself against the Gospel, wages war against the holy synods, contradicts the blessed and holy father, Athanasios the Great; that Gregory who is acclaimed in theology; that imperial robe of the church, Basil the Great; and that golden mouth of the world, that sea of wisdom, he who is rightly called Chrysostom (Golden-mouth). Why am I even saying "this one and that one"? For this blasphemous phrase that opposes God also takes up arms against all the holy prophets, apostles, hierarchs, martyrs, and the words of the Lord himself.[48]

There is no elaboration on this point, no quotations beyond the phrase from the Gospel of John. Later authors, of course, will elaborate greatly, as we will see already in the *Mystagogia* (chapter 5). Florilegia, too, will be produced in great numbers to prove that the Fathers and councils all taught a single procession of the Holy Spirit. For this author, again, as befits an early inventor of anti-Latin polemic, the simple statement is enough.

We return to logical arguments—this time with many of the characteristics of earlier antiheretical texts. He asks the rhetorical question: "The Spirit proceeds from the Son; is this procession the same as the procession from the Father, or opposed to it?" If the procession is the same, then the hypostatic properties are confused—that is, the Father and the Son share something that can be proper to only one of them. And if it is opposed . . . ? Here we see how cleverly the author has set up a binary opposition. Logically we would say that this opposition is not necessary; the procession from the Son could be different from the procession from the Father without being opposed to it. Nevertheless, this is how he has set it up, with the result that he can now accuse the Filioquists of dualism: "How do Manes and Marcions not reveal themselves to us in this phrase, wagging their God-fighting tongues against the Father and the Son?"[49] In other words, if the Spirit proceeds from the Son in a way opposed to the procession from the Father, somehow that must mean that the Son is a second god and opposed to the Father, which would be dualism. This is a conclusion, of course, that no Latin would agree with. It is also a skilled use of a classic heresiological technique: opinions the opponent would never countenance are derived from his doctrine and then assimilated to heresies already identified and condemned.[50]

Next we get an argument made explicit that has been assumed already at different points above: "In addition, if the Son is begotten of the Father but the Spirit proceeds from the Father and the Son, the Spirit would not escape being a synthesis, since it is referred back to two causes."[51] Both Niketas Byzantios and the *Mystagogia*, to give only the early examples, will do much more with this argument, establishing by syllogisms that a single entity cannot have two causes, or that if it does one of those causes must be inferior to the other, and so on. The author of this section of Ep. 2 characteristically leaves the bald statement without elaboration.

We move then to another argument that will return throughout the Filioque literature:

> Moreover, if the Son is begotten of the Father, but the Spirit proceeds from the Father and the Son, what is the novelty concerning the Spirit except that some other entity proceeds from him? So, according to their God-fighting opinion, not three but four hypostases are introduced—no, rather, an infinite number, for the fourth brings forth for them another, and that one yet another, until they will fall into Hellenic polytheism.[52]

The assumption behind this statement is again that if the Father and the Son are both bringers-forth of another entity, then bringing-forth-another-entity must be a characteristic of the essence of the Godhead. Therefore, the Spirit must also be a bringer-forth of another entity. The argument also makes it possible to accuse the Filioquists of yet another heresy: this time, of reintroducing polytheism.

The author now returns to an argument that was already addressed earlier, although he states it a bit differently here: if the coming-forth-into-being of the Spirit is perfect or complete, what need is there for a procession from the Son? The Spirit would need to proceed from the Son only if he were in some way a synthesis of two different entities, and that is blasphemous.[53]

The next paragraph makes clear an argument that has been implicit throughout: "If everything which is not common to the omnipotent, consubstantial, and supernatural Trinity pertains to only one of the three, then, since the sending-forth of the Spirit is not common to the three, it must pertain to only one of the three." Or if they continue to argue that the procession of the Spirit pertains to the Father and the Son together, then they are saying that the procession of the Spirit is a characteristic of the essence of the Godhead, which then means that the Spirit itself cannot be part of the Godhead. "So," he concludes, "they are foremost not only among the impious but also among the mad."[54]

In the end, the Filioque portion of Ep. 2 reveals that its author knows little about Latin arguments in favor of double procession. The possible exception here is his citation of Jn 15:26, which was a common proof text among the Latins who defended double procession. Otherwise, his arguments follow the time-honored heresiological technique of using "logical" conclusions of the other side's assertions to demonstrate that their position is clearly blasphemous and ridiculous, related to previous heresies, and attributable to men who are either not of sound mind, not of sound faith, or both. We will return to these points about heresiology in the conclusion to this book.

In addition, the arguments presented in Ep. 2 are often inchoate and/or so abbreviated as to be incomprehensible without context from other anti-Filioque writers. I am not altogether sure what to make of this beyond the obvious point that this is one of the earliest series of arguments put together against the Filioque. In both the *Mystagogia* and Niketas Byzantios's *Syllogistic Chapters*, we will see expansion of these arguments; in Photios's Ep. 291 we will see elaboration of some of these arguments combined with greater awareness of the pro-Filioque arguments.

Conclusion

Ep. 2 is one of the earliest Byzantine texts to attempt to refute the Latin doctrine of double procession. Probably by Patriarch Photios, to whom it is attributed in most manuscripts, it emphasizes the "absurdity" of the Latin position, using rather loosely constructed logic and the language of earlier Trinitarian controversies. Especially in its longest section, about one hundred lines arguing against the Filioque, it has a significant impact on later anti-Latin polemic, including the *Mystagogia* (see chapter 5, below). This section is not, however, universally attributed to Photios. Thus Ep. 2 reveals both an early stage in Byzantine anti-Filioque literature and the considerable uncertainties involved in studying that stage.

NOTES

1. I have used this as a securely dated, authentic text in more than one work.

2. In what follows, I am in debt to Paul Speck, "Griechischen Quellen." Before Claudia Sode pointed me toward that article, I had reached many of the conclusions presented below, but Speck's argument was convincing and cogent when I was still struggling to put together the pieces. What follows here is a synthesis of (1) Speck's thesis and argument, (2) my own knowledge of what is likely and unlikely in ninth-century theology, (3) my own examination of the manuscript tradition, and (4) insights from other work of Sode.

3. Ep. 2, 5–12 (references throughout are to line numbers of the edition by Laourdas and Westerink).

4. Ep. 2, 13–51.

5. Ep. 2, 52–64.

6. Ep. 2, 65–107.

7. Ep. 2, 108–99; these arguments are discussed in detail below.

8. Ep. 2, 200–76.

9. Ep. 2, 277–305.

10. Ep. 2, 306–21.

11. Ep. 2, 321–41.

12. Ep. 2, 342–87.

13. Ep. 2, 388–99.

14. Speck characterizes it as "an odd hodgepodge of arguments and occasions" (ein sonderbares Sammelsurium von Argumenten und Begebenheiten): "Griechischen Quellen," 355.

15. On Photios's motives for reminding his flock regularly of the dangers of iconoclasm, see Mango, "Liquidation."

16. Appendix 1, below, is an outline of the letter without lines 108–99; see also Speck's outline of the letter in "Griechischen Quellen," 354–55.

17. See Kolbaba, *Byzantine Lists*, 23–31. Reassessment of some of the later lists and of the role of this "Photian" one is going to be necessary in light of these arguments.

18. PG 120:789–94; English trans. of the list of errors in Kolbaba, *Byzantine Lists*, 23–24.

19. See Kolbaba, *Byzantine Lists*, 173–74; Kolbaba, "The Legacy of Humbert and Cerularius: The Tradition of 'The Schism of 1054' in Byzantine Texts and Manuscripts of the Twelfth and Thirteenth Centuries," in *Porphyrogenita: Essays in Honour of Julian Chrysostomides*, ed. Charalambos Dendrinos et al. (Aldershot: Ashgate, 2003), 52–53, 56.

20. Hergenroether, *Photius*, 1:650–51.

21. Speck, "Griechischen Quellen," 356.

22. See Laourdas and Westerink, 1:6–7 for details.

23. E.g., Mt. Athos, M. Iveron, 684. See Laourdas and Westerink, 1: VII–VIII for details.

24. Warren Treadgold, *The Nature of the "Bibliotheca" of Photius* (Washington, D.C.: Dumbarton Oaks, 1980), 18.

25. Treadgold, *Nature of the "Bibliotheca,"* chap. 2.

26. Treadgold, *Nature of the "Bibliotheca,"* 113.

27. Laourdas and Westerink, 4: XVI–XVII.; 5: 128–30, 264–65.

28. See Treadgold, *Nature of the "Bibliotheca,"* 99, on the religious works in the *Bibliotheca*. Of Photios as a religious man, Gilbert Dagron has spoken eloquently: "Upon reading his letters and treatises, it is not a layman promoted by chance to the patriarchate that appears, but an ardent defender of orthodoxy, an admiring disciple of the great patristic scholar and canonist Gregory Asbestas, the initiator of intense missionary activity, and a man of policy [*un homme politique*] careful to affirm the autonomy of the patriarchate against both imperial intervention and Roman authoritarianism" ("L'Église et l'État," 184). On the fate of Photios's iconophile family during iconoclasm, see Mango, "Liquidation."

29. Later Byzantine polemic routinely connected Latins and Armenians. Were they connected this early? Pope Nicholas I's summary of a Greek list of accusations brought against Latins in Bulgaria includes the accusation that Latins sacrifice a lamb at Easter—a practice of the Armenians, condemned by the seventh-century council in Trullo. This seems to suggest that Byzantines were already connecting Armenians and Latins in the ninth century, but the evidence is much too thin to skate upon.

30. As noted in Laourdas and Westerink, 1:40, *apparatus criticus* to lines 1–4, Paris, Bibliothèque nationale, ancien grec 1228, fol. 688, has the title: ἑτέρα ἔκδοσις πε(ρὶ) τοῦ ἁγίου πν(εύματο)ς. And a marginal inscription reads, ἐξεδόθ(η) ἐν τῷ π(ατ)ριαρχ(είῳ) μ(ε)τ(ὰ) τὴν ἐπάνοδ(ον) τῆς ἐξορίας.

31. E.g., Rome, Biblioteca Vallicelliana, MS graecus 12 (B 53), fols. 166v–68r. E. Martini, *Catalogo di manoscritti greci esistenti nelle biblioteche italiane*, vol. 2, *Catalogus codicum graecorum qui in Bibliotheca Vallicellana Romae adservantur* (Milan: Ulrico Hoepli, 1902), 21–25, item 19.

32. Haugh, *Photius and the Carolingians*, 97, 169.

33. See the discussion in *The Homilies of Photius, Patriarch of Constantinople*, intro., trans., comm. Cyril Mango (Cambridge, Mass.: Harvard University Press, 1958), 21–22. Greek text, 21: οὔτε τοῦ υἱοῦ τὴν ἐκπόρευσιν τοῦ πνεύματος συγκληρουμένου; English trans., 276: "nor the Son having a share in the procession of the Ghost."

34. Ernst Dümmler, ed., *Epistolae Karolini Aevi*, MGH Epp. VI (Berlin, 1825), letter 88, p. 459. A portion of this passage is trans. by Bishop, *Nicholas I*, 114–15: "Consider that it is ridiculous to be called Emperor of the Romans, and yet not know the Roman language. . . . Here in the beginning of your letter you call yourself Emperor of the Romans, and yet do not fear to call the Roman language barbarous. . . . Therefore be silent about calling yourself a Roman emperor, since according to you those of whom you claim you are Emperor are barbarians."

35. Ep. 291, 75–80.

36. For a fuller discussion of this generation and the importance of the Seven Ecumenical Councils, see the conclusion to this book.

37. Ep. 2, 110–14.

38. For further discussion of this issue, including its connection to anti-Islamic polemic, see chapter 7 and the conclusion to this book.

39. Ep. 2, 115–17.

40. Ep. 2, 139–40.

41. Ep. 2, 118–21.

42. Ep. 2, 122–31.

43. In the late eleventh century, for example, Theophylact of Ohrid notes that the Latin language may have no way to distinguish between the procession of the Spirit from the Father within the Godhead and his being-sent from the Son to creation: Προσλαλιά τινι τῶν ὁμιλητῶν περὶ ὧν ἐγκαλοῦνται Λατῖνοι [Response to one of his students regarding accusations against the Latins], ed. P. Gautier, *Théophylacte d'Achrida. Discours, traités, poésies. Introduction, texte, traduction et notes* (Thessaloniki: Association de recherches byzantines, 1980), pars. 5, 7; pp. 253–55, 257. In fact, this is classic Greek condescension: Latin does have two words—*processio* and *missio*—that could be used to make the distinction.

44. Ep. 2, 133–38.

45. Ep. 2, 139–40.

46. See chapter 7, below.

47. Ep. 2, 141–44.

48. Ep. 2, 145–59.

49. Ep. 2, 160–65.

50. A few of the innumerable examples can be found in Le Boulluec, *La notion*, 332–60.

51. Ep. 2, 166–68.

52. Ep. 2, 169–74.

53. Ep. 2, 175–80.

54. Ep. 2, 181–92.

CHAPTER 5

The "Treatise regarding the Mystagogia of the Holy Spirit"

Although the *Logos peri tes tou agiou pneumatos Mystagogias* (the *Mystagogia*) has been accepted as Photios's work and discussed as a single piece of datable theological reasoning by a single author for many centuries, it is in fact a much more complicated text than that. While some of its complex history cannot be recovered, it is still crucial to recognize the *Mystagogia* as a composite work, based on earlier treatises against the Latin doctrine of double procession of the Holy Spirit.

The first hint that it is not simply the original work of a single person is that its preface says so: "The arguments by which the arrogance of those men who strive against the truth with unrighteousness[1] are refuted are scattered in many lengthy treatises. Since your most proper and God-loving zeal has begged that a kind of synopsis or outline be made of those arguments, if divine providence looks upon us kindly, may the accomplishment of what you request be not unworthy of your divine desire."[2] One could choose not to believe this author, for the existence of a late ninth- or early tenth-century manuscript makes his text one of the earliest extant treatises against the Filioque. On the face of it, it seems unlikely that he had "many lengthy treatises" to consult. Nevertheless, his text bears out his claim. Places where he ended his use of one source and began to use another are obvious. Moreover, when one analyzes the textual divisions that these seams imply it becomes possible to describe, at least in rough outline, what the source texts looked like. Since those sources would then be among the earliest—if not *the* earliest—examples of Greek treatises against the Latin addition to the creed, this is important. In fact, we can disentangle one exegetical source and another theological source or sources, each characterized by its own ways of approaching the question of double procession, its own tone, and its own sense of audience.

The Textual Tradition—Seams

I have analyzed each chapter of the text, as well as groups of chapters, in terms of several criteria—some more important than others. I will not burden the reader with all of these; what I include here will be burden enough. We can see the seams between different sources of this text, as well as ways that certain groups of chapters seem to fit together, if we look at the following criteria. I will deal with them in order (roughly) of importance.

1. Some chapters are addressed to the opponent/Filioquist; others to an ally.

2. Some chapters deal entirely with definitions of Trinitarian and Christological terms, and with proving that the Filioquist position is untenable in terms of the church's teaching about three persons in one essence, and the properties of each; others deal entirely with exegesis of scriptural terms and/or discussion of patristic, conciliar, and even papal tradition.

3. Some chapters use the verb μυσταγωγέω/*mystagôgeô*, the noun μυσταγωγία/*mystagôgia*, or, in one case, the noun μυσταγωγός/*mystagôgos*; others do not.

4. After establishing some rough divisions of the text, based on these criteria, we will see that those divisions often correspond to a difference of opinion in the manuscripts about how to divide the text and number its chapters.

Finally, we will look in more detail at the sections that result, and I will argue that we have at least three (probably more) sources whose characteristics we can roughly outline.

1. THE ADDRESSEE

The most striking indicator of a seam in the text is a change in its addressee. Some paragraphs are addressed to the "you" of the preface or someone like him—that is, to another Greek who wants to know how to refute the Latins. In these passages, the Latins, the heretics, the enemies, are referred to in the third person. Written for "us," the text discusses "them" and "their" error. These sections are full of lamentation and denunciation in the third person, "O depth of impiety! . . . It is necessary, it seems, that these men who dare all things should not stop even at such an unbearable attack upon God."[3] In contrast, other sections of the text are addressed to a Latin "you," the imagined opponent who teaches double procession of the Holy Spirit. These sections are also full of lamentation, but this time the denunciations are more hortatory, and in the second person: "When you blaspheme with your monstrous contradiction of the enhypostatic and unalterable truth, how will you not be liable to judgment?"[4]

The places where the text switches from one addressee to the other are quite obvious, even disorienting. The reader stops, re-reads, wonders if she parsed the verb incorrectly. But, no, the author has really changed from second- to third-person heretics, or vice versa, abruptly and without warning. For example, after the preface discussed above, addressed to the pious and God-fearing "you" who requested the work, the first chapter reads,

> Above all, the words of the Lord himself are against them, like a piercing arrow that cannot be escaped, thundering down upon and utterly destroying every wild beast and every fox. Which words? The ones where He says that the Spirit proceeds from the Father. The Son mystically teaches that the Spirit proceeds from the Father. Do you seek still another to initiate you, to make you perfect—no, rather, to perfect your impiety—and to promulgate the myth that the Spirit proceeds from the Son?[5]

"The words of the Lord are against *them*" but "*you* seek" encouragement for your impiety? Is this a text written for an ally or an opponent?

What are we to make of these changes? Hergenroether surmised that Photios was both writing to a friend and occasionally imagining his opponent standing before him.[6] This would follow a known pattern in anti-heretical texts. Take, for example, Epiphanius of Salamis, in his famous *Panarion*, a "medicine bag" against various heresies. In his discussion of Noetians (usually labeled as modal monarchianists), he moves several times from clear-cut description of their beliefs to rhetorical address of Noetius, the founder of the sect: "And now your brainless argument has completely collapsed, Brainy!"[7] Closer to Photios's own time and more relevant to this book is the example of Niketas Byzantios, who also sometimes poses questions addressed to an imaginary opponent. This may be what happens at times in the *Mystagogia*—a kind of brief rhetorical address to the idiotic opponent—but at other times the direct address to the opponent is too central to the meaning and spirit of the passage to be dismissed as merely rhetorical. Moreover, the contrast between the sections addressed explicitly to "you, my friend" and those addressed to "you, my opponent" goes beyond the mode of address.

2. THE CONTENT

Closer scrutiny of these places where the addressee changes reveals that other features of the text are unusual in the same places. Take, for example, chapters 3–4 and 6–19. All are addressed to an ally and they speak consistently of "their impiety and their rebellion against God."[8] In chapter 10 the author pronounces it "dreadful that we have allowed their blasphemy to lead us onward to these conclusions."[9] In chapter 18 he calls his opponents "men who dare all things," who do "not stop even at such an unbearable attack upon God."[10] At the beginning of chapter 20, however, the addressee changes. Instead of addressing an ally, the author addresses his opponents: "From whom would you conceal that you flee to the word of the Savior not so that you might find an advocate, but so that you might accuse the Lord Himself, the ageless font of all truth, of contradiction?"[11]

One notable feature of these places where the addressee changes is that the subject changes at the same place. That is, chapters 3–4 and 6–19 deal with theological issues: for example, the distinction between essence or nature and persons in the Trinity; the relationships among the three persons—Father uncaused and unbegotten, Son begotten, Spirit proceeding; cause (αἴτιος, *aitios*) and principle (ἀρχή, *archê*) in the Trinity. But in chapters 20–30 discussion of terms such as essence and person is absent, replaced by claims that Jesus himself "mystically taught" (μυσταγωγέω, *mystagôgeô*) that the Spirit proceeds from the Father. Scriptural exegesis of Johannine passages is used to show that Jesus did say that "the Spirit proceeds from the Father," and never said that "the Spirit proceeds from the Son" or "from me."

In short, with some exceptions that can be explained, chapters addressed to "you, my friend" are primarily theological; chapters addressed to "you, my opponent" are primarily exegetical—interpreting sometimes Scripture itself, sometimes patristic or conciliar tradition.

3. THE *MYSTAGOGY* OF THE HOLY SPIRIT

The use of the verb *mystagôgeô* and the nouns *mustagôgia* and *mystagôgos* correspond to two kinds of chapters: most of the time they appear in chapters addressed to "you, my opponent" and ones dealing with exegesis; rarely they appear in chapters that I hypothesize were composed or at least heavily revised by our author-compiler (e.g., chaps. 1 and 2). These words do not appear in the theological chapters.

Using these criteria to divide the text is not completely straightforward. There are chapters that switch from one addressee to the other and chapters whose subject cannot be neatly categorized. For most of the text, though, we can see a relatively straightforward division into sections. Two large groups of theological chapters, addressed to an ally and not using *mystagôgeô* or its relatives, emerge: 6–19, 31–47. Exegetical chapters, addressed to the opponent and occasionally using *mystagôgeô* or its relatives, fall into similar groups: 20–30, 48–59, 65–89. Once we have these rough divisions of the text, we can see how they coincide with disagreement in the manuscripts regarding the division of the text into numbered chapters.

4. CHAPTER NUMBERING

The manuscripts have different ways of counting chapters or arguments. For example, while Hergenroether's edition, following the fourteenth-century Vatican, Biblioteca Apostolica Vaticana, MS Vaticanus graecus 2195 (Column. XXXIV),[12] divides the arguments about exegesis into ten chapters (21–30), other manuscripts do not divide this exegetical section at all. The most notable of these manuscripts are Vatican, Biblioteca Apostolica Vaticana, MS Palatinus graecus 216; Paris, Bibliothèque nationale de France, MS ancien grec 1228; and Vatican, Biblioteca Apostolica Vaticana, MS Vaticanus graecus 1923. The first is notable because it is the earliest manuscript (C9ex-10in); the second because it is also relatively early (C11) and seems to reflect an early tradition; the last because Hergenroether used it for his edition. In these manuscripts, the text corresponding to Hergenroether's chapters 21–30 constitutes one long chapter numbered 20. Then, where Hergenroether's text begins chapter 31, these other manuscripts also resume counting shorter units of text. The result is that Hergenroether's chapter 31 equals chapter 21 in Pal. gr. 216, Vat. gr. 1923, and Paris. gr. 1228, 32 = 22, and so on.

So, too, what Hergenroether numbered as chapters 48, then 49 to 60, some manuscripts number as 38, then 1–12. In other words, a section that I suggested above was distinctively exegetical, chapters 48–59 in Hergenroether's numbering, is seen by whoever numbered the chapters in Pal. gr. 216, Vat. gr. 1923, and Paris. gr. 1228 as a separate section. And the third of the exegetical chunks of text, chapters 65–89? They are numbered in the three manuscripts from 1 to 20. I attempt to make all of this clearer in tabular form in appendix 2, below.

In conclusion, a close study of various criteria in the text and its manuscript tradition reinforces our suspicion that the text really is, as its author claimed in his preface, a compilation of earlier works. Now the questions are, what were his sources? And how did he use them?

The Textual Tradition—Sources

The best clue we have for answering these questions is the fortuitous existence of one of his sources—or perhaps of another text that used the same source. Chapters 31–37 correspond to the central paragraphs on the Filioque from Ep. 2. Whether the chapters of the *Mystagogia* are based on Ep. 2, Ep. 2 is based on the *Mystagogia*, or both are based on some common source, the overlap is unmistakable. For details see appendix 3, below. The author-compiler of the *Mystagogia* attempted to smooth the transition between this material and what precedes it, for while chapter 31 echoes some language of Ep. 2, it also differs markedly. Starting in chapter 32, however, the two texts are often identical. The compiler of the *Mystagogia* has inserted here arguments from a particular treatise, the same treatise that appears (in part? originally? at much the same time?) in Ep. 2. In doing so, he has perhaps revealed some of his modus operandi. Faced with a relatively coherent short treatise against the double procession of the Holy Spirit, he inserted it into his composition with few changes. He changed it most at the beginning and the end, where he tried to smooth the transition from a different source with a different subject and a rather different tone.

If we assume that he treated other sources similarly, we may be able to use this knowledge of his methods to reveal the other sources upon which the *Mystagogia* is based. These sources are not known to be extant, which makes an educated guess about their form and content important for an analysis of the *status questionis* at the time of Photios.

SOURCE 1

One source—hereafter called Source 1—is addressed to "you," the heretics the text refutes. It dwells on scriptural exegesis and conciliar and patristic tradition. The scribes, as we have seen, have differences of opinion about whether it should be divided into chapters. When the paragraphs with the characteristics of Source 1 are isolated—that is, if we take them out of the whole and treat them as a separate text—repetitions, abrupt transitions, changes of addressee, and so on, largely disappear. I conclude that the author-compiler of the *Mystagogia* had, among his sources, a single coherent text that dealt primarily with matters of tradition—scriptural, conciliar, and patristic. The author of this source, addressing himself to his opponents, displays little interest in theological concepts related to the one essence, three persons, and unique hypostatic properties. Instead he explicates Johannine and Pauline Scriptures in which Jesus and Paul speak to their followers about the Holy Spirit, he dismisses claims that the Latin Fathers taught double procession, and he adduces the evidence of councils and popes who have affirmed the conciliar creed of Constantinople—that is, without the Filioque. Moreover, this text has a legitimate claim to be called the *Mystagogia of the Holy Spirit*. The verb *mystagôgeô* and the noun *mystagôgia* appear ten and nine times, respectively, in Hergenroether's edition. Significantly, they occur—with two possible, ambiguous exceptions—only in the sections of the *Mystagogia* that are addressed to the author's opponent. Neither of these words is common, and the author uses them only to describe rather specific kinds of teaching: the direct teaching of the Lord as recorded in Scripture, the teaching of Paul, and the teaching of councils and acknowledged Fathers of the Church. The word *Mystagogia* as the title of the extant text is, I would argue, based upon these exegetical chapters and their subject—the discussion of the *Mystagogia* of God, which is to say his own explicit revelation and his revelation through Spirit-inspired Fathers and councils. What follows is a brief synopsis of this reconstructed treatise.

Chapter 2 is the beginning. Perhaps significantly, this chapter is numbered as chapter 1 in some manuscripts. "The Son mystically teaches [*mystagôgeô*] that the Spirit proceeds from the Father. Do you seek still another to initiate you, to make you perfect—no, rather, to perfect your impiety—and to promulgate the myth that the Spirit proceeds from the Son?"[13] The rest of the chapter's high-flying rhetoric proposes that the teaching of Jesus himself, as recorded in the Scriptures, is clear about the procession of the Holy Spirit. Therefore, what can possibly be the excuse of you people who advocate double procession? What can save you if you cannot be persuaded by the Word of God Himself? Chapters 3 and 4 do not take up the subject of what Jesus "mystically taught"; they deal instead with theological questions and are not part of Source 1. Chapter 5 begins the next section of Source 1, for it picks up where chapter 2 left off. It addresses "you heretics"; it continues to introduce the topics the author of Source 1 will cover; it uses the word *mystagôgia*. And it continues the theme of authority by moving from Scripture to Fathers and then councils. (For a detailed summary of these arguments, see below.) Chapters 2 and 5 are, then, an introduction to a treatise on the *mystagôgia* of the Holy Spirit. From the structure of this introduction, the reader expects the rest of the treatise to analyze the teaching of the Scriptures, then the teaching of the councils, and then the Fathers. But chapters 6 to 19 do not deal with these topics; they return to theological reasoning and to addressing an ally about "their" false teaching. This section is not part of Source 1; I will return to it below. Instead, chapter 20 logically follows chapter 5: it begins with the next statement addressed to "you" heretics and continues the exegetical method of Source 1.[14] Chapter 30 ends with some concluding words, as if this argument were coming to a close. It is indeed an end of sorts, the end of the exegesis of Gospel passages: "What could be more brilliantly clear than these undefiled words? What could more clearly show that 'He shall receive from mine' brings us to the person of the Father and preaches with holy words that the Spirit receives the operation of graces from the Father as a cause? . . . Therefore is not every excuse for your impiety, from whatever source, cut away? Will you still dare to contrive quibbles and falsehood against the truth or to scheme against your own salvation?"[15] So far, then, Source 1 has an introduction (chapters 2 and 5) that outlines the subjects of the treatise—"the Lord's own words," the writings of Paul, the councils, the Fathers. Then it has a section of Gospel exegesis (chapters 20–30). All of these chapters are addressed to the author's opponents.

In the middle of chapter 31 the text has another seam—a return to addressing the author's ally, a return to theological discussion, and the beginning of the section that corresponds to Ep. 2. Again, these chapters are not a part of Source 1 and are discussed in detail below. In chapter 46 the author-compiler again addresses his opponent, and the text shows some signs of confusion and patching, as it did in chapters 30 and 31. But chapter 46 has more than change of addressee to mark it as a return to Source 1. Before the seam in chapter 30, Source 1 was discussing the implications of this scriptural exegesis for the person (πϱόσωπον, *prosôpon*) of the Father: "'He shall receive from mine' brings us to the Father's person." Chapter 46 not only returns us to exegesis, but also picks up the discussion of the theological implications of the preceding Gospel passages:

> For these and similar reasons, then, you ought—even if belatedly—to receive again an awareness of your impieties, join together in thought with the catholic and apostolic Church instead of your much-deluded superstition, be purely initiated into piety, and learn again how to believe with all your mind and with undoubting understanding that each person of the consubstantial and divinely ruling Trinity is, according to a logic beyond understanding (ἀφϱάστῳ λόγῳ), joined together in an inseparable communion of nature, while also, according to the logic of person (τὸν τῆς ὑποστάσεως λόγον), each preserves, with respect to one another, the unchanging character of the hypostatic properties.[16]

The passage chosen for exegesis at this point is Galatians 4:6: "God has sent the Spirit of his Son into your hearts crying, 'Abba, Father'." This exegesis, concerned to show that "the Spirit of the Son" does not mean the same thing as "the Spirit that proceeds from the Son," continues through chapter 59. Finally, the scribes again saw some sort of separate block of material here, sometimes numbering chapters 49–58 as chapters 1–12.

At chapters 60–61[17] there is another break between Source 1 and another source or sources, but it is not as abrupt or obvious as the break at chapter 20. While it continues to analyze what it means to call the Spirit "of the Son," the addressee is an ally and the discussion is more theological and less scripturally based. I suspect that, although their location here makes sense in terms of subject, these chapters were originally part of a different work or were added by the final author-compiler of the text as we have it.

Chapter 65 returns to authority[18] and it follows the outline we might have expected from the introductory matter in chapters 2 and 5: namely, first we had Jesus' own statements; then other Scripture; and now the teaching of the Fathers. It is difficult to sort out sources here: the subject for chapters 65–68 is clearly the authority of the Fathers, but the addressee is inconsistent. Confusion here about the addressee and more than the usual amount of repetition possibly indicate a conflation of two or more sources. Still, the author of Source 1, who is concerned primarily with exegesis and authority, is dominant here, and he mostly addresses his opponents. Chapters 69 to 89[19] are then consistently addressed to an opponent and continue discussion of the Fathers, up to and including relatively recent popes. What Hergenroether numbers chapters 67–84 some other manuscripts number 1–20. From chapter 85 on, material from Source 1 has again been combined in some way with other material. Chapter 90 introduces a series of arguments—some repeating the earlier material in the *Mystagogia*, some new—that seems to have been tacked on to the end. This continues to chapter 95.[20] Chapter 96 is a closing address to the same person as chapter 1.[21]

In sum, Source 1 comprised a series of arguments against the Filioque based primarily on citing Scripture and tradition. Its author assumed that it was enough to point out that no Scripture, no Fathers, no councils, and no popes (including quite recent ones) proclaimed that the Holy Spirit proceeded from the Son. It is an argument from silence—none of them said the Holy Spirit did *not* proceed from the Son, either—and it will never convince the other side. Nevertheless, it will also become venerable, the basis for one stream of Greek Orthodox thinking about the Filioque down to the present. Chapter 95 is the rhetorical conclusion to this argument:

> But you still do not wish to see what sort of precipices you are cast over and what sort of pits of the soul's destruction you are thrown into by your unwillingness to be persuaded by Christ or his disciples, to follow the ecumenical councils, or to pay attention to logical teachings—even those drawn from the holy Scriptures. Rather, you have accused our shared Lord, slandered the noble Paul, risen in rebellion against the holy and ecumenical councils, and disparaged the Fathers. Banishing your own archpriests and Fathers, who are truly Fathers, from your mind, you consign them to the ravens, and you are shamefully silent about reasonable examination. And everything that is salvific for you has been swallowed up in the passion for your dangerously misleading proposition. But instead of us, let David the psalmist and ancestor of God cry out to you: "Take heed, you senseless ones among the people; you fools, when will you think?" [Ps 93:8] Otherwise, the common enemy of our race, having surrounded us with many traps, will carry off your souls "as a lion, ravenous and roaring" [Ps. 21: 13], "and there will be none to rescue you" [Ps 49:22].

Note, as in chapters 2 and 5, the implied organization of the argument: Jesus' words, Paul's words, the councils, and the Fathers.

THE OTHER SOURCES

The other source or sources used by the compiler of the *Mystagogia* are rather different and frustratingly difficult to sort out. On the one hand, they resemble one another in their emphasis on theological arguments akin to those we have already seen in Ep. 2. If the Spirit proceeds from the Son, then the Father and the Son share something (being προαγωγός/*proagôgos* or προβολή/*probolê* of the Spirit) that the Spirit does *not* share. But in the Trinity all characteristics or appellations must apply either to only one of the persons/hypostases or to all three. There can be nothing shared by two that is not shared by the third. Therefore, since to make the Son a sender-forth of the Spirit is to make the Father and Son share a characteristic (sending-forth-the-Spirit) that the Spirit does not share, it is obviously blasphemous.

On the other hand, while these chapters share a kind of theological method and central concern, they also show signs of having been patched together from other sources. The most definitive piece of evidence for this has already been discussed: the excerpt that is the same as the Filioque section of Ep. 2. There are other indications, as well. What happens if one tries to reconstruct the outline of this source or these sources? Conclusions are tentative and arguable. But, again, it seems worth pointing out possible divisions in the text and their origins. One part of these separate sources comprises the preface, the afterword, and some parts of the chapters that coincide with seams in the text. The preface and afterword are straightforward: they are the work of the person who compiled the text as it has come down to us. He promises his friend and addressee that he will bring together the arguments against the Filioque from where they are "scattered in many lengthy treatises." In the end, he laments his lack of books and secretaries, and pronounces this work the best he can do. Chapters that coincide with seams, including chapters 31, 38, and 45, often continue the subject of preceding chapters, but in markedly different ways. They often begin by addressing the heretics and end by addressing an ally, or vice versa. They often combine bits from exegetical arguments with theological ones. These are places where the author-compiler saw a connection and tried to make it clear, possibly by adding some of his own material, possibly by inserting what seemed relevant from other texts he had, probably both.

Chapters 3 and 4 seem to be united to one another and distinct from other units of the text. Sandwiched between chapter 2 and chapter 5 (which I argued above are introductory chapters for Source 1), these chapters do not begin from chapter 2's implied promise of explaining how "the Lord's own words" refute the double procession of the Holy Spirit. Instead, chapter 3's abrupt beginning suggests that an introduction, perhaps even some preliminary arguments, preceded it.

For if both the Son and the Spirit are produced from one cause, the Father—even if one comes as one proceeding and the other as one begotten—and if again the Son is producer of the Spirit (as this blasphemy proclaims), then how would the myth not follow logically that the Spirit is also the producer of the Son? For if both come forth from that cause equal in honor, and if the Son is a necessary cause of the Spirit, but the Spirit is not [a necessary cause] of the Son, would not the preservation of absolutely equal rank require each acting as cause equally for the other?[22]

Chapter 4 continues this argument, but then chapter 5 begins: an account, as chapter 2 promised, of "the Lord's own words." Other evidence, too, points to the independence of chapters 3 and 4. They appear alone in Vienna, Österreichische Nationalbibliothek, MS theol. gr. 249 (Lamb. 60), fol. 79r–v, under the name of Metrophanes of Smyrna. This is a sixteenth-century manuscript, but it may reflect some sort of earlier, independent tradition of these two chapters. There is a small but early tradition of attributing the whole of the *Mystagogia* to Metrophanes—a point I will return to below when discussing authorship.

I would adduce more examples of this sort if I thought the reader could bear it. There is more information in appendix 5, below, for the stalwart. Suffice it to say that it looks as if the author-compiler has integrated arguments from other sources much as he integrated the section related to Ep. 2. It may be impossible, however, to sort out these sources, and one does begin to worry that the differences and similarities are merely in the eye of the beholder. I hope that all will become clearer when a critical edition is achieved.

Author and Date

Was the author-compiler of the *Mystagogia* Photios himself? There is not and will never be conclusive evidence on this point, but there can be such a thing as overwhelming circumstantial evidence. The more I have studied the text and the manuscript tradition of the *Mystagogia,* and the more I have read of Photios's other works, the more reasons I have found for suspecting that he did not compile the *Mystagogia* as we have it.

Could Photios have written that prefatory statement about arguments "scattered in many lengthy treatises"? We know of only one other long treatise refuting the Latins in his time: the work of Niketas Byzantios discussed below. As noted above, Photios was himself the author of two of the first—if not the first two—attempts to refute the double procession of the Holy Spirit, and neither of those attempts could be considered lengthy, even in our terms, let alone in Byzantine terms.[23] If, on the other hand, someone a decade or so later than Photios's Ep. 291 had written this preface, he might have made precisely this claim.

Is the inclusion of the paragraphs from Ep. 2 proof that Photios wrote the *Mystagogia*? Rather the opposite. A number of points are relevant here. First, as argued in chapter 4, above, we might doubt that Photios wrote the Filioque refutation of Ep. 2. Second, even if he did write it, he nowhere else quotes himself in this way *in his polished works*. See, for example, the discussion of the composition of the *Amphilochia* in chapter 2, above; it is the *unpolished* material, perhaps compiled by someone other than Photios, that quotes earlier material. In Ep. 291, for example, he is addressing the same issues as he addressed in Ep. 2 (if indeed Ep. 2 is entirely Photios's work). But he has a different addressee, his purposes are different, and it is years later. So although he uses some of the same arguments against the double procession of the Spirit as he used—if he was the author—in Ep. 2, he does not quote himself.[24] Even if he did quote himself here, why would he do so in this piecemeal way? Would he not mention that he had made these arguments previously? Most importantly, I repeat the crucial point that the portion of Ep. 2 included in the *Mystagogia* is precisely that section that circulated independently.[25] If Photios wrote the *Mystagogia* between the end of his second patriarchate and his death, what sources would he have had available? Clearly his own two letters on the procession of the Holy Spirit would have been first and foremost. But the author of the *Mystagogia* does not use Ep. 291 in any direct way, and Ep. 2 forms the basis for only seven chapters (chaps. 31–37 out of 96) in the middle of the work. Moreover, the *Mystagogia*'s version of arguments found also in Ep. 291 are much less sophisticated than Ep. 291's versions.

What do we know about Photios's style and how it relates to this question of authorship? Photios lived during the intellectual recovery and reform that followed Byzantium's survival of the Islamic invasions and the final resolution of the iconoclast controversy in 843.[26] While the late sixth and early seventh centuries had seen a desperate struggle for survival and meaning, a period of relative peace followed in the ninth through eleventh centuries. Intellectual activity in the late eighth through early tenth centuries was focused on recovering and preserving the long heritage of Greek literature. The period saw much collection of ancient material; much copying of manuscripts in a new, faster, more legible script; much emphasis on proper grammar and vocabulary; much reformation of syntax and style. "Proper" here meant well-attested in the classics; "reformation" meant a return to classical style.

Photios was one of the leaders in this movement.[27] A prolific writer, he was, among other things, the author of both a *Lexicon*[28] and a catalogue of all the books he had read, with synopses, known as the *Bibliotheca*.[29] Among the works Photios had read and studied were classical rhetoricians and grammarians, and his style was deeply influenced not only by those works but by the classical reading list of his early education. Soaked in and saturated with classical and late antique style, Photios naturally adopted many of its ideals. The translator may despair at the intricately constructed sentences, the word-play, and other features of Byzantine style that do not translate well. But his arguments are cogent, clearly developed, and logical. They are not, of course, unassailable—we are often talking about polemical texts written by a man who is sincerely exercised by the opposition within his patriarchate of the "Ignatians," by unwarranted (in his view) interference from Rome, and by the errors Latin missionaries are teaching. Still, even his most emotional letters are carefully, even painstakingly, crafted. The *Mystagogia*, in contrast, is none of these things.

This argument alone is far from sufficient to disprove Photios's authorship. The unpolished bits of the *Amphilochia*, the *very* long letter to the Khan of Bulgaria[30]—these are examples that can be adduced of Photios not living up to his own stylistic ideals. Nevertheless, the style of the *Mystagogia* reinforces my doubts about Photian authorship.

Perhaps the most interesting and important source of doubt, however, is that the *Mystagogia* is not universally attributed to Photios in the manuscripts. Hergenroether knew this and thought it insignificant. To him it was beyond doubt that Photios had written the *Mystagogia*. He pointed to the references to Pope John VIII, the inclusion of the central paragraphs from Ep. 2, and the tradition of the manuscripts. The earliest extant manuscript that contains the *Mystagogia*—Biblioteca Apostolica Vaticana, Pal. gr. 216—dates to the late ninth century, but Hergenroether thought it was a later product. It was therefore all the easier to dismiss that manuscript's attribution of both the *Mystagogia* and some chapters against the Manichaeans *not* to Photios, as in all the other manuscripts, but to one of his bitterest enemies, Metrophanes, metropolitan of Smyrna. As Hergenroether put it, "Who would not recognize that this inscription is false, when so many other manuscripts differ?"[31] But the Palatinus manuscript is not the only one to see Metrophanes' hand in this composition. A thirteenth-century manuscript, Bologna, Biblioteca Universitaria, MS gr. 2412 (olim 585), also attributes the *Mystagogia* to Metrophanes. Modern scholars may have been unquestioning about the attribution of the *Mystagogia* in its entirety to Photios; medieval scribes were less sure.

This could have had something to do with Photios's reputation in the centuries following his death, which was *not* wrapped up with anti-Latin sentiment. As Frances Dvornik puts it, "None of the historians of the tenth century see in Photius the main author of the schism or the champion of the national Byzantine Church against Roman authority. . . . The historians do not even credit Photius with championing the Byzantine faith on the Filioque against the Latin 'heresy'."[32] Successors and disciples of Photios did not emphasize the issue. Take, for example, Photios's student Nicholas, who became patriarch of Constantinople in 901 (901–7, 912–25). Loyal to his teacher, he went into voluntary exile at the time of Photios's second deposition. Yet, as Dvornik notes, his confession of faith includes no reference to Photios's conflicts with the Latins or to the Filioque. Other disciples of Photios who wrote of him as if he had been canonized likewise did not mention anything about the Roman Church.[33] Another man who moved in these high intellectual and political circles in Constantinople, Arethas, archbishop of Caesarea in Cappadocia, is probably referring to the difference between Latins and Greeks regarding the Holy Spirit when he says, in his confession of faith upon becoming archbishop, that the Logos and the Spirit both come forth from the Father—"the one by generation and the other by procession, whatever that genesis and procession may mean."[34] The earliest known extant notice of Photios in a Synaxarion of the church dates to the tenth or eleventh century; in it, he is named as "Photios, our holy father and archbishop." A twelfth-century Synaxarion refers to him as "the miracle-worker." Again, nothing here indicates that he was remembered as defender of the faith against the Latin heresy of double procession.[35]

In later centuries, when conflict between papal legates and patriarchs of Constantinople heated up for many reasons, Photios was still not invoked, nor was the procession of the Holy Spirit much discussed. Keroularios freely borrows verbatim from Photios Ep. 2 in his own synodal edict of 1054—notably the emotional introit—but he has little interest in the Filioque. More strikingly, he does not mention Photios, nor does Humbert of Silva Candida.[36] In fact, the opening salvo in a series of polemical exchanges in 1053 and 1054 is fired by the archbishop of Bulgaria, Leo of

Ohrid.[37] If we would expect anyone both to know about the important issues dividing the churches and to raise the most important ones, it is Leo. Yet he nowhere mentions Photios, and his main grievance is with the use of unleavened bread in the western Eucharist. Photios is still missing in a series of controversial works produced between ca. 1089 and 1112: Eustratios of Nicea, Theophylact of Ohrid, John Phournes, and others, writing in some detail about the procession of the Holy Spirit, do not invoke Photios as their predecessor. Later in the twelfth century, Nikolaos of Methone seems to have used the arguments of the *Mystagogia* extensively, but he does not attribute those arguments to Photios nor invoke Photios's name.

Granted that this is an argument from silence, hazardous and shaky at the best of times, it still seems evident that tenth- to twelfth-century Byzantine theologians were barely aware of Photios's work regarding the Holy Spirit. They either did not know the work at all, as seems likely in most cases, or if they did they never acknowledged that it was by Photios. Why not? Perhaps because they did not know it as Photios's work? To whom might they have attributed it?

Metrophanes of Smyrna left only faint marks in the historical record. Born early in the ninth century, he was among the most vocal and devoted supporters of Patriarch Ignatios I and therefore one of the most committed enemies of Photios. He was exiled in 860 for his refusal to commemorate Photios as patriarch, and again in 879/80 for the same offense. As far as we know, he died without being reconciled to the patriarch—one of perhaps two men to do so. Extant is a letter to Manuel, the logothete of the drome, in which he excoriates Photios; it is one of those texts that Dvornik characterizes as "obviously inspired by hate, and unaccountable on the current assumption of purely religious fervor."[38] There is no mention in the sources of his having produced a work on the procession of the Holy Spirit, but then there is no mention in the sources of Photios having done so, either, until the twelfth century. Perhaps his scant fame and reputation as an enemy of Photios, combined with Photios's later reputation as a defender of orthodoxy, led to the transfer of credit for the *Mystagogia* from a relatively unknown figure to the great patriarch himself.

Did Metrophanes have a reason to write such a work? Perhaps. Again a great number of possibilities must be piled together, and we will never be sure. During his first exile the metropolitan of Smyrna went to Cherson, where he met and interacted with Constantine-Cyril the Philosopher and his brother Methodios. These missionaries to the Slavs were among the earliest to be aware of the Frankish use of the Filioque; Methodios is generally considered to be one of the first Byzantines to object to it. Metrophanes' name was known to both Popes John VIII and Nicholas I, and he may have traveled to Rome to plead Ignatios's case. In travels such as these, with contacts such as these, he had adequate opportunity to discover the Frankish use of the Filioque and to have a friend ask him to refute it.

Yet, after all of that, it is still possible that Photios, in his old age, asked by a friend, put together every argument he could think of against the Filioque and that he used a copy of his own (?) encyclical letter (?) to the eastern patriarchs to do so but did not have a copy of his letter to the archbishop of Aquileia. Being in a hurry, perhaps, or in his dotage, lacking secretaries and books, he did a sloppy job—did not clean up the repetitions and changes of addressee, but just stuck a bunch of stuff together and added an introduction and conclusion. It still seems unlikely that this is the case. Even with the evidence of the *Bibliotheca* and the *Amphilochia,* it seems far-fetched to imagine Photios as if he were an undergraduate with a paper due in three hours.

In the end, I think it possible, even likely, that Photios wrote a treatise against the Filioque. In fact, I would go further: I think that he wrote a treatise on the *Mystagogia of the Holy Spirit*—a work heavy on exegesis and light on theological argument. That treatise was then used, with others, to form the text as we have it now. In short, if I had to guess—an educated guess, but a guess for all that—I would say that Source 1 was written by Photios, and it is for this reason that the whole compilation came to bear his name. There are some other aspects of Source 1 that support the idea of Photian authorship. It is in Source 1, for example, that we get both an insulting reference possibly aimed at Pope Nicholas I and complimentary references to "my John"—Pope John VIII—and his successor Hadrian III. I join Dvornik and others in seeing these references as strong evidence for Photian authorship.[39]

The Arguments—Source 1

As detailed above and in appendix 5, below, Source 1 comprises chapters 2, 5, 20/21–30, 48–59, 65–68 (edited by author-compiler), 69–89.

"Above all, the words of the Lord himself are against them, like a piercing arrow that cannot be escaped."[40] The first evidence that our author adduces against the Filioque is going to come from sayings attributed directly to Jesus in the Gospels. He begins by alluding to the passage "where

He says that the Spirit proceeds from the Father" (Jn 15:26). He then
addresses an argument he attributes to his opponents. In Jn 16:15b, Jesus
says, "That is why I said the Spirit will take from what is mine and make it
known to you." The author of the *Mystagogia* claims that "you," my opponents, have taken this statement, the Spirit will "take/receive from *mine*" as
if it meant "the Spirit will receive from *me*." Moreover, you are construing
"take/receive" [*lambanô*] as synonymous with proceed [*ekporeuô*].[41] "Even
children who are just beginning their grammar" know that *ex emou* and *ex
tou emou* mean, respectively, "from me" and "from mine": "For the phrase
'from me' means the one speaking, while 'from mine' means some person
other than the one speaking." More specifically, "from mine" must mean
"another person, united by familial bonds with the speaker, but wholly
different in terms of hypostasis." From whom could the Spirit receive
anything if not from the Son? Obviously, only from the Father. So, if you
had understood the grammar correctly, you would know that what Jesus
said meant "the Spirit will receive from my Father."[42]

Now our author turns to the context of Jn 16:15b. "It is time," he writes,
"to hear from the beginning" what the Lord teaches about the Holy Spirit,
for his teaching begins earlier in the Gospel. In Jn 14:12, Jesus tells his
disciples that he is going to the Father. In Jn 16:7 he notes that his leaving
them is filling them with sorrow and tells them that they should not grieve:
"But I tell you the truth: It is for your good that I am going away. Unless I
go away, the Counselor will not come to you; but if I go, I will send him to
you." Then in Jn 16:13–15 he adds,

> But when he, the Spirit of truth, comes, he will guide you into all truth. He
> will not speak on his own; he will speak only what he hears, and he will tell
> you what is yet to come. He will bring glory to me by taking from what is
> mine and making it known to you. All that belongs to the Father is mine.
> That is why I said the Spirit will take from what is mine and make it known
> to you.[43]

Having introduced all of these passages, the author now interprets them
for his readers, stressing several basic principles of Trinitarian theology, but
not directly addressing the Latin "error" again. Only in the conclusion of
this section does he argue that the overall meaning of the passage, with its
emphasis on how the Father, Son, and Spirit are one and glorify one
another, shows clearly that when the Son says, "He will receive from mine,"
he means "from my Father." "What could more clearly show that 'He will

receive from mine' brings us to the person of the Father and that he preaches with holy words that the Spirit receives the operation [ἐνέργεια, *energeia*] of graces from the Father as a cause?"[44] The second part of this argument about Jn 16:15b, that receive and proceed are not synonyms, is hardly developed here; one sentence in chapter 21 addresses it: "For to receive something from someone for the sake of another necessity can not by any means be equated in accurate definition with procession into essence."[45]

Having finished his exegesis of Jesus' own words, the author of the *Mystagogia* now turns to the apostle Paul. The supporters of double procession, he writes, adduce Gal 4:6 as proof that they are right: "God has sent the Spirit of his Son into your hearts crying, Abba, Father." They say, "If Paul, that expert regarding right dogma, says that the Spirit proceeds from the Son, how will those who do not accept this [nevertheless] accept Paul as the sacred instructor [*mystagôgos*] of heavenly things?" First of all, the author of Source 1 writes, it is not we who impugn Paul on this point, but you. For you say that although the Lord explicitly said, "The Spirit . . . proceeds from the Father" (Jn 15:26), Paul contradicted him by saying that the Spirit proceeds from the Son.[46] In any case, you are wrong. Paul never says that the Spirit *proceeds from* the Son. He says that the Spirit is "of the Son," and "God forbid that he should be something alien!"[47] A series of chapters follow to establish the absurdity of thinking that "of the Son" and "proceeds from the Son" mean the same thing. For example, God is the Father "of the Son," but that certainly does not mean that the Father proceeds from the Son. Saying that the Spirit is "of the Son" refers to his being consubstantial with the Father and the Son. So, likewise, the Son is "of the Spirit" and the Father is "of the Son and the Spirit," and so on. Also, if the Spirit being "of" something means that he proceeds from it, what do we do about the following phrases: the Spirit is "of wisdom," "of understanding," "of knowledge," "of love," "of adoption," "of judgment," "of fullness," and so on. Clearly Paul did *not* mean that the Spirit proceeds from the Son; rather, that he is consubstantial with the Son.[48]

Having proved his point about Paul to his own satisfaction, the author now turns to the next source of authority: the Fathers. Again he begins with his opponents' argument: "They oppose Ambrose, Augustine, Jerome and some others to the teaching of the church, for they say that these men taught that the Spirit proceeds from the Son and that one ought not to accuse the holy fathers of impiety."[49] He confronts this argument in a number of ways.

First, he asks the same question he asked about the apostle Paul: Who insults the Fathers? You who say that they taught something that contradicts Jesus' own words? Or we who deny that the Fathers contradict our Lord in any matter? Obviously *you* are at fault here. Besides, *if* any of these illustrious Fathers professed that the Holy Spirit proceeded from the Son, he made a mistake. Only if he persisted in his error when corrected did he become a contumacious heretic. In bringing up his error and holding it up as doctrine, it is you who are shameful. "I do not say that what you maintain was taught plainly by them," he writes, "but even if it was, you ought to keep quiet about it, for they were only human and could fall into error as can any of us. To proclaim their error to the world is to imitate Ham, who revealed his father's nakedness—no, actually, it is worse, for Ham merely told his brothers of Noah's nakedness, while you proclaim the errors of your fathers to the world. You ought, instead, to act like the good sons of Noah, who covered their father's nakedness.[50]

Second, he questions the authenticity of their evidence: "Augustine and Jerome said that the Spirit proceeds from the Son. And how are we to receive this and give it credence when so much time has passed that their treatises may have been treated fraudulently?"[51] From the Council of Chalcedon to the Council of Nicea in 787 and on down to the fifteenth-century Council of Florence, accusations that one's opponents had forged documents, interpolated statements into patristic florilegia, and practiced other, similar kinds of mendacity, were ubiquitous. The author of Source 1 here follows a venerable tradition.

Third, you might be taking something said by one or more of the Fathers out of its historical context. Sometimes they wrote things that were, strictly speaking, not orthodox; they might do this in the heat of apologetics against the pagans, in condescension to their audience, or by overcompensating to refute heretics. For example, the apostle Paul himself told the Athenians on the acropolis that their altar "to an unknown god" was actually an acknowledgment of the god he was going to tell them about. Did he really believe this? Would Paul really have said that the one God, the God of the Jews, was somehow one of the many pagan gods? Obviously not. And then there are the Fathers: Dionysios of Alexandria, opposing Sabellius, "almost stretches out his hand to Arius"; St. Basil, condescending to his flock, holds back from proclaiming that the Holy Spirit is God.[52]

Fourth, there are your Fathers who explicitly agree with the rest of the church about the procession of the Holy Spirit. By confirming the councils, whose creeds did not have the Filioque, Pope Damasus and others maintained the orthodox faith. Pope Leo I, whose letter was the basis of the decisions of the Council of Chalcedon, through his legates, subjects to anathema any who alter the creed.[53] After other examples, the author of the *Mystagogia* adduces a story that, in various forms, will be popular with anti-Filioque writers for a long time to come:

> Recently—not even two generations have yet passed—that renowned Leo, who also did miracles for which he is glorified, removed every heretical pretext from everyone. For Latin, when professing the holy teaching of our Fathers, because the poverty of the language means it cannot stretch as broadly as the Greek, often did not accurately, purely, and appropriately fit the words to the meaning. And because the poverty of words does not allow [Latin] to interpret the meaning with accuracy, it produced a suspicion of diversity of faith in many people. Therefore, this divinely wise man had an idea—and the motivation for doing so at this point was, in addition to the aforementioned factors, the heresy which is now proclaimed freely and openly but was then whispered in the city of Rome. And this idea was to command that the Romans say the holy creed of the faith in the Greek tongue. For by this divinely inspired plan the inadequacy of the [Latin] tongue would be restored to fullness and harmony, and heterodoxy was removed from the suspicion of the pious—indeed, he quickly cut off at the root the newly sprouted pollution of the Roman polity. Therefore he not only posted notices and edicts in Rome that the sacred symbol of our faith was to be chanted in the mystic rite in the way which it had been from the beginning in synodal statements and decrees—that is, it was to be proclaimed in the Greek tongue even by those who used the tongue of the Romans—but also sent sermons and synodical letters throughout all the provinces which accept the high-priesthood and rule of the Romans on account of piety, that they were to think and to act the same.[54]

This same Pope Leo also knew that

> there were in the treasuries of the princes Peter and Paul, stored away among the other treasures from most ancient times, when piety flourished, two shields, which recorded in Greek letters and words the holy proclamation of our faith so often mentioned. He judged that these should be read aloud before the Roman people and displayed to the view of all, and many of those who saw this and read the shields are still living.[55]

This is not quite an *accurate* account of Pope Leo's interaction with the Franks (see chapter 3, above), but it shows that the Byzantines of the ninth century knew of the tension between popes and Franks on this point.

Probably the last paragraph from Source 1 follows: a reference to "my John," Pope John VIII, with whom Photios had had his differences, and to his legates sent to a council in Constantinople in 879. There the creed was recited and assented to without the Filioque. So, too, the latest pope, Hadrian, had sent Photios a letter upon his enthronement, in which he too confessed that the Holy Spirit proceeds from the Father.[56]

The Arguments—the Theological Sources

As detailed above, the remaining chapters of the *Mystagogia* are harder to characterize. It is not possible to see them as remnants of a single, integral text the way that the chapters on scriptural exegesis fit together. Moreover, they are repetitive, often elliptical in their arguments, and in general hard to follow. To get a sense of this—especially of the repetition—one has to read the text, available in a very good English translation.[57] In what follows, I outline the main arguments found in the *Mystagogia*, but I cannot over-emphasize the way in which such a summary must make the text into something it is not—it is *not* a systematic, step-by-step theological treatise. In this it contrasts greatly with Niketas Byzantios, a point I will return to in chapters 7 and 9.

There are three clusters of issues that the *Mystagogia* raises in its criticism of double procession. Because they are related to one another, and intertwined in the text itself, it is not possible to completely disconnect them. Still, for purposes of something like clarity, I will talk about the following groups. First, to say that the Spirit proceeds from the Father and the Son is to posit two causes in the Trinity. Two causes in the Trinity means two gods, which is polytheism. Second, there are various arguments about how double procession confuses the hypostases of the Trinity. That is, each person (usually *hypostasis*, rarely *prôsopon*) in the Trinity has both traits it shares with the other two (characteristics of the essence—usually *ousia*, rarely *physis* of the Godhead), and hypostatic properties that are peculiar to it (*idiôma* or *idiôtês*). Everything predicated of any one of the persons must therefore either be predicated of both of the others (and therefore an essential property of the Godhead) or be predicated of that hypostasis alone (and therefore a hypostatic property). To make the sending-forth of the Spirit common to the Father and the Son is to violate this rule, for two hypostases will share a trait not shared by the third. Third, and a logical consequence of the second, this positing of a double cause or a double producer of the Spirit makes the Spirit inferior to the Father and the Son.

Two causes or principles implies two gods, which is polytheism.

Besides the things already said, if two causes (*aitia*) are perceived in the divinely sovereign and superessential Trinity, where then is the much-hymned and God-befitting power of the monarchy? How will godless polytheism not riotously rush in? How will the superstition of Hellenic error not be reintroduced, in the cloak of Christianity, by those who dare to say these things?[58]

This argument was discussed in detail in chapter 4 above. The author of the *Mystagogia* does not give this point the crucial, central role that the author of the Filioque section of Ep. 2 does. It is neither his first argument, nor one of the most repeated and developed. Especially in comparison to Niketas Byzantios's emphasis on this issue, the *Mystagogia*'s concern about two causes is relatively muted.

Double procession confuses/mixes the hypostases.

For if whatever is common to the undifferentiated, indivisible, simple, and unitary community [of the Trinity] belongs to the Spirit and to the Father, it also pertains to the Son. Likewise it is impossible not to confess that whatever is attributed to the Spirit and the Son must also pertain to the Father. Nor indeed can anything whatever that pertains to the Son and the Father be absent from the Spirit.[59]

This is the central point around which the author of the *Mystagogia* arranges his other arguments. Sometimes, as here, he merely states this as a fundamental point of Trinitarian doctrine. At other times he expands on the point, showing that to violate this principle is to fall into heresy in various ways. For example, to attribute the procession of the Holy Spirit to both the Father and the Son is to "confuse" the hypostases. Something that is a property of only one hypostasis is made a property of another or perhaps even an essential property.[60] This can be called "Sabellianism" because, in our author's opinion, it sees the Father and the Son as really being the same hypostasis.[61] Or it can be worse: for example, if the procession of the Spirit from the Son is different from the procession of the Spirit from the Father, do we not have two opposed principles in the Godhead? And is that not what Mani and Marcion preached?[62]

Double procession implies the inferiority of the Spirit.

The author sees inferior status for the Spirit as a logical consequence of confusing the three hypostases. So, he argues, if the Father is the cause of the Son and the Spirit, and the Son is now the cause of the Spirit, then the Spirit can only be equal by being the cause of something else. What could that something else be? Is the Spirit cause of itself?[63] What nonsense! Is the Spirit cause of the Son?[64] Equal nonsense. Is the Spirit the cause of a fourth hypostasis?[65] Why not just admit that we are returning to polytheism? The alternative is to say that the Spirit is not the cause of something else in the Godhead. Then we have a different problem. The Spirit will then be inferior to the other two persons. He will be inferior simply because, by not sharing something that the Father and the Son share he is neither consubstanial with them nor equal to them.[66] He will be inferior because anything that has more than one cause is a composite, a synthesis.[67] Or—one of my favorites—by coming into being by the Son, the Spirit will be a grandson of the Father.[68]

Conclusion

The *Mystagogia* joins Ep. 2 as one of the earliest Byzantine attempts to refute the Filioque. The ideas of the author(s) of the theological source(s) differ little from those of the Filioque section of Ep. 2. Both are troubled by the same issues, although the *Mystagogia* writer is more aware of the scriptural justifications offered by the Latins than was the author of Ep. 2. That said, he still shows no great awareness of Latin theological positions and tends to follow the aporetic-logical method that characterized Ep. 2. His access to more than one previous treatise allows him to create an overwhelming accumulation of all of the arguments against a given position—a time-honored heresiologists' method. The more arguments, the more heresies to which one can compare the opponent's position, even while also decrying its "novelty."

The author of Source 1 presents a different way of approaching the question, one based primarily on exegesis of Scriptures, appeal to conciliar creeds, and the assumption that the scriptural or creedal statements that the Spirit proceeds from the Father mean *only* from the Father. Source 1 thus represents, much more clearly than the other sources, the middle-Byzantine type of conservatism. Convinced that only verbatim adherence to traditional statements of councils and Fathers can prevent strife within the church, the Byzantine authors insist on such adherence. In the eyes of this type of conservative, the Frankish addition to an ecumenical creed is, as Ep. 2 puts it, "the crown of all evils."[69]

Finally, again like Ep. 2, the *Mystagogia* has significant textual problems and therefore reinforces our uncertainty about the origins of the earliest Byzantine criticism of the Filioque

NOTES

1. Echo of Rom 1:18, "those men who hold the truth in unrighteousness."

2. PG 102:280. The claim that someone begged the heresiologist to write his refutation is a *topos*.

3. PG 102:297.

4. PG 102:300.

5. PG 102:280–81.

6. PG 102:267.

7. Epiphanius of Salamis, *Panarion*, ed. Karl Holl, *Epiphanius*, vols. 25, 31, 27 of *Die griechischen christlichen Schriftsteller der ersten drei Jahrhunderte* (Leipzig: J. C. Hinrichs, 1915, 1922, 1931–33), 57,4,12; trans. Frank Williams, *The Panarion of Epiphanius of Salamis, Books II and III,* Nag Hammadi and Manichaean Studies 36 (Leiden: Brill, 1994), 93.

8. PG 102:288.

9. PG 102:292.

10. PG 102:296.

11. PG 102:297–300.

12. Josef Hergenroether, *Praefatio* to his edition of the *Mystagogia,* PG 102:269–72.

13. PG 102:281

14. Note the full argument above for chapter 20 as one of the places where a seam in the text is obvious.

15. PG 102:312.

16. PG 102:324.

17. PG 102:340.

18. PG 102:344.

19. PG 102:348–80.

20. PG 102:384–89.

21. PG 102:389–92.

22. PG 102:281–84.

23. Daniel Callahan began and Claudia Sode finished showing that accounts of an early ninth-century Filioque controversy in Jerusalem are legendary and based largely on the work of an eleventh-century Latin forger; see Callahan, "The Problem of the 'Filioque' and the Letter from the Pilgrim Monks of the Mount of Olives to Pope Leo III and Charlemagne: Is the Letter another Forgery by Adémar of Chabannes?" *Revue bénédictine* 102 (1992): 75–134, and Sode, *Jerusalem, Konstantinopel, Rom. Die Viten des Michael Synkellos und der Brüder Theodoros und Theophanes Graptoi* (Stuttgart: Franz Steiner, 2001), 163–202.

24. See appendix 4, below, for some examples of overlapping ideas (and a few verbatim parallels) between Ep. 291 and *Mystagogia*.

25. See chapter 4, above.

26. For more on this revival and Photios's role as one of its second generation, see Nigel Wilson, *Scholars of Byzantium*, rev. ed. (London: Duckworth, 1996), 65–119; Paul Lemerle, *Le premier humanisme byzantin; notes et remarques sur enseignement et culture à Byzance des origines au Xe siècle* (Paris: Presses universitaires de France, 1971), 205–35.

27. Wilson, *Scholars*, 89: "We now come to the man who must probably be reckoned the most important figure in the history of classical studies in Byzantium. . . . To church historians he is famous as the man who widened the gulf between the Greek and Roman churches, the enduring consequences of which are enough to make him one of the leading figures in European history. His importance in the history of scholarship is of the same order."

28. *Lexicon*, ed. Christos Theodoridis, 2 vols. (letters A–M) (Berlin: de Gruyter, 1982, 1998).

29. Photios, *Bibliotheca*, ed. I. Bekker, 2 vols. (Berlin, 1824–25); Photios, *Bibliothèque*, ed. René Henry, 9 vols. (Paris: Société d'éditions les belles lettres, 1959–77). See chapter 4, above, and Treadgold, *Nature of the "Bibliotheca,"* for full discussion and bibliography. English trans. J. H. Freese, *The Library of Photius*, Transactions of Christian Literature, ser. 1, Greek Texts (London: SPCK, 1920); N. G. Wilson, *Photius, the "Bibliotheca": A Selection Translated with Notes* (London 1994).

30. Paul Speck doubts that Photios is the author of Ep. 1 to the Khan, as well; see "Die griechische Quellen," 352–53.

31. PG 102:266: "Sed tamen hanc inscriptionem quis non falsam agnoscit, quam tot alii codices refellunt?"

32. Dvornik, *Photian Schism*, 392.

33. Dvornik, *Photian Schism*, 386–88.

34. "ἥντινα δήποτε ταύτην τὴν γέννησιν ἢ τὴν ἐκπόρευσιν ἐννοεῖν": R. J. H. Jenkins, B. Laourdas, Cyril Mango, "Nine Orations of Arethas from Cod. marc. gr. 524," *Byzantinische Zeitschrift* 47 (1954): 25, lines 22–23 (repr. in Jenkins, *Studies on Byzantine History of the 9th and 10th Centuries* [London: Variorum, 1970], art. 6).

35. M. Jugie, "Le culte de Photius dans l'Église Byzantine," *Revue de l'orient chrétien*, ser. 3, 3 (1922–23): 107.

36. PG 120:789–94; Dvornik, *Photian Schism*, 392.

37. Leo of Ohrid, Letter to John of Trani, *On azymes*, PG 120:835–43. For an outline of this letter, see Mahlon H. Smith III, *And Taking Bread . . . Cerularius and the Azyme Controversy of 1054* (Paris: Éditions Beauchesne, 1978), 174. Smith's footnotes contain English translations of selected passages from this work.

38. Dvornik, *Photian Schism*, 5.

39. E.g., Dvornik, *Photian Schism*, 196 n. 2.

40. PG 102:280.

41. PG 102:300–301.

42. PG 102:301–4.

43. PG 102:304–5.

44. PG 102:305–12.

45. PG 102:300.

46. PG 102:328.

47. PG 102:328.

48. PG 102:328–37.

49. PG 102:344.

50. PG 102:344–52. On the origins of this image of Ham and Noah in heresiological texts, see Gray, "Covering the Nakedness."

51. PG 102:352.

52. PG 102:352–60.

53. PG 102:360–73.

54. PG 102:376–77.

55. PG 102:380.

56. PG 102:380–84.

57. *'On the Mystagogy of the Holy Spirit,' by Saint Photios, Patriarch of Constantinople,* trans. Holy Transfiguration Monastery (Astoria, N.Y.: Studion, 1983).

58. Quotation from chap. 11, PG 102:292; also found in various forms in chapters 12, 14, 42.

59. Chap. 6, PG 102:288; see also chaps. 9, 10, 15–19, 35–36, 46–47, 62, 64.

60. Chap. 19, PG 102:297.
61. Chaps. 9 and 15, PG 102:289, 293.
62. Chap. 35, PG 102:316.
63. Chap. 6, PG 102:288.
64. Chap. 3, PG 102:281–84.
65. Chap. 37, PG 102:318.
66. Chaps. 8, 17, 32, 34, 38, 40, 41.
67. Chaps. 4, 7, 31, 33, 43, 44, 45, 63.
68. Chap. 61, PG 102:340.
69. Ep. 2, 101–7.

CHAPTER 6

Photios's Ep. 291
"To the Archbishop of Aquileia"

The one piece written against the doctrine of the Filioque that is certainly by Photios is Ep. 291. This letter circulates in a different set of manuscripts from Ep. 2, and has neither the external nor the internal evidence needed to date it precisely.[1] Nevertheless, there is no reason to doubt its authenticity, for it is everywhere attributed to Photios and the style in which it is written is either Photian or an incredibly clever imitation.

Date and Context

Ep. 291 refers to John VIII as being "among the saints," which dates it to after that pope's death in December 882.[2] Hergenroether argues that it must have been written before the accession of Pope Hadrian III (17 May 884) because it does *not* mention him, and he is mentioned in a similar context in the *Mystagogia*. Of course, if the *Mystagogia* was not written by Photios and/or is as heavily interpolated as I have suggested above, this evidence is not conclusive.

The context of such a letter, however, seems clear. Photios returned to the patriarchal throne in 878, and from that time through the 880s he and Emperor Basil I strove to repair Byzantine relations with the bishops and rulers of Italy. According to the Venetian chronicler John the Deacon sometime around January 878 an imperial mission to the doge of Venice granted him the title of protospatharios and gave him rich gifts. In return, the doge sent bells to Constantinople for the emperor's new church.[3] In the autumn of 878 or the winter of 878–79 Photios wrote to John VIII, announcing his return to the patriarchal throne and expressing his desire to restore peace between Constantinople and Rome.[4] In the same period, he wrote to John, archbishop of Ravenna, reproaching him for lack of support during Photios's times of trouble. This may indicate that Photios had previously pursued some kind of informal alliance with western bishops who were unhappy with Nicholas I and might also explain the paragraph of Ep. 2 that refers to complaints Photios has received from certain western bishops regarding the "tyrannical" behavior of the pope.[5]

In the early months of 880, a synod in Constantinople resolved the last issues of the so-called Photian Schism. John VIII's legates and Photios agreed that the pope and the patriarch would recognize each other's suspensions, depositions, and excommunications.[6] The same council promulgated the creed without the Filioque and pronounced anathema on anyone who changed it.[7] In the aftermath of this synod, Photios wrote to John VIII and to a number of bishops in Italy.[8] To Marinus, bishop of Caere (now Cerveteri), formerly a deacon and legate to the council that condemned Photios in 869, he wrote that he wished peace, that he would repay Marinus's past injustice with friendship, and that as a token of that friendship he was sending some pieces of the True Cross, encased in gold.[9] A similar letter went to Gauderic, bishop of Velletri, also formerly an enemy.[10] To Zachary, bishop of Anagni and papal librarian, who had been a papal legate to Constantinople in 861 and had assented to the condemnation of Ignatios, Photios sent thanks for his undying support and promises of any gift he might request.[11]

This series of patriarchal letters are probably connected to Byzantine imperial actions in the west. Although evidence is more intermittent than we would like, scattered pieces of information reveal that the emperor in Constantinople was interested in the western regions around this time. In 876, the Lombard ruler of Bari asked the emperor to take over the defense of that city against Muslim raiders. Basil I responded by installing a military governor (*strategos*) there. Around 880, the same emperor probably sent a mission to the Croats and Serbs.[12] In his letter to Basil in August 880, Pope John thanked the emperor for "having sent your fleet and placed it at our service for the defence of the land of St. Peter."[13] Throughout the 880s, the Byzantine general Nikephoros Phokas led the work of reconquering Byzantine Italy—a series of campaigns that returned most of southern Italy to imperial jurisdiction. All in all, the Byzantines were deeply involved in

Italy in this period. They were making an attempt, largely successful, to return the shores of the Adriatic to imperial control.[14] All of this gave the patriarch as patriarch many reasons to seek *rapprochement* with Italian churchmen and the patriarch as imperial official strong motives for seeking peace with Italians in general.

When John VIII died in December 882, his successor was that Marinus who had been Photios's enemy. We know little of Marinus's reign, but one thing Dvornik shows clearly: the tradition that Marinus refused to announce his election to Photios and that he and Photios excommunicated one another is false, a legend propagated by Photios's enemies.[15] In fact, Photios's attempts at reconciliation seem to have borne some fruit. Not only did Marinus accept Photios as patriarch, but he also kept the previous pope's appointee as papal librarian: Zachary of Anagni, who, as we have seen, was a long-time supporter of Photios and perhaps only one representative of a "pro-Greek" party at the papal court.[16]

This, then, is the general Italian context in which Photios wrote his letter to the archbishop of Aquileia. A more specific context is also necessary. Because there were two bishops in two places claiming to be the legitimate archbishop of Aquileia, and because Photios's letter is addressed simply to the title and not to a named individual, scholars have generally been reluctant to assign the letter to one or the other of these archbishops and have disagreed when they have assigned it. To understand these arguments we must first understand the history of this contested see.[17] Around the end of the fourth or beginning of the fifth century, the province of "Venetia et Histria," which included the lagoon of Venice, was subject to the metropolitan jurisdiction of Aquileia. During the Lombard invasion of 568–69, Paulinus, bishop of Aquileia, fled to Grado, a late Roman fortress on an island in the lagoon south of Aquileia, which, like the other islands and the fringes of the Italian coast here and in Istria, remained under Byzantine control. Meanwhile, the rest of the diocese of Aquileia ended up in Lombard hands and therefore developed separately from the archbishopric on Grado. Still, there was one archbishop of Aquileia at this point—the one on Grado.[18]

Being under Byzantine rather than Lombard rule meant that the church of the lagoon operated with considerable autonomy, as did the government; both were developing toward that independent duchy of Venice so familiar in later ages. Then came yet another imperial attempt to heal some of the schisms which had followed the Council of Chalcedon. This attempt by Justinian I (527–65) resulted in the posthumous condemnation of three writers ("the Three Chapters") whose works were particularly hated by those who opposed the decisions of Chalcedon. The popes were coercively persuaded to go along with the imperial decision, and the Second Council of Constantinople in 553 sealed the decision. But some of the churches of the west were not willing to follow the popes, especially since they knew that papal consent had been coerced. Initially, both the bishop on Grado and the bishop on the mainland were among these dissenters, but Grado, under imperial rule and imperial protection, was also more vulnerable to imperial pressure. The bishops of the lagoon eventually agreed to condemn the Three Chapters and returned to communion with Rome and Constantinople. Already weakened by separate political jurisdictions, the ties between Grado and Aquileia were severed by this difference. When the metropolitan Marciano, who had been resident in Grado, died in 610, the mainland church elected one successor, an opponent of Constantinople 553 and its decisions, while the church of Grado elected another, who accepted the council and its condemnation of the Three Chapters. The see had two bishops—a schism by any definition.[19]

When, in 698 or 699, the mainland church returned to communion with Rome, this double occupation of the cathedra of Aquileia ought to have ended. It did not. By the time of Pope Gregory II (715–31), in fact, Aquileia and Grado were recognized as separate dioceses, each with its own bishop. In 723–25, Gregory defined the authority of Aquileia as coterminous with the Lombard polity (it extended "finibus . . . gentis longobardorum existentibus"), while recognizing an election to the see of Grado without protest. He referred to Grado's suffragans as "the bishops of Venetia and Istria" ("episcopi Venetiae seu Istria"). We have, then, a see of Aquileia on the Lombard mainland and a see of Grado encompassing the islands and Istria.[20]

The eighth century saw a competition between Aquileia and Grado (or, as those on Grado would have it, Old Aquileia and New Aquileia), with neither willing to recognize the other. Additional conflict resulted from the mutability of political boundaries: "finibus . . . gentis longobardorum existentibus" did not describe a well-defined and permanent border. Moreover, the Istrian Peninsula, claimed by the archbishop of Grado, was ruled first by Lombards and then by Franks, making it a place that Grado controlled with difficulty and Aquileia coveted. The next significant change occurred at the peak of Carolingian power, when the bishop of Grado seems to have accepted that he had no claims to the mainland territories now under the bishop of Aquileia. This was only practical, since the Carolingians controlled those territories and wanted them left undisturbed. In their stead, this bishop of Grado pursued greater control and recognition of his jurisdiction over Istria. He did so by choosing sides in an ongoing struggle between Carolingians and Byzantines, thereby inaugurating what Rando calls a period of strong philo-Carolingian policy. The Carolingians were successful in their expansion initially, and there were rewards for the bishop of Grado, Fortunatus. But all of his plans to root the episcopate of Grado firmly in Istria under Carolingian protection were thwarted when Byzantium and the Franks made peace at Aquisgrana in 810–14. The *status quo ante*, including Byzantine control of Venice, was restored. Fortunatus died in exile.[21]

Competition between Grado and Aquileia continued in the ninth century, exacerbated by a period of restoration and reformation in Aquileia. The beginning of this restoration dates to the reign of Charlemagne and his close relationship with Paulinus, the patriarch of Aquileia, whom he had appointed to this vital see.[22] It continued under Paulinus's successors, who attempted to make Aquileia's authority real in places where it had previously been nominal. Conflict with Byzantine Grado was inevitable. At the Synod of Mantua in 827, the archbishop of Aquileia and the other bishops of his diocese officially pronounced that the first bishop elected in Grado in 610 was illegitimate, a heretic and an ambitious *poseur* who tried to turn a *castrum* into a *civitas*, when the rightful *civitas* was Aquileia. In other words, there had never been an independent metropolitanate of Grado; the whole of it was under Aquileia, which had only one legitimate line of bishops. The same synod granted to the patriarch of Aquileia the right to ordain bishops in Istria, previously an accepted right of Grado. Theoretically, then, this synod was immensely important: it recognized the metropolitan of Aquileia; it denied the status of metropolitan to Grado; it gave Istria back to Aquileia. In fact, the situation was rather different. The popes continued to send the pallium to Grado, thereby recognizing its metropolitan status. On the other hand, one important factor did change on the ground: Istria was severed from Grado, thereby determining a future in which the see of Grado would encompass only the lagoon and its islands. Instead of being, as they used to be, the bishops "of Venezia and of Istria," the bishops of Grado became the bishops of "the metropolis of the Venetians." The see of Grado now corresponded, geographically, to the duchy of Venice. Nevertheless, its bishops continued to call themselves the archbishops of Aquileia.[23]

One final piece of information may be useful here: under that Paulinus who was a friend and client of Charlemagne, a council was held in Friuli in 796 or 797. Concerned with refutation of the ever-threatening heresy of Adoptionism, the council dealt still more with the question of the Filioque. A firm supporter of the Carolingian addition to the creed, Paulinus himself developed a justification for that addition by arguing, first, that the doctrine of double procession was correct and denial of it heresy and, second, that the addition to the creed was therefore legitimate because when the Fathers of the Ecumenical Councils forbade any addition to the creed they meant only no addition that contradicted their teaching. In fact, it was not only permitted but positively recommended that additions be made to the creed when new heresies sprung up that must be refuted, for the best way to eliminate heresy was through the creed.[24] Paulinus's arguments are interesting and have tremendous implications, but they are not our subject here. Instead, what is important to help us determine to which "archbishop of Aquileia" Photios wrote is that the archbishops of Aquileia were proponents of the Filioque. Dependent as they were upon the Franks—in fact, some of the archbishops were themselves Franks—this is no surprise.

So, when Photios wrote to the archbishop of Aquileia in 883 or 884, to whom did he write? Around the time this letter was written, Walpert was archbishop of Aquileia on the mainland, while first Pietro and then Victor II presided on Grado. Hergenroether concluded that Photios's addressee was probably Walpert, on the mainland, for three reasons.[25] First, the archbishop on the mainland was, to speak properly, the only archbishop of Aquileia, and the Byzantines knew that. Although the addressee is called "archbishop of Aquileia or Venice" in some manuscripts, these are later manuscripts, and the "or Venice" phrase is almost certainly an interpolation. Second, the patriarchs of Grado had excellent relations with Rome in this period and needed Rome's support in a struggle with the doge. Meanwhile, the archbishops of Old Aquileia were frequently in conflict with Rome and had more reason to seek a Byzantine alliance to counterbalance the popes. Finally, the archbishop and rulers of Grado/Venice were more closely connected to the Byzantines, while Walpert was the successor of Paulinus, one of the preeminent defenders of the Filioque. Therefore, Hergenroether argued, it is more likely Walpert to whom Photios wrote, since he was refuting the Franks.

The first of these points is fragile, at best. The Byzantines continued, for reasons of their own, to act as if the proper archbishop of Aquileia was the one on Grado. So, for example, the person who placed a title on Peter

of Antioch's letter to the archbishop of Grado in the middle of the eleventh
century used the following formula: "Peter, by the mercy of God Patriarch
of God's City, Great Antioch, to the Reverend Lord and our spiritual
brother, the most holy Archbishop of Grado, or rather Aquileia."[26] Since,
by the eleventh century, Grado could be considered Aquileia only in an
antiquarian sense, and yet it was so considered, Hergenroether's argument
is thin at this point.

Hergenroether's second point depends entirely on one assumption:
that Photios was, at the time he wrote Ep. 291, still in open conflict and
schism with the popes in Rome. For Hergenroether this was a given, and it
was obvious to him that Photios raised the issue of Filioque only in order to
stir up trouble. Dvornik demolished these assumptions. After 880, Photios
was in communion with the popes. He and John VIII had reconciled their
differences, and the rest of Photios's tenure as patriarch saw peace between
popes and patriarch. Moreover, the popes at this point were also opponents
of the Filioque as an addition to the creed. With the Franks and other
westerners, they believed that the doctrine of double procession was correct,
but they rebuked the Franks for adding it to the creed. Whether Photios
knew of this doctrinal point is questionable, but he certainly knew that the
Church of Rome, and probably the patriarchs of Grado, had not added the
Filioque to the creed. The natural alliance, then, would be between the
patriarch of Constantinople, the papacy, and the archbishops of Grado.

Finally, Hergenroether's argument that the letter was more likely written to the archbishop of Aquileia on the mainland because that archbishop
was a known defender of the Filioque completely ignores the most obvious
point in the letter: it is written to someone who agrees with Photios, not to
someone against whom he is arguing. The whole of Ep. 291 is an attempt
to persuade a powerful figure in the western church to join the eastern
church in speaking out against this illegitimate interpolation and all of its
implications.

Other evidence also points in the direction of Grado. Venice was
always in closer contact with and sympathy with the Byzantines than was
Old Aquileia; again the example of Peter of Antioch writing to Domenico,
patriarch of Grado, in the middle of the eleventh century might be adduced. Clearly there was a sense in Constantinople that Grado could be a
mediator of sorts between Byzantium and other western churches. Finally,
the letter reports that the ambassador of the archbishop is himself a bishop.
The patriarchs of Grado in this period routinely used their suffragan bishops as ambassadors to Constantinople.

In sum, although this is yet another of those points that cannot be proved beyond a shadow of a doubt, the weight of the evidence points overwhelmingly toward the patriarch of Grado as recipient of this letter. The recipient is, then, a relatively friendly face with both adequate reason to oppose Frankish intervention in the churches and known connections to Constantinople. At last, then, we can turn to the letter itself.

The Arguments

Given a friendly addressee in the west, the mild tone of Ep. 291 is not surprising. There are, for example, no attacks on all westerners as men of darkness. Moreover, Photios knows some of the western arguments in favor of the double procession of the Holy Spirit and addresses them directly and in a reasonable, albeit polemical, manner. The letter begins cordially. Photios greets the archbishop of Aquileia as "your blessedness" and rejoices that God has provided "lights and guides in western regions as in eastern ones" and set them "upon the height of the archiepiscopal thrones to ever lighten and illuminate the souls and minds of many." These greetings are followed by a long series of praises for the archbishop's messenger.[27] Then Photios gets to the point:

> But when we so understood your divine virtue and gloried and took pleasure in its actions, we took great hope from it for the destruction of the thing which has now come to our ears—would that it were not necessary, for it is a disease not of the body but of the soul—and we thought it necessary to utterly uncover this illness. For it has come to our ears that some of those in the West—I do not know how to say this without sorrow—either because they are not trained well in the words of the Lord, or because they have no account of the synodical definitions and dogmas, or because they overlook the precision from the synods, or because they have minds that have become hardened to such things, or I do not know how else someone would say it, nevertheless therefore—would that it were not so!—it has come to our ears that some of those in the West introduce [the idea] that the all-holy Spirit proceeds not only from God the Father, but also from the Son, and they work thence a great harm through this saying for those who are persuaded by them.[28]

Hergenroether made much of the word *now* (*nun*) in the first sentence of that paragraph. For him, it was more proof of Photios's duplicity, for

Hergenroether believed that Photios had known about and condemned the Filioque more than a decade earlier in his encyclical letter, Ep. 2. This letter characterized westerners as men of darkness and wild beasts. Now, seeking favor with western bishops in order to undermine the papacy, he pretended to have learned of Filioque only "now" or "recently." He did not want western bishops to know how vociferously he had attacked their doctrine earlier.[29] But if Ep. 2 is not to be relied upon—either in its date or in its text[30]—then we need not so rashly accuse the patriarch of dishonesty and duplicity. A skilled politician he was, surely, and eager to court members of the western hierarchy. But he was not trying to undermine the popes in this period and it may also be true that he had only recently heard of the Filioque. More likely, he may have heard only recently that the use of the Filioque in the Eucharistic creed was more widespread than the eastern Franks who were proselytizing in Bulgaria.

Considering his western audience, the opening of Photios attack on the double procession of the Spirit is a masterstroke. He invokes as his first authorities Scripture and popes. Those who advocate double procession of the Spirit, he says, battle against the Lord's own words and against the traditions of all of the great archiepiscopal thrones, including Rome. For example, two popes named Leo were opposed to the Filioque: Pope Leo I, whose letters were the foundation of the decisions of the Fourth Ecumenical Council; and Pope Leo III, who struggled mightily against attempts of some men to introduce the Filioque in Rome. So the Roman Church has always been in agreement with the rest of the churches on this issue.[31]

After more lamenting about the horrors of this "illness" that has infected the Latin Church, Photios now moves on to Scripture (John 15:26, "the Spirit, who proceeds from the Father"),[32] but does not dwell on this point, moving instead to the argument that was also the first argument of Ep. 2. To teach that the Holy Spirit proceeds from the Father and the Son is to teach two causes in the Trinity, which is a kind of polytheism. Moreover, it suggests that the Spirit would be imperfect if he proceeded from the Father alone. If the Spirit needs to proceed Filioque because he needs something from the Son, then the Spirit becomes a compound, a synthesis, imperfect (for, of course, all perfect things are simple). Or perhaps, Photios suggests, those who say that the Spirit proceeds from both the Father and the Son "would also not hesitate to say that the Spirit is a grandson. . . . For if the Son comes forth from the Father through begetting and the Spirit from the Son through procession, he is established in the rank of grandson." Then there is another problem (this one not in Ep. 2): there is no "before" or "after" in the eternal relations within the Godhead. Therefore, if the Spirit proceeds from the Son, He must do so at the same time as the Son is begotten of the Father. But if the Spirit proceeds thus, then the Spirit not only proceeds from the Son but is begotten with the Son.[33] This argument seems to become dear to Photios's heart, for he will return to it in a subsequent paragraph.

For now, though, he turns to one of the arguments made by those who advocated the Filioque. "I hear that they even dare to attack Paul and the common Lord and teacher by proposing that the divine Paul is in agreement with their own heresy. For they say that Paul was referring to procession when he said, "God has sent the Spirit of his Son, crying out in your hearts, 'Abba, Father'." [Gal. 4:6] These people are merely displaying their own ignorance, Photios writes. Paul says, "the Spirit of the Son." But why would that mean that the Spirit proceeds from the Son? If "of the Son" is equivalent to "proceeds from the Son," then the Father also proceeds from the Son, for he is consistently called "the Father of the Son." Then again, if being "of" something is the same as "proceeding from" something, then the Spirit proceeds from wisdom, from knowledge, and from power, for Scripture calls him "the Spirit of wisdom," "the Spirit of knowledge," and "the Spirit of power."[34]

Returning to questions of essence and person, Photios again raises the issue of what it does to the Spirit to say that he proceeds from two separate persons. Now, he says, we recognize that two separate persons can come forth from two other persons. Indeed, two persons can come forth from one other person, as when two children are born of the same mother. But it is utterly beyond imagination that a single person can come forth from two separate persons. So, if the Spirit comes forth from the Father and the Son, two persons, then the Spirit himself must be two persons "one proceeding from the Father and the other from the Son." That is heresy.[35]

From this point on, Ep. 291 proceeds to argue always with scriptural, patristic, or conciliar authority as the basis. It is a very different procedure from Ep. 2. To Latins who say that John 16:14 (The Spirit "will receive from mine and announce to you.") means that the Spirit proceeds from the Son, Photios replies, first, Jesus says, "He will receive," not "He will proceed." Second, Jesus says, "from mine," not "from me." It is clear to anyone who knows how to read that "receive from mine" is not equivalent to "proceed from me."[36]

Some Latins also invoke Ambrose, Augustine, Jerome, and other church fathers, drawing passages from them in which they refer to the Spirit proceeding from the Son, and saying that we must "not dishonor the Fathers by accusing them of heretical doctrine." Photios replies with an argument we have already seen in the *Mystagogia*. The Fathers, he says, sometimes did not teach with complete accuracy. They said things, under pressure of circumstances, that were not entirely correct—sometimes out of ignorance, sometimes condescending to their audience, sometimes trying to avoid harmful controversy. Sometimes they overstated their position as they attempted to refute heretics. So, out of condescension, Paul became a Jew to the Jews. So, too, Dionysios of Alexandria, fighting Sabellianism nearly crossed the line into Arianism. And so on. It is not the authority of a single Father—or even of a few Fathers—that makes a teaching accurate, for individual Fathers were only human. They erred, they slipped up. So what they relied on, and what we rely on, is the consensus of a great number of the Fathers, especially when that consensus is embodied in the creeds of the synods. And all such creeds say that the Spirit proceeds from the Father.[37]

So, the Lord himself says that the Spirit proceeds from the Father; previous popes have agreed—Leo I, Leo III, Hadrian I, John VIII and his legates.[38] All of these recited with us a creed without the Filioque; all of these subscribed to synods whose creed did not have the Filioque. If some small number of Fathers wrote that the Spirit proceeds from the Father and the Son, they erred. It is not we who insult them by saying this, but the heretics who insult them by drawing attention to it. They are like Ham, son of Noah, who, seeing his father's nakedness, went and told his brothers about it. The letter ends here with a prayer that we might all avoid Ham's sin and Ham's curse.[39] In one manuscript there is a postscript: "For a small blessing and reminder, and as a symbol of our love and affection in the Lord, we have sent pieces of the honorable and life-giving wood placed in a golden *tupos*."[40]

Conclusion

While Photios argues in Ep. 291 that the theological principle of one *ousia* in three *hypostases* necessarily eliminates double procession, he puts more emphasis on Scripture and church fathers, with special reference to the popes. His arguments resemble those of Source 1 of the *Mystagogia* more than they resemble Ep. 2 and the theological source(s) of the *Mystagogia*. This is another argument for Photios having written Source 1.

More interesting, perhaps, is the degree to which Photios now knows some of the arguments of his opponents. Again like the *Mystagogia*'s Source 1, he deals with Johannine Scripture and Galatians 4:6—both proof texts used by Ratramnus of Corbie, among others, in the ninth century. Both Haugh and Hergenroether argue that Photios had read some form of Ratramnus's work on the Holy Spirit.[41] I originally thought that a chapter of this book would be sufficient to cover the issues raised by such claims, but I have come to question almost every assertion made about knowledge of Latin, translation of Latin texts, and related issues in the ninth century. The question of what Photios knew of Latin doctrine, when, and how, is embedded in much larger questions about Greek and Latin language in Constantinople in the ninth and tenth centuries, and those larger questions deserve a book of their own. For now, I hope it suffices to say that Photios does seem to address real Latin arguments here, bracketing for the moment the question of how he knew about them.

Finally, Photios introduces a note of condescension toward Latin language and learning—a trait characteristic of middle Byzantine literature, including the *Mystagogia*, though lacking in Ep. 2. Speaking of Leo III's efforts to stop the spread of the Filioque to Rome, he writes, "so that the immaculate teaching of our piety might never in any way whatsoever be debased by a barbarous tongue, he commanded those in the west to glorify and theologize the Holy Trinity in the Hellenic tongue, just as it had been said in the beginning." In his discussion of John 16:14—the difference between "receive from mine" and "receive from me"—he says that the problem of these men is that they "neither understand the words known to all nor have in hand a way of learning them." The implication is that not knowing Greek is equivalent to not knowing "the words known to all." It is interesting to note that Byzantines seem not to have realized that this suggestion was insulting. Instead, it is most often in moderate, conciliatory works—even, as in Ep. 291, in works written to and for "Latins"—that they raise this point. They seem to see it as a way of letting the "Latins" off the hook, so to speak, exonerating them of any blame for their erroneous doctrine. They just cannot help it, poor things. "Latins," of course, were less likely to see it that way and more inclined to fulminate against Byzantine arrogance.

NOTES

1. Laourdas and Westerink, 3:VI.

2. Hergenroether, *Photius,* 2:634.

3. F. Dölger and P. Wirth, *Regesten der Kaiserurkunden des oströmischen Reiches von 565–1453,* vol. 1, *Regesten von 565–1025* (Munich, 1924; repr. Hildesheim: H. A. Gerstenberg, 1976), 501; John the Deacon, "La cronaca veneziana del diacono Giovanni," in *Cronache Veneziane antichissime,* ed. Giovanni Monticolo (Rome, 1890), 125–26.

4. Venance Grumel, *Les regestes des actes du Patriarcat de Constantinople,* vol. 1, fasc. 2–3, *AD 715–1206,* 2nd ed., ed. Jean Darrouzès (Paris: Institut français d'études byzantines, 1989), 546 [513].

5. On John of Ravenna, see Bishop, *Nicholas I,* 20–22, 307–18. On the reference in Ep. 2, see Grumel, *Regestes,* 547 [514], and Ep. 2, 321–41.

6. Grumel, *Regestes,* 551 [520].

7. Grumel, *Regestes,* 552 [521].

8. For a fuller account of these letters and their context, see Dvornik, *Photian Schism,* 202–9.

9. Grumel, *Regestes,* 554 [523]; Ep. 272, Laourdas and Westerink, 2:221–22.

10. Grumel, *Regestes,* 555 [524]; Ep. 273, Laourdas and Westerink, 2:222–23. On Gauderic, see Dvornik, *Photian Schism,* 204–5.

11. Grumel, *Regestes,* 556 [525]; Ep. 274, Laourdas and Westerink, 2:224

12. Dölger and Wirth, *Regesten der Kaiserurkunden,* 503.

13. MGH Epp. 7, Epp. Karolini Aevi 5, 229; trans. Dvornik, *Photian Schism,* 209.

14. Gay, *L'Italie méridionale,* bk. 2.

15. Dvornik, *Photian Schism,* 216–25.

16. Dvornik, *Photian Schism,* 224.

17. The following account is based primarily on Daniela Rando, *Una chiesa di frontiera. Le istituzioni ecclesiastiche veneziane nei secoli VI–XII* (Bologna: Il Mulino, 1994).

18. Rando, *Chiesa,* 13.

19. Rando, *Chiesa,* 13–14.

20. Rando, *Chiesa,* 14–15.

21. Rando, *Chiesa,* 14–18.

22. On Paulinus in general, see Carl Giannoni, *Paulinus II, Patriarch von Aquileia: Ein Beitrag zur Kirchengeschichte Österreichs im Zeitalter Karls des Grossen* (Vienna: Mayer, 1896).

23. Rando, *Chiesa*, 17–20.

24. Paulinus, Patriarch of Aquileia, *Concilium Forojuliense*, PL 99:286–87.

25. Hergenroether, *Photius*, 2:633–39. Beck, *Kirche und theologische Literatur*, refers to the letter as "to Walpert," but discusses the attribution no further.

26. PG 120:755.

27. Ep. 291, 1–34.

28. Ep. 291, 35–48.

29. Hergenroether, *Photius*, 2:634.

30. See chapter 4, above.

31. Ep. 291, 63–107.

32. Ep. 291, 108–18.

33. Ep. 291, 119–52.

34. Ep. 291, 153–81.

35. Ep. 291, 182–203.

36. Ep. 291, 204–44.

37. Ep. 291, 245–365.

38. This is a reference to the Photian Council of 879–80, held in Constantinople. At this council, the papal representatives signed a strong statement about the inviolability of the creed, in which it was clearly stated that "this Creed cannot be subtracted from, added to, altered or distorted in any way" (Mansi 17:516, cited in and translated by Haugh, *Photius and the Carolingians*, 126–27).

39. Ep. 291, 366–409.

40. Ep. 291, 410–12; Venice, Biblioteca Nazionale Marciana, MS gr. 153, fol. 194v.

41. Haugh calls Ratramnus, *Contra Graecorum opposite Romanam Ecclesiam infamantium*, PL 121:223–304, "the most ambitious and theologically significant work against the Greeks" (*Photius and the Carolingians*, 107–31). Hergenroether, *Photius*, 2:642–44.

For Those Who Skimmed Chapters 4–6

In chapter 3 I suggested that many readers would want to skip or at most skim the chapters that present the technical details of the transmission of Photios's works on the Filioque. This interlude summarizes the conclusions of those chapters for readers who took that advice.

Three works addressing the Latin addition to the creed have traditionally been attributed to Photios of Constantinople: his second letter (Ep. 2), the *Treatise Regarding the Mystagogia of the Holy Spirit* (*Mystagogia*), and letter 291 (Ep. 291). Of these, Ep. 2 and the *Mystagogia* have features which make their attribution uncertain. Ep. 2 seems to be a compilation of excerpts from several different letters or treatises, and the detailed argument against the Filioque which comprises lines 108–99 seems to have been composed separately (see appendix 1, below). These lines appear also in *Mystagogia*, chapters 31–37 (see appendix 3 and appendix 5, below). Moreover, the author of these lines reveals no knowledge of Latin arguments in favor of double procession. He uses the time-honored aporetic method to refute their theology: that is, beginning from their assertion that the Spirit proceeds from the Son he draws the "logical," blasphemous, heretical, ridiculous, and absurd conclusions from that assertion— conclusions with which no Latin theologian would agree. For these and other reasons, my conclusion is that the arguments found in Ep. 2 are very early but can be neither securely attributed to Photios nor dated to 867, the date usually given to Ep. 2.

The *Mystagogia* is a composite work, compiled from at least two, probably three, and maybe more than three sources (see appendix 5, below, for details). Its sources include Ep. 2 but not Ep. 291. Photios is probably the author of one of those sources, which is largely exegetical and traditional in content, arguing that Scripture, the Fathers, and even recent popes have taught the procession of the Spirit from the Father alone. Another source is more theological in nature, arguing that to say the Spirit proceeds from the Son is to imply two principles in the Godhead, inferiority of the Spirit, confusion of the three persons in the Trinity, and other such heresies. While the exegetical source may be from Photios's pen, the compilation as a whole is likely to be someone else's work. It is still an important text, for its existence in a late ninth- or early tenth-century manuscript makes it one of the earliest Byzantine refutations of double procession.

On the other hand, there are no reasons to question the attribution of Ep. 291 to Photios: its style, its context, and its arguments all fit the traditional attribution of the letter to the patriarch of Constantinople in the 880s. This letter reveals rather more knowledge of Latin arguments than Ep. 2 or the *Mystagogia,* as well as a clear knowledge that the papacy had not yet accepted the addition to the creed; the Filioque was still the practice of Iberian and Frankish churches, but not of Rome.

In sum, we have in these three works three of the earliest refutations of the Latin doctrine of double procession. All date to the late ninth or early tenth century. None shows extensive knowledge of Latin arguments, although Ep. 291 shows some awareness—perhaps of the arguments of the ninth-century Frankish theologian Ratramnus of Corbie. Together they reveal that the Byzantine response to the Latin addition was twofold from the beginning: first, there are various exegetical and traditional arguments based on Scripture and tradition; second, there are arguments about the relations among the three persons of the Trinity based on the language of the Trinitarian controversies of previous centuries (one *ousia,* three *hypostases,* etc.). The latter arguments especially allow these early Byzantine objectors to the Filioque to pursue the classic heresiological technique of comparing the Latins to a variety of earlier heretics: Arians, Sabellians, Pneumatomachians, and more.

With these conclusions in hand we are prepared to look at two more non-Photian texts of the ninth century that reveal Byzantine objections to the double procession of the Holy Spirit and other Latin practices.

CHAPTER 7

Niketas Byzantios's "Syllogisitc Chapters"

Ἄπαγε τῆς τοιαύτης πολυθείας ἐξ ἡμῶν τὸ βλάσφημον, ἐπειδὴ ἡμῖν
ἀρχὴ μία τὸ σεβαζόμενον καὶ εἷς Θεός.

(Far be the blasphemy of such polytheism from us, since the one revered
by us is one principle and one God.)[1]

The fourth text against the Filioque that can be securely dated to
the ninth century is by a little-known figure usually called Niketas
Byzantios.[2] One of many Niketases in the middle Byzantine period, he left
behind a body of work that coheres in style and substance. We can consequently be relatively certain of the accuracy of the attributions. His modern
fame stems primarily from his composition of some of the earliest refutations of Islam—perhaps the earliest to be composed in Greek and in
Constantinople, rather than in Syriac or Arabic and/or in Palestine, Syria,
or Persia. Allegedly in response to two letters addressed to the emperor
and patriarch by a Muslim who claimed that the superiority of his religion
could be established by reference to reason alone and by logical refutation,
Niketas composed two letters that sought to prove the superiority of
Christianity in the same terms. Later, he combined similar (and sometimes
the same) apologetic arguments with a sura-by-sura criticism of parts of the
Qur'an. All three of these works are seminal in the history of anti-Islamic
polemic, as has been detailed by both Adel-Théodore Khoury and Karl
Förstel.[3] His work is also an important witness in debates about when the
Byzantines had a Greek translation of the Qur'an.[4]

120

Less famous are Niketas's "syllogistic chapters . . . against those who impiously and atheistically add and say and teach in the holy symbol of the orthodox faith of the Christians concerning the all-holy and life-giving divine Spirit 'and in the Holy Spirit, the Lord, the Giver of Life, who proceeds from the Father and the Son'—instead of from the Father alone."[5] Regardless of its relative obscurity, however, this treatise is also one of the first of its kind, and it deserves to take its place with the *Mystagogia*—perhaps ahead of the *Mystagogia*—as one of the earliest attempts to refute the idea of the double procession of the Holy Spirit. As such, it gives us an invaluable glimpse of some of the specifically ninth-century circumstances that went into the making of Latin heretics.

The Textual Tradition

Two thirteenth-century manuscripts of this text exist.[6] Such a late date for the earliest extant manuscripts might lead to skepticism about the author-ship and dating of the piece, but the style of the treatise and some of its arguments are definitive. There can be little doubt that the author of this text is the same as the author of the anti-Islamic texts contained in Vatican, Biblioteca Apostolica Vaticana, MS Vaticanus graecus 681, which dates to the late ninth or early tenth century.[7] Specifically, the author is a skilled logician who is concerned with logical consistency rather than with literary style. As Karl Förstel, editor of the anti-Islamic texts puts it, his work has few "literary qualities," and "[a] comparison with the expositions of Photios regarding the same themes allows the narrow, purely technical character of Niketas' style to emerge clearly."[8] One might put this more positively: because Niketas eschews literary flourishes in favor of logical clarity his arguments are often lucid or even perlucid where other ninth-century texts leave us wondering. Besides his emphasis on Aristotelian logical principles, this author also relies, but not heavily, on the works of John Damascene, Gregory of Nazianzus, and Basil of Caesarea—or perhaps on a florilegium on the Holy Spirit that contains their work.[9] The most striking characteristic of his work, moreover, is an optimistic view of the potential of human reason and logical training; this optimism is so marked that his asides about the unknowable nature of God and his brief discussions of apophatic theology seem perfunctory. As Adel-Théodore Khoury puts it, "Despite his declarations about the limitations of his attempt, his tone betrays an imperturbable confidence."[10] Förstel and Khoury write about Niketas's anti-Islamic works, but their comments apply equally to his anti-Filioque treatise. From his title *Syllogistic Chapters* onward, Niketas signals his intention to show the *logical* absurdity of the Latin position. While he occasionally cites Scripture as well, he does so far less than Photios and other authors of the texts so far surveyed—especially far less than Source 1 of the *Mystagogia*.

Author and Date

About Niketas Byzantios we know very little except that he "lived in the times of the Emperor Michael [842–67], Son of Theophilos, surviving until the very reign of the Lord Emperor Leo the Wise [886–912]."[11] This places him firmly in the period after the Restoration of Orthodoxy in 843 and makes him a contemporary of Photios. In addition to the anti-Islamic works already mentioned and the treatise against the Filioque, he wrote a polemical letter against the non-Chalcedonian Armenians. It is remarkable that a figure with such important and seminal output should be otherwise unknown, but it is still virtually unquestionable that a single author, living no later than the early tenth century, wrote these works.

The Arguments

Niketas's prologue contrasts sharply with the *Mystagogia*. Far from compiling arguments from previous treatises, he implies that he was either the first or among the first to hear of the Latin doctrine of double procession. When he heard about it, he says, "I lamented, I could not bear it, and, moved by burning and divine zeal, I tried to provide for the refutation and overturning of this impiety." Yet fear at first kept him from the task—fear that he would "mutilate" dogma and be unable to sustain the argument. In the end, he proceeded because of "the impending danger from silence," but only after "having called upon the life-giving and divine Spirit himself—the Spirit concerning whom the contest has come upon us—with the Father and the Son, that the Father might favor us, the Son work with us, and the Spirit inspire us—rather, hoping that a single illumination from the single godhead might come to be." "For refutation and the overturning of this impiety, the correction of those who have fallen away from the truth, and the confirmation and assistance of those who have continued to be nourished by piety," he wrote these "syllogistic chapters."[12] Allowing for a certain authorial conceit in Niketas's implicit claim that he is the first to write on this issue, it nevertheless seems likely that his arguments throughout are his own. In terms of both style and substance, they seem to have come from the same pen, and there are no indications that he was writing with earlier treatises against the double procession of the Holy Spirit in front of him. What he did have before him were some treatises or perhaps a florilegium on the Trinity—for this the edition's critical apparatus is invaluable.

The list of things he had read conforms to the sources he cites in his anti-Islamic works, which were almost certainly written before the Filioque treatise. Challenged by Muslim accusations that the Christians had three gods, Niketas had already developed some of the arguments that he would use against the Latins. Most notable here is the point that usually strikes western theologians first: Niketas's utter insistence that there can be only one principle (ἀρχή/*archê*) in the Trinity. Whatever the possible patristic sources of this insistence—discussed briefly below in the conclusion to this book—Niketas's emphasis on a single principle comes directly from his knowledge of Muslim anti-Christian polemic. The Muslims, confronted by the Christian doctrine of a Trinity, accused the Christians of polytheism. Against them, Niketas argued that Christians recognized three persons in the Godhead, but only one principle.[13]

Niketas begins with a premise that is now familiar to us: every name and operation which belongs to the Godhead as a whole belongs to each of the three hypostases equally: for example, Lord, Emperor, Lord of Lords, Life, Light. He throws in an interesting consideration here, however, which is characteristic of his way of proceeding. He notes that there is one sense in which all of these titles and all of the human words for these operations are inadequate. In apophatic ways of talking about God, in fact, we say that he is not-Lord, not-Emperor, not-Lord of Lords, and so on. But we can leave aside these apophatic ways of talking about God, Niketas argues, because they are not about logic, but rather about the ultimate impossibility of understanding God: *apophasis* of this sort acknowledges that when we speak of the goodness or sovereignty of God, "these things belong to the divine nature but they do not wholly reveal it."[14] Niketas here distinguishes between two kinds or two levels of theology. There is a kind of theology of the unknowable things, which can only be spoken of apophatically: they are *not* like anything we know in creation. Niketas has virtually nothing to say about this level of theology after this point. Then there is a kind of theology that involves logic and human reason. On this level, Niketas insists, we *can* say true and adequate things about God. In the end, his nod to apophatic theology is rather perfunctory.

He returns then to his argument: some names and operations are equally true of all three hypostases in the one essence or nature[15] of the Trinity. Other names and operations "are said singly and separately about one of the divinely ruling persons," as when we say that the person of the Father is ungenerated, has paternity, and so on, while the Son is generated and the Spirit proceeds.[16] Finally, there are some things that are said of two persons and not of the third, but we will find that these common ways of speaking do not really mean the same thing. So, for example, the Father is uncaused while the Son and the Spirit are caused. But this does not really mean that the Son and the Spirit share some characteristic not shared with the Father, for they are caused *in different ways*—the Son is caused "as the begotten one and the son [οἶον τὸ γεννητὸν καὶ τὸ γέννημα], the Spirit as one made to proceed and sent forth [οἶον τὸ ἐκπορευτὸν καὶ πρόβλημα]."[17]

In the course of making this argument about how the Son and the Spirit are caused by the Father in different ways, Niketas has included a central tenet of his argument: that the unique person of the Spirit is characterized by its being "the one made to proceed and sent forth." It is as the person "made to proceed and sent forth" that the Spirit is distinguished from the Father and the Son. Given that both "being made to proceed" and "being sent forth" are passive characteristics, Niketas's next step is to demonstrate that only the Father or only the Son must be the actor here: only one person can cause the Spirit to proceed and send the Spirit forth. Or, as he puts it, there can be only one sender-forth (προβολεύς/*proboleus*) of the Spirit and the sending-forth (προβολή/*probolê*) of the Spirit can be a characteristic of only one person. Otherwise, if the Son shares with the Father the character of sender-forth and the characteristic of sending-forth, then the Father and the Son will share a characteristic that the Spirit does not have. Unless, of course, you are ready to say that the Spirit, too, is a sender-forth. But see the absurdity of that position: is the Spirit the sender-forth of itself? Or is the Spirit the sender-forth of some other person, which would then render the Trinity a Quaternity? The blasphemy, Niketas likes to say at the end of each argument, is obvious.[18]

What if our interlocutor should say that the Spirit is sent forth by both the Father and the Son, just as the Son and the Spirit are both caused by the Father, but in different ways? How could this be? Would the Spirit then have two sendings-forth? To say that it does is to imply that the Spirit is composite, or a synthesis in some way, and "a multitude of such absurdities follow." Here Niketas reaffirms one of his first principles: what is said to be a characteristic or operation of two persons in the Trinity *in the same way* must be a characteristic of the third. But when a characteristic or operation is said to be true of two persons, but *in different ways*, as when the Son is caused as one begotten and the Spirit as one sent forth, the statement may be true.[19]

Now, the Fathers teach us that the Father is generator of the Son and sender-forth of the Spirit. They teach, furthermore, that the Spirit proceeds from the Father and rests upon the Son, and that from the Son it is distributed and received by all creation. What if the Spirit proceeds from the Son, as these impious opponents of ours say? Well, then, the Spirit would somehow have to proceed from the Father, rest upon the Son, and proceed from the Son at the same time. This would require two Sons—one to make the Spirit proceed and one to have the Spirit resting upon him. "But if this is so, there is a son of the Son and therefore a grandson appears."[20]

If, as they say, the Spirit proceeds from the Father and the Son, does it proceed eternally and without time? Or does it proceed first from one and then from the other? If the latter, this is clearly blasphemous, for nothing in the Trinity has priority and posteriority, but all happens eternally and without time. So if the Spirit proceeds from the Father and the Son, it must do so eternally and without time. What then? Does it proceed from both as from a first cause (πρωταιτίως/*prôtaitiôs*)? If so, then their blasphemy is again obvious, for there would then be in the Trinity "two persons that are both principles and without a principle according to cause" (δύο ἀρχικαὶ καὶ ἄναρχοι κατ᾽ αἰτίαν ὑποστάσεις). To bring two uncaused causes and two principles into the Trinity is to make two gods, which is to restore polytheism.

It is worth stressing again that Niketas first developed the argument that three persons in the Trinity does not mean three principles or causes in his anti-Islamic polemic, as a defense against the Muslim charge of Christian tri-theism. So, clearly the Spirit cannot proceed from the Father and the Son, without time and eternally, as from two first causes. Then what? Do they mean that the Spirit proceeds from the Father and the Son, without time and eternally, but as from two different kinds of causes: a proximate and remote cause or a prior and secondary cause? But does not everyone agree, even in common speech, that a first cause is greater than a secondary one? Then they have introduced superiority and inferiority into the Trinity, which is anathema.[21]

So how are they going to argue that the Spirit can proceed from Father and Son, given all of the absurdities we have just demonstrated? Let us examine another possibility. Is the Spirit's sending-forth by the Father perfect or not? If not, and a further sending-forth by the Son is necessary, then neither the Father nor the Spirit is perfect. But if the Spirit's sending-forth by the Father is perfect, then there is no need of a sending-forth by the Son.[22]

Our opponent raises two more points. First, we say that the Father wills (εὐδοκέω/*eudokeô*), the Son operates (ἐνεργέω/*energeô*), and the Spirit cooperates (συνενεργέω/*sunenergeô*). Do we not imply thereby that either the Son and the Spirit share something—operation—that they do not share with the Father? Or that the Son is imperfect because he needs a cooperator (συνενεργός/*sunenergos*) while the Father shares his willing with no one? Second, what prevents the Father, who can do anything he wills, from sharing the sending-forth of the Spirit with the Son?[23] To their first question we answer as follows: when we say that the Father wills, the Son operates, and the Spirit cooperates, we are talking about operation and not essence. In their essence, all three persons do all of these things; but in their operation within creation, they are said to will, operate, and cooperate. God the Father does not need the Son's operation, nor the Son the Spirit's cooperation, but they will it thus.

To their second question we say, yes, God can do all things, *except negate himself*. The Father alone is properly cause, principle, father, and sender-forth. These things are proper to the Father's person, and therefore cannot be shared because if they were shared the Father would not be who/what he is. They also cannot be negated because they are what the Father is.[24] Again Niketas's logic is impeccable once one has accepted his premises: namely, that the sending-forth of the Spirit is one of the Father's hypostatic properties; that the sending-forth comes from a principle; that there can be only one principle in the Trinity. Given these premises, double procession of the Spirit mixes up hypostatic properties and makes two principles in the Godhead.

From this point on, many of the arguments are only slightly different versions of these points, often with additional analogies or different logical principles adduced. For example, Niketas argues again that if the Spirit proceeds from both the Father and the Son, the Spirit has two causes. Two things are blasphemous about attributing two causes to the Spirit. First, it implies that the Father was not a sufficient cause, and therefore not perfect. Second, we know that anything that has two causes must be a composite or synthesis; Niketas gives a series of examples from life. Therefore, if the Spirit has two causes, it must be a synthesis, which is unthinkable. God is One.[25] This conclusion was already reached above, on different grounds, but Niketas seems determined to offer every possible variation of his logical arguments against double procession. Similarly, Khoury has concluded regarding Niketas's *magnum opus* on the Qur'an: "We do not think that Niketas wished only to write a book of religious propaganda. Such a work would have been very much more efficacious if it had been composed in Arabic. Niketas intended to furnish, for Byzantine polemicists and all writers of religious propaganda, an official document containing all useful information about the Qur'an and the teaching of Islam."[26] In this case, too, Niketas writes more for the sake of confirming the orthodox than for converting or persuading the heretics.

It is also important to note that Niketas's way of restating some conclusions bears little resemblance to the repetition in the composite text of the *Mystagogia*. Niketas does not repeat exactly the same arguments; one may sometimes have to read a chapter more than once to see how it differs from a previous one, but the differences are always there. Moreover, transitions from one chapter to the next are smooth, and references to previous chapters are germane. When he says the equivalent of "and here is another argument," he really does introduce a new argument, building logically from the previous ones and leading into the following ones. He seeks always to show, in the words of "a certain wise man" whom he quotes in both this work and the anti-Islamic Ep. 1, "where one absurdity is given, a myriad will follow."[27]

Another of his arguments should sufficiently demonstrate the kind of repetition which Niketas practices. He has already established, by about halfway through the work, that the idea of the Son as sender-forth of the Spirit is blasphemous for various reasons: because it implies that the Father cannot send forth the Spirit perfectly on his own, and so on. In chapter 6, he begins a new series of logical propositions to prove exactly the same thing—that is that dual procession is a blasphemy—but he does so by bringing up a whole new set of issues. Let us ask our opponents, he says, how the Spirit is related to the Father. Is it to the Father inasmuch as he is father and begetter? Or is it in some other way? Obviously, they will say that it is some other way—namely by sending-forth—because if the Father were related to the Spirit as father, the Spirit would be a second son. Now, our opponents say that the Son is also sender-forth of the Spirit. Let us ask them, then, whether he is related to the Son inasmuch as the Son is son and begotten one. Or is he related to the Son in some other way? That is, is the Son related to the Spirit as sender-forth? If they say he is *not,* then obviously we are finished here: they have admitted that the Son is not sender-forth of the Spirit, and therefore that the Spirit does not proceed from the Son. But if they say that the Son *is* related to the Spirit as sender-forth, just as the Father is, then we have some new questions for them. If the Son is sender-forth of the Spirit, then the Son is both caused by the Father and a cause of the Spirit. Is he sender-forth of the Spirit as a cause? Or sender-forth of the Spirit as a caused being? If they say he is sender-forth of the Spirit as a cause, then they have posited two causes in the Godhead and made the Spirit a multi-caused being, and we have already established that that is blasphemy of the worst sort. If they say that he is sender forth of the Spirit as a caused being, and the Son is caused by generation as a son, then they are saying that the Spirit is caused by the Son inasmuch as he is a son, which makes the Spirit a grandson. We need not say more. Clearly the Holy Spirit does not proceed from the Son in the same way as the Holy Spirit proceeds from the Father. QED.[28]

Conclusions

We are fortunate to have Niketas's work to compare to the texts attributed to Photios. His attachment to logic and his skill in using it contrasts with Photios's more literary style. The resulting arguments are often clearer and more convincing. As a side benefit, Niketas's works reveal a great deal about Byzantine use of logic in the period of "the Macedonian Renaissance" or "the Age of Photios."

If only we had more precise dates for all of these texts, we might also be able to trace their possible influences on one another. For example, Niketas's argument that to posit the double procession of the Spirit is to make him the Father's grandson is the clearest and most logical statement of an argument that appears also in Ep. 291 and the *Mystagogia.* Who made this argument earlier? We simply cannot know at this point, but it does seem that an exchange of ideas was taking place in Constantinople.

Most importantly, Niketas's person and work embody a crucial link between the Byzantine invention of Muslim infidel and the invention of Latin heretics. This point is discussed in detail below in the conclusion to this book.

NOTES

1. Niketas Byzantios, Ep. 2, 150–53; Förstel, *Niketas von Byzanz.*

2. *Oxford Dictionary of Byzantium*, s.v. "Niketas Byzantios."

3. Khoury, *Théologiens*, 110–62; Khoury, *Polémique*; Förstel, *Niketas von Byzanz.*

4. Erich Trapp, "Gab es seine byzantinische Koranübersetzung?" *Diptycha* 2 (1980/81): 7–17; Khoury, *Théologiens*, 119–20.

5. Hergenroether, *Monumenta*, 84–138.

6. Munich, Bayerische Staatsbibliothek, MS gr. 229. Venice, Biblioteca Nazionale Marciana, MS Antico 530 (319).

7. Förstel, *Niketas von Byzanz*, XXIV; Ioannes Mercati and Pius Franchi de' Cavalieri, *Codices Vaticani Graeci*, 3, codd. 604–866 (Vatican City: Biblioteca Apostolica Vaticana, 1950), 143–45.

8. Förstel, *Niketas von Byzanz*, X.

9. Förstel, *Niketas von Byzanz*, XII.

10. Khoury, *Théologiens*, 113.

11. Hergenroether, *Monumenta*, 84, from Munich 229.

12. Hergenroether, *Monumenta*, 84–87.

13. A note on translation: where Niketas uses variations on the word $α\ddot{ι}τιος$, I have translated with variations of the English word "cause"; where he uses variations of the word $ἀρχή$, I have used variations of "principle."

14. Hergenroether, *Monumenta*, 88.

15. Niketas usually refers to the common "nature" (φύσις); he uses "being" (οὐσία) less often.

16. Hergenroether, *Monumenta*, 88.

17. Cf. Niketas, Ep. 2, 117–26; Förstel, *Niketas von Byzanz*, 182: "Thus some things that we say truly [about God], in the manner of theology, are said about the three persons together and in common, as they are one essence [οὐσία] or divinity and one God. For example, I say the names God, the Lord, the lover of mankind, and many others which are enumerated because we are speaking of the unity, as has been demonstrated. Other things, though, [that we say truly, in the manner of theology, about God] are said individually, as they are first and properly [properties] of the persons. For example, Father, Son, Holy Spirit; these are enumerated because we are speaking according of things proper to the individual person. For the enumerating of the things said properly of the individuals is not said of them commonly, as we have already shown. At times, however, there is found some term that applies to two of the divinely ruling persons, as, for example, the being-caused."

18. Hergenroether, *Monumenta*, 88–89; for a similar argument, see 93–94.

19. Hergenroether, *Monumenta*, 89–90.

20. Hergenroether, *Monumenta*, 90–93.

21. Hergenroether, *Monumenta*, 94–95.

22. Hergenroether, *Monumenta*, 95.

23. Hergenroether, *Monumenta*, 96–97.

24. Hergenroether, *Monumenta*, 97–99.

25. Hergenroether, *Monumenta*, 100–102.

26. Khoury, *Théologiens*, 118–19.

27. Chap. 8, Hergenroether, *Monumenta*, 107: "καὶ γὰρ ἑνὸς ἀτόπου δοθέντος τὰ μυρία ἕψεται, σοφός τις ἔφη." Cf. Niketas, Ep. 1, 74; Förstel, *Niketas von Byzanz*, 160: "ἑνὸς ἀτόπου δοθέντος μυρία ἕψεσθαι."

28. Chap. 6, Hergenroether, *Monumenta*, 102–4.

CHAPTER 8

The Letter of Pope Nicholas I
(858–67) to Hincmar of Rheims

S ome of the most fascinating documents to survive from the ninth-century struggles between the popes, on the one hand, and the patriarchs and emperors in Constantinople, on the other, are the letters of Pope Nicholas I. Dvornik's *Photian Schism* and Jane Carol Bishop's dissertation, "Pope Nicholas I and the First Age of Papal Independence" provide a detailed and reliable history of this correspondence—so detailed and reliable that it would be futile for me to repeat it. Instead, I want to look at only one of those letters and for two specific reasons. First, Nicholas reveals in this letter that he has received, secondhand, a text criticizing certain doctrines and usages of the Roman Church. In discussing this text, he becomes an indirect witness to some of the accusations Greeks were leveling against Latins in Bulgaria in the late ninth century. Second, the letter exemplifies the process of dividing the eastern and western, Roman and Constantinopolitan, Latin and Greek churches as it occurred on the western side. This book is primarily about wall-building from the Greek side, but it seems important—given that the history of mutual condemnation and blame sometimes continues today—to realize that some thought-leaders on the Latin side were also working to separate "us" from "them" and to unite "us" more thoroughly. One could use innumerable papal letters of the period to illustrate this Latin invention of Greek heretics; I use this one because its other content is also useful.

On 23 October 867, Pope Nicholas I wrote a letter to Hincmar, metropolitan of Rheims and "our other brothers, the archbishops and bishops in the kingdom of Charles."[1] He tells the story of his recent dealings with the emperors and patriarch in Constantinople, complains about their behavior and the calumnies they have brought against the Church of Rome, and asks Hincmar to move quickly either to compose refutations of the Greek insults or to commission someone else to do so.[2] He begins by presenting the problem as twofold. The emperors (Michael III and Basil I) and so-called patriarch (Photios) are angry, first, because Nicholas has refused to approve of the deposition of Ignatius and promotion of Photios. Second, they are "jealous" because Khan Michael of the Bulgars had chosen to submit his church to Rome rather than to Constantinople. The troubles had begun with the deposition of Ignatius, when Rome echoed with a "clamor of evils" from Constantinople.[3] The emperors (at that point Michael III and Caesar Bardas) and those who obeyed them had arranged the removal of Ignatius, and some were "begging and praying without cease that we should investigate." So, in 860, Nicholas sent two envoys, Radoald, bishop of Porto, and Zachary, bishop of Anagni, to Constantinople.[4] "Against our prohibition," he tells Hincmar, these envoys condemned Ignatius and took communion with Photios. They then returned to Rome with an envoy from the emperors, Leo *a secretis*. This is most emphatically not what Nicholas wanted them to do and the letter gives the impression that he excommunicated both Radoald and Zachary as soon as he understood what they had done. He also refused to accept the agreement they had signed and sent Leo back to Constantinople with a letter in which "we agreed to neither the deposition of Ignatius nor the promotion of Photius."[5] The emperor replied immediately (865) by sending Michael the protospatharius "with a letter full of insults" to Rome. The pope says that the insults to him personally did no harm, "but we were not silent about the insults against the church." His letter back to the emperor (28 September 865) defended the church of Rome and tried "to return this emperor and his followers . . . to the right path . . . in this affair"—that is, the matter of Photios and Ignatius. Then, "so that these matters could be reported more fully to that emperor and to the other faithful," Nicholas held a synod which, among other things, agreed to send yet more hortatory letters to Constantinople.[6] But now it was not the season for a sea voyage, and Nicholas says that he feared for his envoys also "on account of the well-known envy of those Greeks." Fortunately—"who can say how much joy and exultation filled us!"—Nicholas was soon informed of a legation from the Bulgarian Khan. The joy stemmed from the

Khan's explicit acceptance of obedience to Rome and papal instruction regarding the rudiments of the faith from the pope. It also stemmed from the possibility that a legation could now go to Constantinople by way of Bulgaria, thus avoiding the sea voyage.[7] An embassy went to Bulgaria and spent some time there; other legates who intended to go on to Constantinople accompanied it. But when the second part of the legation tried to move on to Constantinople it was met at the border by imperial officials who "strove to extract from our envoys, if they wished to be received by them [the emperors], against every rule and contrary to every custom, a *libellus* of the faith" in which they anathematized some things they believed. The officials also refused to accept the letters unless they were directed to Photios, "him whom they call the ecumenical patriarch."

Meanwhile, another important document had entered the picture. While the papal delegation was in Bulgaria, the emperors wrote to the khan. According to Nicholas, the khan straightaway ordered that the letter "be passed on to us through our legates." When Nicholas examined the letter, he was appalled. It accused the Roman Church of a number of errors: fasting on Saturdays, saying that the Holy Spirit proceeds from the Father and the Son, prohibiting clerical marriage, allowing confirmation only by bishops, mixing chrism from *aqua fluminis*, not fasting properly during Lent, offering and blessing a lamb on the altar at Easter, shaving their beards, and ordaining a deacon as bishop when he has not yet held the office of priest. This list, more than any other part of these events, led Nicholas to write to Hincmar. He wants Hincmar and the other Frankish bishops to write refutations of these Greek insults because they have been made not just against Rome, but "against the whole church throughout the area that is distinguished by its use of the Latin tongue." The western regions, he insists, have never been found to disagree with the see of blessed Peter. So let some one of your suffragans write in opposition to these accusations, and then send his work to us so that we can do a better job of "opposing their venom," and so that everyone will know that you are in no way divided from the head, that is the see of Peter.

Nicholas then begins a defense himself, noting that there are two kinds of accusations made by the Greeks: some are just plain lies, and some are true but have been Roman customs for a long time without contradiction by anyone in the Roman Church or indeed in the west. Saturday fasting was discussed and legitimated in the time of Pope Sylvester. The double procession of the Holy Spirit was taught by "many illustrious men, especially

Latin men." But then Nicholas seems to get distracted from these details to what is always for him the crucial point:

> No wonder that they should pretend such things, since they even maintain and boast that when the Emperors moved from the Roman city to Constantinople, the primacy of the Roman See was also transferred to the Church of Constantinople and that the privileges of the Roman Church changed hands together with the royal honours, so much so that the usurper of that same Church Photius calls himself in his writings archbishop and universal patriarch.[8]

Consider, then, all of the things these emperors and their illegitimate patriarch have done: they have repeatedly accused and criticized the Roman Church which received authority "from Peter her patron and founder and is considered uncorrupted throughout other regions of the world." It was from Rome, too, that "the Christian religion began to be spread." Boniface, for example, considered himself Rome's representative, and through his work the universal church grew rapidly under St. Peter. How dare they, then, shut out ambassadors from the apostolic see and refuse to accept the pope's letters? With a flash of humor, Nicholas notes that if it were proper for patriarchs and emperors to refuse letters, "nobody would lead a more tranquil life than we would, freed from all those legates and letters that daily cause us great and tiring labor." How dare they, too, require a statement of faith from the legates? "Have we ever been the inventors of any novelty? Have we handed down any things other than those that pertain to their salvation and to the common condition of the church? Were any of us ever heretics? For although we do not deny that we are sinners," we have never fallen into error. They, in contrast always have schisms and errors. So we have sometimes demanded *libelli* from them, but there is no precedent for them demanding such from us. They have no right—Nicholas repeats this; it is crucial for him—because nobody has a right to demand anything of that sort from representatives of the pope, for the pope judges others. The superior judges the inferior, not vice versa.

For all of these reasons, then, Nicholas announces his intention to convene a council that includes the Frankish bishops, but in the meantime he is asking them to compose their rebuttals of the Greek accusations. He adds another reason to do so—because he knows that the emperors and patriarch have written to the patriarchs of Alexandria and Jerusalem, the western bishops must respond for the good of those eastern Christians, "oppressed by the Hagarenes," who may otherwise have to obey the Byzantine emperor. After another call for unity and repetition of the request that Hincmar pass this letter on to the other bishops "in the kingdom of our son Charles," Nicholas ends his letter.

The list of accusations against the Roman Church that Nicholas repeats in his letter to Hincmar may be our earliest evidence of the circulation of such a list among the Greeks and the Slavs they were trying to convert not only to Christianity but specifically to eastern Christianity. Even if all parts of Photios's Ep. 2 date to 867 (see chapter 4, above), the list Nicholas saw must have been earlier than Photios's. It was also longer. Nicholas's paraphrase of it is worth quoting in full:

> For they try to reprove our church in particular, and all churches which use the Latin tongue in general, because we fast on Saturdays and because we say that the Holy Spirit proceeds from the Father and the Son, while they confess that it proceeds only from the Father. Moreover, they say that we abhor marriage because we prohibit priests from choosing wives, and they try to bring a charge against us because we prevent those priests from anointing the foreheads of the baptized with chrism. They also falsely charge us with mixing that chrism from *aqua fluminis*. They labor no less to accuse us because we do not stop eating meat eight weeks before Easter and stop eating eggs and cheese seven weeks before Easter, as is their custom. They lie, too, as is indicated by the attached writings, in saying that at Easter we offer and bless a lamb, in the manner of the Jews, on the altar beside the Lord's body. Then they exert themselves again to reprove us because our clerics shave their beards and theirs do not and because a deacon can be ordained as a bishop without having ever held the office of priest—and that when . . . the very one they call their patriarch was, from lay status, precipitously tonsured and made a monk, then with a single bound reached the height of the episcopate by imperial favor and imperial might.

Each of these Greek complaints about Latin doctrine or practice has a long history ahead of it, but that has been detailed elsewhere and need not be repeated.[9] I will save further analysis of these particular complaints for the conclusion, which analyzes thematically the ways that Byzantine heresiology was beginning to form its picture of the Latin heretic.

Here I want rather to focus on the ways that this letter reveals how the wall (still not very high or solid) between Greek and Latin Christians could be built up from the Latin side as well as the Greek. Building such a wall is both about making distinctions between "us" and "them" and about convincing "us" that we are a unit. For often we are not (yet). In this letter Pope Nicholas depicts a unified western church, the church in which everyone speaks Latin, and sets it over against the church of the Greeks. Where in fact Byzantine polemic against western practices had been focused on small groups of missionaries, Nicholas portrays an attack on the whole of the western church. He speaks of "those things . . . that are brought against us—no, rather, against the whole of the west—iniquitously by the emperors of the Greeks, namely Michael and Basil." He stresses that "they try to reprove our church in particular, and all churches which use the Latin tongue in general" for the faults mentioned. He demands that the bishops of Charles's realm help with the rebuttal of these Greek accusations: "[I]t is fitting for you above all to labor, brothers, because these opprobria are alleged in common, just as we showed previously, against the whole church throughout the area that is distinguished by its use of the Latin tongue." The western regions, he says repeatedly, have always agreed with the see of St. Peter, Prince of the Apostles. The letter is rife with words such as *universalis, communis, unanimiter, omnis generaliter quae lingua Latina utitur ecclesia, conlaborare, concordia.*

The reality was a bit more complicated. In fact Nicholas had clashed with Frankish bishops, including Hincmar himself, a number of times and for a number of reasons. The bishops and the secular rulers in Frankish lands had ambitions for the independence of their church that did not match Nicholas's ideas of the pope's prerogatives.[10] Against his claims to papal monarchy, Hincmar and others adduced a collegial model of the episcopate. Nicholas was determined to assert and practice to the utmost the papal right (as he saw it) to hear appeals against any bishop in the western church; Hincmar's denial of this right caused two serious disputes between the pope and the bishop.[11] Nicholas also angered some important Franks with the legation he sent to Bulgaria in 866–67. As soon as it arrived in Bulgaria, its leader, Formosus of Porto, dismissed and sent packing the Frankish delegation already there, a delegation carefully prepared and sent by Louis the German.[12] In this context Nicholas's reference to St. Boniface, his conversion of the north, and his consistent submission to the see of St. Peter was a pointed one.

Dvornik surmises an even more direct connection between the pope's insecurity about the Franks and his insistence on unity. There is considerable evidence that the Byzantine court and the Frankish court of Louis II were experiencing some sort of *rapprochement* in the 860s. This culminated in Byzantine recognition, at a synod in Constantinople in 867, of Louis's right to be called "emperor." Was there a chance that the Franks and the Byzantines might "join hands in their opposition to Nicholas"? Given the "coolness" that grew to "an undercurrent of bad feeling" between Louis II and Nicholas I, Nicholas may well have thought so.[13]

Letters related to Byzantium were not, of course, the only times that Nicholas made strong statements about the unity of the church and the pope's position as monarch in that single church. Bishop sees all of Nicholas's actions throughout his pontificate as being aimed at "one basic goal. He wanted the papacy to have monarchial control over the whole of the Christian church."[14] Still, this goal was far from achieved in Nicholas's time, and his statements on this matter again remind us of heresiological texts: they describe an ideal rather than the real situation.

But divisions in the western church were not only about Nicholas's strong pretensions for his office. He was a principled and obstinate man whose strictness toward and expectations of his subordinates could make him enemies. We need not doubt Ep. 2's claim that Photios had received complaints about Nicholas's "tyranny." One bishop at odds with him complained that "[h]e numbers himself an apostle among the apostles, and makes himself emperor of the whole world."[15] One of Photios's later letters led Dvornik to speculate that he had expected Archbishop John VIII of Ravenna and some other western bishops to support him in his quarrels with Nicholas; John had been a thorn in Nicholas's side since the beginning of his pontificate.[16]

Nicholas's writings also reflect the growing barriers to understanding between east and west in ways less evident in this particular letter, where he cites the words of previous popes only briefly. In letters to Byzantium he had used his predecessors as his primary authorities against Photios and in favor of papal intervention repeatedly. Bishop notes, for example, that in his first letter to Emperor Michael III he quoted three popes and cited the papal decrees of eleven.[17] He rarely cites anyone except his predecessors, and even when he does his references reveal no substantial knowledge of Greek fathers. He cites councils that took place in the east only when he can praise them for their deference toward Peter and his successors in Rome.[18] Perhaps he did not realize that these references carried little weight in Constantinople; perhaps he simply did not care. Moreover, his arguments for papal primacy must have seemed ludicrous in Constantinople, not only to patriarchs but also to emperors. He wanted them to recognize the principle that the Pope, not by imperial permission but by right of law, should participate in—indeed, decide—all questions of deposition of bishops and patriarchs in the Constantinopolitan church. . . . His second letter showed that he conceived of very different roles for Michael in his relations with the Roman and with the Constantinopolitan church; the Emperor stood protectively over the latter, but he went for advice to the former.[19]

These principles form another barrier preventing the prelates in Rome and the prelates and emperor in Constantinople from understanding one another and arguing on the same ground. This is well before the twelfth century when claims of papal primacy were more concretely manifested in the west and more clearly understood in the east,[20] but it is already a significant obstacle to peace.

Some rhetorical features of this letter show other ways in which the pope, while encouraging the Frankish bishops to feel more connected to Rome, also encourages them to feel more distant from Constantinople. Very early in the letter he labels the emperors against whom he struggles: "But among the other things that immerse us in immense labors, those things seem to trouble us especially which are brought against us—no, rather, against the whole of the west—iniquitously by the emperors of the Greeks, namely Michael and Basil." To call the emperors "emperors of the Greeks" is to deny them their proper title—emperors of the Romans—and, by so doing, to remove any suggestion that they have rights in the regions that were once the western empire, including Rome. Nicholas was a Roman patriot, and his sense that the emperors ought not to interfere in Rome may have been purely visceral. His use of the wrong formal title for the emperors, however, must have been deliberate. Even when he addresses them more politely, not using the phrase "emperors of the Greeks," he does not call them "emperors of the Romans," either.[21]

Because this book concentrates on the process by which some Byzantines sought to invent Latin heretics, I have spent little time on the other side of the wall: the Latins who were inventing Greek heretics. Much could be done here, though it seems a job for someone who works on the Latin west rather than the Greek east. For this book, Nicholas's letter to Hincmar serves as an example both of the multiplication of complaints on each side and of the ways in which the Latin world was going to build its side of the wall.

NOTES

1. MGH *Epistolarum VI, Karolini Aevi IV,* Nicolai papae epistola 100, 600–609.

2. Details of these events in Dvornik, *Photian Schism,* 70–131.

3. Such rumors were also mentioned in an earlier letter to the eastern patriarchs; Dvornik, *Photian Schism,* 98.

4. On Radoald, see Dvornik, *Photian Schism,* 88–91, 96, 102, 130; Bishop, *Nicholas I,* 19, 24, 26–27, 32–33, 35, 146–47, 189, 224, 229–30, 259–63. On Zachary, see Dvornik, *Photian Schism,* 88–91, 96, 97–98, 101–2, 131, 181, 202–3, 224, 258 n. 4; Bishop, *Nicholas I,* 24, 26, 259–62.

5. Nicholas's account here is, at best, a simplified version of what happened; at worst, it is a distortion. In fact, he excommunicated and deposed Zachary only in 863 (at the synod in Rome, see n. 6, below) and Radoald only in 864; Dvornik, *Photian Schism,* 97–98, 101–2. Milton V. Anastos disagrees with Dvornik at some crucial points: see "The Papal Legates at the Council of 861 and Their Compliance with the Wishes of the Emperor Michael III," in *Armos: Timetikos tomos ston Kathegete N. K. Moutsopoulo gia ta 25 chronia pneumatikes tou prosforas sto Panepistemio,* 2 vols. (Thessaloniki: Aristoteleio Panepistemio Thessalonikes Polytechnike Schole, Tmema Architektonon, 1990), 1:185–200 (repr. in *Aspects of the Mind of Byzantium: Political Theory, Theology, and Ecclesiastical Relations with the See of Rome,* ed. Speros Vryonis, Jr., and Nicholas Goodhue [Aldershot: Ashgate, 2001], art. 6).

6. The synod met in Rome, probably in late summer 863; Dvornik, *Photian Schism,* 97–98.

7. Dvornik, *Photian Schism,* 113–14; Bishop, *Nicholas I,* 27–28.

8. Dvornik, *Photian Schism,* 124.

9. Kolbaba, *Byzantine Lists.*

10. The history of Frankish ambivalence toward Rome—on the one hand, a reverence for St. Peter that is almost unlimited; on the other, consistent clashes with the papacy over the specifics of Roman jurisdiction (or lack thereof) in Frankish lands—has been detailed in many works, as have the papal attempts to resolve that ambivalence in their favor. This is, for example, one major theme of Bishop, *Nicholas I;* see especially 58–62, 121–73, 188–92. Most importantly for this study, there had been disagreement between Rome and the Frankish rulers about the iconophile decisions of the Seventh Ecumenical Council, Nicea 787, and about the Filioque since the reign of Charlemagne. See chapter 2, above.

11. Bishop, *Nicholas I,* 37–44, 278–84, 318–36.

12. Dvornik, *Photian Schism,* 114.

13. Dvornik, *Photian Schism,* 120–23 ("join hands," 123); Bishop, *Nicholas I,* 118, 141–57 ("coolness," 143; "undercurrent," 153).

14. Bishop, *Nicholas I*, 236; she argues this point in detail, 236–56.

15. Cited and trans., Bishop, *Nicholas I*, 4.

16. Dvornik, *Photian Schism*, 120, 129–31; details about John and Nicholas are in Bishop, *Nicholas I*, 20–22, 307–18.

17. Bishop, *Nicholas I*, 83; the reference is to Letter 4 (PL edition), Letter 82 (MGH edition), 438–39.

18. Bishop, *Nicholas I*, 82.

19. Bishop, *Nicholas I*, 107.

20. Jean Darrouzès, "Les documents byzantins de XIIe siècle sur la primauté romaine," *Revue des études byzantines* 23 (1965): 42–88.

21. Bishop, *Nicholas I*, 109–10.

Inventing Latin Heretics in the Ninth Century

There are two broadly defined ways to approach the contents of the Greek works discussed above, regardless of their authorship. The first would be to analyze the theological arguments themselves: their content and its history; their logic or lack thereof; their continuation or development of tradition; the Latin theology to which they may be responding. Given, however, that these are probably the earliest anti-Filioque arguments,[1] the natural direction to go in studying the tradition of which they are part is forward in time, tracing their influence in the centuries that follow. This needs to be done. Among other things such a study would permit a more nuanced understanding of how Byzantine theological reasoning does or does not change under Latin pressure from the tenth century on—one of my own primary interests. Still, it is not a task for this book. Too much reassessment of the dating and manuscript traditions of later texts needs to be done before we can answer these questions. One example may suffice: Francis Dvornik states that Eustratios of Nicea, one of the most important Byzantine theologians in the early twelfth century and a product of the period in which philosophical methods in theology had first been reborn and then punished rather severely, "probably also made use of Photius' *Mystagogy*."[2] I am not entirely sure that this is true, but I do know that Eustratios's texts against the double procession of the Holy Spirit are laden with technical terms taken from grammar, logic, and rhetoric. If he uses the *Mystagogia*, it would be interesting to see what he does with it, for its method differs markedly from his. Did he perhaps use Niketas

Byzantios's text instead? A nice dissertation topic, but not something that can be covered in a book about the ninth century.

The second way to approach the Photian texts is to see them within the broad corpus of heresiology and therefore look backward for ways to understand them. This has the advantage of being possible in the current state of the field. It is also interesting to look at heresiological themes and methods observed in earlier ages and their impact on these early attempts to refute the "heretical" doctrine of double procession of the Holy Spirit. Finally, analyzing the heresiological aspects of the texts allows us to look at them largely in their own ninth-century context, perhaps thereby achieving a balance between the historian's task and the dangerous distortions of hindsight.

As discussed in the introduction above, "orthodox" writers began to define "heresy" and to sketch out certain characteristics of "heretics" and "heresiarchs" in the second century. By the end of the period I discussed there, after the resolution of the controversy about "iconoclasm," orthodox writers possessed an armory of weapons against the heretics. These weapons could then be deployed against most deviance, including differences that we might define rather as "ethnic" or "political," for such matters were not always separated in the Middle Ages. In the case of the Filioque and other differences between Latins and Greeks mentioned in Ep. 2, ninth-century Byzantines faced real differences that had not (yet) been defined as heresy. Like second-century heresiologists and rabbis who "invented" Judaism and Christianity "in order to explain the fact that there were Jews and Christians,"[3] some ninth-century Byzantines thought that they needed to explain why there were Latins (Franks?) and Greeks. To do so, they drew on traditions of heresiology that were embedded in the culture and education of their society—so embedded that using them probably felt natural. Still, using them against western Christians, adherents of the Seven Ecumenical Councils, perhaps did not feel natural, and these early texts show considerable ambivalence and some awkwardness in dealing with the Latins as heretics.

The ways in which heresiological commonplaces of long ancestry could be used are obvious throughout these texts. The fundamental principle is simple: heresy is never harmless. It is always malignant because it is always the product of "the enemy of the human race" and his servants: "It seems that there are never enough evil deeds for the evil one, nor any end of the inventions and machinations which he has been accustomed, from the beginning, to move against the human race."[4] In Ep. 2, Photios (assuming it is he)[5] brings this heresiological generalization up to his own day: after Jesus had come and defeated him, the Evil One moved against Christians by inspiring heresiarchs (Marcion and Mani, Arius and Eutyches, et al.). When those had been defeated by "the seven holy and ecumenical synods" some people hoped that the peace would last forever.[6] But alas! Now come these men from the west to the newly baptized Bulgars, striving "to destroy them and to separate them from the right and pure doctrines of the blameless faith of the Christians." These heretics are like wild animals in the Lord's vineyard. The *Mystagogia*, too, talks of the devil sowing evil seeds in the souls of those who added to the creed.[7] Heresy is a disease of the heretics, who also infect others.[8]

A second constant feature of heresiology is the use of aporetic argument: the denunciation of "some possible consequences of the doctrine being combated by presenting them as inevitable. One must make them seem to be manifest errors even though the adversary would never admit to such ideas."[9] The language used in such cases is often the language of compulsion: in a single chapter of the *Mystagogia* we have both "Their novel argument will compel them to preach [this heresy]" and "your principle then demands." This is one of the most common ways of proceeding in all of the texts presented here. An example from Ep. 291:

> For those who teach that the all-holy Spirit proceeds from the Father and from the Son certainly introduce two principles, and the monarchy in the Trinity will be long departed. For obviously there are two causes proclaimed by those who speak in this way, from which thing also the one principle is rent into two principles—may this blasphemy be turned onto the heads of those who caused it! Moreover, if the procession of the Spirit from the Father is perfect, what need is there for a second procession, since perfection is already perceived in the Spirit from its coming forth from the Father? But if it is imperfect—who will endure such an irregularity? For first the one who dares to say this has thrown an imperfect thing into the utterly perfect Trinity. And then he helps to prepare the perfectly made Spirit from two imperfect causes—no indeed he creates a synthesis, as from some two causes. And then—O! intemperate tongue and ignorant opinion—the Spirit proceeds imperfectly from each.[10]

In the next paragraph, Photios goes further: to say that the Spirit proceeds from the son is to make the Spirit a grandson. No Latin theologian would support such propositions, of course, but these arguments are not composed for Latin theologians. It is sufficient to demonstrate to *our* satisfaction that *their* position is not merely wrong, but obviously wrong, ridiculously wrong, demonically wrong.

Part of that demonstration can take the form that Le Boulluec calls assimilation. Using deduction of the sort just described, the heresiologist demonstrates that the implications of the heretical teaching are not only ridiculous but also the repetition of some earlier heresy already condemned by the church, ideally centuries ago and in an ecumenical council. So, for our author or authors, the Latin insistence on clerical celibacy makes them Manichaeans.[11] In fact, the Latins in question are not dualist about marriage. Parts of the Latin Church have embraced clerical celibacy at this point for reasons that are far from Mani's. But this is not important to the heresiologist. If he sees a similarity between Manichaean contempt for marriage and Latin disapproval of clerical marriage, the Latins become Manichaeans. Consequently, they can now be accused of all sorts of other Manichaean ideas.

Assimilation works for other groups as well. In both Ep. 2 and the *Mystagogia* it is argued that two causes or principles in the Trinity necessarily mean two gods, and therefore return the heretics to polytheism. At least that is what two principles mean if the two principles work together. The other alternative is to have two principles opposed to one another—and that would be Manichaeism. Or perhaps the people who teach double procession think that the Holy Spirit is inferior to the Father and the Son; that, of course, is Macedonianism (Pneumatomachianism). Or maybe they mean that the Father and the Son are really the same *hypostasis*; that would be a new and monstrous kind of Sabellianism or semi-Sabellianism.

All of these labels are distortions, but that does not matter. To have labeled the "other" as a heretic, and specifically as a kind of heretic that has already been identified and anathematized by the church, is to exclude him definitively. There is no need even to hear his case. His heresy is obvious; he must not be allowed to infect others.

Having taken the known and indisputable teaching of the heretics and pushed it to what are said to be inevitable and blasphemous conclusions, the heresiologist can now look at those conclusions and argue that the heretics are mad, audacious, arrogant, proud, and mendacious. Finally, having demonstrated that the heretics in question are both just like other heretics in their teaching and just like other heretics in their character, we can perform the final assimilation: all heretics are alike, period: "Even if each pretends to battle with the other (for such is the harvest of impious seeds) nevertheless they both lead to the same crime of imperfection."[12]

Finally, it should not surprise us to find in these texts both an insistence on the authority of the Fathers and a fully developed technique for dismissing any statement of a Father that would seem to strengthen the opponents' case. As outlined in chapter 1, above, from the fifth century onward the orthodox churches relied increasingly on a narrowly defined group of "Select Fathers."[13] Further, they limited even which writings of a designated Father could be adduced as authoritative. The development of florilegia on various topics allowed the omission of patristic statements that might cause difficulty. Such narrowing, the closure of a canon of Fathers and their accepted works, was not uncontested, however. Opponents could simply develop their own canon, sometimes from the works of the same Fathers. Another set of strategies for confuting opponents had to be developed—the challenge to their florilegium's contents.[14]

The first and most obvious challenge was an accusation of forgery. As the author of the *Mystagogia* put it, "[They say that] Augustine and Jerome said that the Spirit proceeds from the Son. And how are we to accept this and give it credence when so much time has passed that their treatises may have been treated fraudulently?"[15] If the texts are not forgeries? Not everything an apostle or a Father said has equal weight. Some things were said when the Father was "attacking the madness of the Hellenes or bringing battle against some other heretical teaching or condescending to the weakness of his audience or some other such thing as human life presents."[16] This argument for considering context, broadly construed, in the use of scriptural and patristic quotations is neither unique nor new. In scriptural exegesis especially it is one of the most basic principles. Yet when used by the heresiologist it inevitably applies to specific passages from the opponents' florilegium rather than to his own. Nobody in the ninth century seems yet to see this feature of the florilegium as a fundamental challenge to its evidentiary value. If the Fathers were wrong sometimes, so that other criteria must be used to prioritize their statements, we are nevertheless a long way from laying down systematic rules for their priority. Abelard's *Sic et Non*, after all, is neither a ninth-century book nor a Byzantine one.

So far, then, the anti-Filioque texts fit without innovation into the traditional treatments of heresy and heretics described in chapter 1, above. But they are also products of their own time in some concrete ways. The most basic of these is their subject: in calling the Filioque heresy, these authors are raising a new issue. The first question one must answer, then, is whether there is a fundamental difference between the Trinitarian theology of those who inserted the Filioque into the creed and those who opposed them. It has often been asserted that there is such a difference between the Trinitarian theology of the Cappadocian Fathers, which has immense influence in the east, and the theology of Augustine, which plays a similar role in the west. John Meyendorff writes,

> As time went on, it became increasingly clear that the Filioque dispute was not a discussion on words—for there was a sense in which both sides would agree to say that the Spirit proceeds "from the Son"—but on the issue of whether the hypostatic existence of the Persons of the Trinity could be reduced to their internal relations, as the post-Augustinian West would admit, or whether the primary Christian experience was that of a Trinity of Persons, whose personal existence was irreducible to their common essence.[17]

There are a number of problems with such a statement, theological as well as historical. First, and most strikingly, the authors who wrote against double procession in the ninth century did not stress that "the primary Christian experience was that of a Trinity of persons," although they insisted upon distinguishing the three hypostases, as orthodox theologians must. Rather, they stressed that there is a single principle (*archê*) or cause (*aitios*) in the Godhead: namely, the Father. The author of Ep. 2 insists that to say that the Holy Spirit proceeds from the Son "introduces two causes into the Holy Trinity" and thus "dissolves the monarchy into diarchy."[18] Similarly, even when invoking the three persons of the Godhead separately Niketas Byzantios stresses their oneness: "having called upon the life-giving and divine Spirit himself, . . . with the Father and the Son, that the Father might favor us, the Son work with us, and the Spirit inspire us—rather, hoping that a single illumination from the single godhead might come to be."[19] It is by no means clear that Meyendorff's characterization of the essential theological difference between "Orthodox East" and "post-Augustinian West" exists in these texts.

Second, as was amply developed at a recent conference on "Orthodox Readings of Augustine,"[20] the claim that Augustine or his followers "reduced" "the hypostatic essence of the Trinity . . . to their internal relations" is problematic, at best. In the centuries since Augustine's time theologians have developed many ways of conceiving of the three persons in the Trinity and their single essence. Different formulations have often led to controversy, but equally often have been accepted as varied ways of trying to express the inexpressible or explain the inexplicable.

Moreover, such differences cannot be characterized in a straightforward way as "eastern" or "western." Differences among eastern theologians or among western theologians are as common as differences between eastern and western ones. In other words, if a fundamental difference in Trinitarian theology exists as one of the essential and defining markers of eastern theology vis-à-vis western, that difference has proved remarkably difficult to define.

Nor are definitions made clearer by invoking an entity called "the post-Augustinian West," which is conceivable only from a particular, modern and Orthodox, perspective. The fundamental error behind such a label is probably the reason that even theologians who adopt it cannot agree on the precise nature of the difference, other than to posit a straightforward distinction between Cappadocians (as if they agreed on a single formulation) and Augustine (as if he were consistent in his own works and as if he were the west's only theologian). One might note, as well, that to attribute the allegedly fundamental difference to Augustine alone is to follow the venerable—or infamous—heresiological tradition of ascribing heresy to a single, larger-than-life figure. Such essentialism and demonization works well for polemic but should be rather less convincing to historians of doctrine.

Finally, there is the quintessential historian's problem: nobody has pinpointed a moment—or even a decade or century—in which this allegedly fundamental difference developed. Note, for example, in the quotation above, Meyendorff's vague chronology: "as time went on . . ."

For all these reasons, the quest for a single fundamental distinction in theological reasoning has proved fruitless—and I would wager that it will remain so. What we can do is look for specific moments when the east reacts negatively to western Trinitarian formulations and then analyze the nature of the reaction. The first such moment occurs in the ninth-century texts here studied, and it is not a reaction to Augustine's *De Trinitate* or to "the post-Augustinian West" in general. Rather, specific, identifiable historical circumstances led the Franks to add the Filioque to the creed and led the Byzantines to react against that addition. In the centuries after Augustine and the Cappadocians, continuing beyond the period when Franks rejected the decisions of Nicea 787, the western churches combated various kinds of subordinationism ("Arianism," "Adoptionism"). These battles—not profound meditation on the Trinitarian theology of Augustine—led to the western addition of the Filioque to the creed. For a time the eastern church was unaware of this addition. But when Byzantines became aware, they did so in various contexts that explain their immediate and vociferous rejection of the double procession of the Holy Spirit.

First, in the aftermath of the Restoration of Orthodoxy (843) it had become crucial for Byzantines that the decisions of the Seven Ecumenical Councils be accepted without question. As discussed in chapter 1, above, this was not a new idea: the reliance on conciliar creeds for closure, a definitive statement of orthodoxy that was to be maintained without change or discussion, had begun by Second Constantinople (381). There was, however, a renewed urgency to this insistence on "the things already received in synodical judgments."[21] We are in the world that created *The Synodikon of Orthodoxy* and a feast to honor "the Restoration of Orthodoxy."[22] The ideal of Byzantine elites at most points in their long history was balance, equilibrium, and order; for Photios and others of his epoch it was common sense to see such balance as resting on the undisturbed and unchangeable decisions of "the Fathers." To go any farther than the theology of the councils was to upset the balance and raise *stasis* in the church, which is to say in the empire. For Photios and most other church leaders and imperial officials of his time, many of whom had suffered a fair amount from such *stasis*, the mere idea of changing the creed was appalling. Change was by definition "adulteration."[23] Their reactions were predictable: a refutation of the Frankish addition and its meaning through citation of tradition and aporetic argument. Whether Photios wrote all three of the anti-Filioque texts attributed to him or not is less important than the fact that someone in the late ninth or early tenth century did. Methodios, apostle to the Slavs, or Metrophanes, Photios's sworn enemy, would have reacted in much the same way.

Meanwhile, accurate knowledge of Islam and Muslim criticism of Christian teaching had finally reached the educated people of Constantinople. It would be some time yet before western Europeans confronted Islam as Niketas Byzantios did when he not only criticized Islam but also penned a kind of *apologia* for Christianity. Above all he had to refute the Muslim claim that Christians worshipped three gods. He did so by asserting repeatedly that there is no plurality of *causes* in the Godhead. Although there are three persons/hypostases there is only one principle or cause, God the Father.

What happens when someone who has been writing this sort of anti-Muslim polemic turns his attention to the Filioque? He has been emphasizing repeatedly that the oneness of the triune God is seen in the way that the Father is the uncaused cause of the other two persons. There may be three hypostases in the Trinity, but there is only one principle. Imagine his horror upon finding that the Latins have introduced a relation into the Trinity (the Spirit's relation to the Son by procession) that implies that the Son is the cause of the Spirit, thereby making two causes or principles in the Godhead. His arguments against this are ready-made. He has already shown the Muslims (he thinks) that the Christian God is and must be only one principle. Now he has to show the Latins the same thing. That is why it was possible to quote from one of Niketas's anti-Islamic works at the beginning of a chapter on his anti-Latin work.

As far as I know—and I would love correction here—this point has not been stressed in previous histories of the Filioque controversy. There has mostly been a divide between scholars who study polemic against Islam and those who study polemic against the Latins. Different languages and different bodies of knowledge are required for the two tasks. With few people reading both the anti-Muslim polemic and the anti-Latin, the parallels have largely gone unnoticed and unexplored. I have noticed them; exploring them has seemed beyond the scope of this study.

That the target of these writings is specifically the *Frankish* west is another way in which these texts are of their time. Ninth- and tenth-century Byzantine authors aim at the Franks because they are aware that it is only in the Frankish lands that the creed is included in the Mass and contains the Filioque. The popes have not yet accepted the addition to the creed, and their statements on the matter have been unequivocal and public enough that the Byzantines know of them. In general, Photios sees bishops south of the Alps as allies in the fight against the addition to the creed. Ep. 291, addressed to an Italian bishop, begins its refutation of the Filioque with examples of popes who opposed the addition to the creed. The *Mystagogia* dedicates a substantial section to showing that past popes and other Fathers as well as current popes and their legates recited the creed properly. Not only does this argument drop out when the popes accept the Filioque in the early eleventh century, but it also saves the appearance of unity between Constantinople and Rome, between pope and patriarch. The emphasis on papal objections to the Filioque, rather than on equally strong papal objections to the Byzantine missions in Bulgaria, is important. It allows Constantinopolitans to believe for another century or so that the problem is not the Romans of the west but rather the barbarians of the north.

On the other hand, we must not take the claim that all of the disturbance came from "outside" at face value, either. While it is a fact that the

Filioque was a western innovation, Ep. 2 portrays the Bulgars as "the beloved, newly planted vineyard" of the Lord which is overrun by the wild boars from the west—a striking image for anyone who knows the damage a boar can do to the landscape, newly planted or not.[24] We know, however, that far from lying fallow without tillers sent from Constantinople, Bulgaria had welcomed—in fact, its khan had actively sought—Frankish missionaries. The khan alternated between seeking an alliance with Rome and proclaiming his allegiance to Constantinople. This is not the kind of internal threat that "Latinophile" emperors and churchmen will pose later in the empire's history; it is still a threat that is less alien and uninvited than Photios suggests. The heretics are within as well as without, as has been true from the earliest days of the church, and the heresiologists still try, whenever possible, to give the opposite impression.

Here the determination of the author(s) of Ep. 291 and the *Mystagogia* to place all blame on some unnamed group of western men who are not from Rome comes in again. The popes were sometimes wary of east-Frankish initiatives in central Europe, but they certainly knew about and supported the missions in Bulgaria. They corresponded with the khan and tried mightily to win his allegiance to Rome. Again, to give the impression that the popes had nothing to do with those who brought the Filioque into the church is to distort the picture—whether this was a conscious distortion or a genuine blind spot in the Byzantine Church is an open question.

A corollary of the idea that heresy comes from outside the church is the idea that there was orthodoxy first. The Catholic and Apostolic Church, in agreement and at peace after the Seven Ecumenical Councils, is an unquestioned entity, solid and unchanging. The heresy is new. Again, the idea is old enough to hardly need restating. But again in the context of the Filioque in the ninth century there are some interesting variations on the theme. First, of course, there is the undeniable fact that the heresiologist is correct: the original creed did not contain the Filioque. His case is unassailable. Still, he emphasizes certain concerns specific to his context. He considers it crucial that everyone recognize the priority of the Byzantine missionaries in Bulgaria: they planted the vineyard; the evil men from the west came only late and as destroyers. Modern historians have complicated this picture. The conversion of the Bulgars was a messy business, with missions from more than one direction at the same time, alternately welcomed and expelled by the khan. Ep. 2's account of their conversion obliterates all such ambiguity.[25]

Our author or authors also emphasize whenever they get the opportunity the *Seven* Ecumenical Councils. After the Restoration of Orthodoxy in 843, the supporters of icons were anything but certain that their victory was permanent. After all, there had been another council that claimed the title of "ecumenical"—that of the iconoclasts in 754—and the decisions of that iconoclast council had been reaffirmed as the truly ecumenical ones in 815. It becomes a kind of reflex among orthodox writers in the decades after 843 to stress that there were seven ecumenical councils, with the Council of Nicea in 787 as the seventh, and that what came out these councils was the universal opinion of "the catholic and apostolic church."[26] We do not know when, precisely, the Byzantine court became aware that the Franks objected to the decisions of Nicea, but by the end of the ninth century they knew both that the Franks disagreed with them and that the popes had sometimes supported the Franks in this disagreement. The author of the text I have called Source 1 for the *Mystagogia* is probably familiar with Latin arguments supporting the use of Filioque. The repeated assertion in these Photian works of the authority of "the Seven Ecumenical Councils" and the agreement of "the catholic and apostolic church" on all issues of importance is not a straightforward depiction of reality. It is a depiction of the world as certain Byzantine churchmen would like it to be. In that world, heretics are not merely mistaken; they are not men of good intention misled and eager to overcome their mistakes. They are, rather, willfully blind, audacious, too proud to submit to authority. For these works, even when the heresy is seen as an illness—potentially a more charitable vision because it allows for a kind of unwilling heresy—the illness is "voluntary."[27]

Here too not all is traditional, however. Beyond the usual malevolence of heretics, Ep. 2 posits a connection between the geographic origins of the heretics and their error. The western missionaries in Bulgaria are not only "impious and ill-omened men" but also "men rising up from the darkness (for they are offspring of the western region)."[28] Although the *Mystagogia* includes many favorable references to "the West"—the western fathers and popes who never preached or accepted the Filioque—it too contains some of these geographic insults: "Look, you blind men, and listen, you deaf men, you who live in the heretical West, whom the darkness holds."[29] Ep. 291, addressed to a western bishop, does not explicitly make the same connection between the west and darkness; in fact, it frequently praises western leaders, past and present. They are "lights and guides in western regions as in eastern ones, [whom God] sets . . . upon the height of the archiepiscopal thrones to ever lighten and illuminate the souls and minds of many."[30] The compliment might, however, seem a bit backhanded. The frequency with which Photios refers to "enlightening" the west implies the cliché that connects the western regions and darkness. He also emphasizes repeatedly that it is "some of those in the west" who have "introduced" this error. In many ways, this emphasis on western darkness and error is simply a logical conclusion: heresiological logic says that the error comes from outside, and in this case the error does come from outside and specifically from the northern regions of the west. What could be more obvious than a connection between "western" and "heretical" in such a situation? The source of error has often been geographically identified, of course, especially with reference to the "Saracen-minded" iconoclasts (see chapter 1, above). Nonetheless, identifying "the western lands" as the source of error is a new development in Byzantine antiheretical endeavors. As discussed in chapter 3, above, the prestige of the papacy was high at this point because of its support for icon veneration. Photios was only one generation removed from men who had taken refuge in Rome from iconoclast emperors.

But these works never attack Rome. Their focus is on "some of those in the west" who promulgate a creed with Filioque. And while they do not specify that these men are Franks or some other kind of barbarian, they regularly employ topoi that allow the reader to understand exactly that. This error, like iconoclasm, is the product of a kind of barbarism. These men who teach the Filioque are not only compared to wild beasts; they also have all sorts of other barbarous qualities. Most importantly, they do not even know Greek, and therefore fundamentally misunderstand one of the crucial scriptural passages. In Jn 16:15 Jesus says that the Spirit "will receive from mine and make it known to you." This was indeed one of the proof passages used by Ratramnus of Corbie, one of those who responded to Nicholas I's request for a refutation of Greek accusations (see chapters 6 and 9, above). In both the *Mystagogia* and Ep. 291 Photios speculates that those who make such an argument lack even basic grammatical training: "Do you see," he writes, "how you have not mastered even the things proper to children? For even children who are just beginning their grammatical education know that, on the one hand, 'from me' means he who utters the phrase, while, on the other hand, 'from mine' reveals another person, united with bonds of family with the speaker, but wholly different in terms of substance."[31] The link between adequate knowledge of the Greek language and proper theological understanding is emphasized again when the

Mystagogia tells the story of Pope Leo III and his rejection of the Filioque (see chapter 6, above). In this story, the pope himself recognizes that Latin's "poverty of words" is not adequate for the creed and orders everyone in the west, even those who "used the tongue of the Romans," to recite the creed in Greek. The historicity of this account is problematic. As Claudia Sode has shown, it is part of a number of questionable stories surrounding Leo III, the Franks, and the Filioque, and Photios has some of the details wrong.[32] In the end, though, it is true that Leo III explicitly reprimanded the Franks for reciting the creed with the Filioque (although he told them that the theology of double procession of the Holy Spirit was correct). Either Leo III or Leo IV also posted the creed without the Filioque in two Roman churches, probably in both Greek and Latin.[33]

Less important than the existence and nature of epigraphic creeds in Rome, however, is the attitude that lies beneath Photios's account. Greek is really the only proper theological language; translation into "the tongue of the Romans" is problematic and can be used by heretics to spread their error. The inferiority of Latin as a philosophical language is a topos of ancient and modern writers; there is nothing new in that. But the claim that Latin is inadequate in some way that can lead directly to heresy, and that a pope recognized that fact, is rather different. The claim epitomizes middle Byzantine attitudes toward Latin intellectual prowess. There are those, like Pope Leo, who recognize the inferiority of Latin and make up for it by promulgating the creed in the original Greek. And there are those who do not recognize the inferiority of Latin, and therefore fall into error.

We stand, then, at the beginning of a new (or at least recast) antiheretical topos, specifically applied to the west and forged in the condescending superiority of middle Byzantium. Some writers will find it possible for the rest of Byzantine history to condescend in this way. Ironically, it is often a way to exonerate the Latins: perhaps the poor things just do not understand. But such condescension can be more biting, as it is in the *Mystagogia*, and serves also, as so many heresiological devices do, to reinforce the heresiologist's and his audience's sense of group cohesion and superiority.

In the end, the ninth-century anti-Filioque texts display both mastery of heresiological technique and considerable ambivalence about applying that technique to western Christians, the popes in particular. Beginning to invent Latin heretics, they begin with Franks—northern barbarians—not with the popes, defenders of orthodoxy. It will be some time before they attribute such heresy to the head of a united "Latin" Church.

NOTES

1. There is a single exception: Maximos the Confessor addressed a letter to Marinus, a priest on Cyprus, in 645/46. Maximus seems to have been dealing with a pope (probably Theodore I, 642–49) who had mentioned double procession in a letter to the east. Maximos defends the pope, "although he is not quite happy about it." He also says that he tried to discuss the matter further, but language differences caused too much difficulty. Alexakis, *Codex Parisinus Graecus 1115*, 72, 75–77.

2. Dvornik, *Photian Schism*, 396.

3. Boyarin, "Semantic Difference," 77.

4. Ep. 2, 5–7; Laourdas and Westerink, 1:40.

5. See chapter 4, above.

6. Ep. 2, 15–19; Laourdas and Westerink, 1:40. This is not the only place where such an optimistic view is expressed; see Photios's *Homily XVIII*, in Mango, *Homilies of Photius*, 306–15.

7. E.g., *Mystagogia*, chap. 17, PG 102:296.

8. E.g., *Mystagogia*, chap. 21, PG 102:300.

9. Le Boulluec, *Notion*, 1:176: "Il est souvent nécessaire aussi de denouncer des conséquences possibles de la doctrine combattue en les présentant comme inéluctables. Il faut les faire passer pour des erreurs manifestes alors meme que l'adversaire n'admettrait jamais de telles idées."

10. Ep. 291, 119–31.

11. Ep. 2, 73–79; Laourdas and Westerink, 1:42.

12. *Mystagogia* chap. 44, PG 102:324.

13. See chapter 1, above, for bibliography.

14. For example, the case described by Gray, "Forged Forgeries."

15. *Mystagogia*, chap. 71, PG 102:352.

16. *Mystagogia*, chap. 72, PG 102:352. For further discussion of this passage see chapter 5, above.

17. Meyendorff, *Byzantine Theology*, 94.

18. Ep. 2, 110–14; Laourdas and Westerink, 1:44.

19. Hergenroether, *Monumenta*, 87.

20. The conference was held 14–16 June 2007 at Fordham University. The papers are to be published.

21. Ep. 2, 24; Laourdas and Westerink, 1:41.

22. J. Gouillard, "Le Synodikon de l'Orthodoxie," *Travaux et Mémoires* 2 (1967): 1–316. Gouillard, "Nouveaux témoins du Synodicon de l'Orthodoxie," *Annalecta Bollandiana* 100 (1982), 459–62.

23. Ep. 2, 105; Laourdas and Westerink, 1:43.

24. Ep. 2, 61–64; Laourdas and Westerink, 1:42.

25. Speck, "Die griechischen Quellen."

26. On this phrase in the documents from Nicea 787 see Auzépy, "Manifestations," 91–92.

27. *Mystagogia* chap. 2, PG 102:281.

28. Ep. 2, 57–58; Laourdas and Westerink, 1:42.

29. *Mystagogia*, chap. 81, PG 102:306.

30. Ep. 291, 30–34; Laourdas and Westerink, 3:140.

31. *Mystagogia*, chap. 22, PG 102:301; cf. Ep. 291, 227–44, Laourdas and Westerink, 3:146.

32. Sode, *Jerusalem, Konstantinopel, Rom,* 183, 186, 196–99. Callahan, "The Problem of the 'Filioque'," passim.

33. Leo's meeting with a Frankish delegation in early 810, in which he reprimands them for adding to the creed and reciting the creed during Mass: PL 102:971–76, most of it trans. Haugh, *Photius and the Carolingians,* 81–85. Details about the history of this "epigraphic creed" in Peri, "Il simbolo epigrafico."

Reconstruction of the Central
Paragraphs of Ep. 2 without Lines 108–99

The westerners in Bulgaria are teaching newly baptized Christians . . . (57–67)

1. to fast on Saturday (67–69);

2. not to fast properly during the first week of Lent (69–73);

3. to insist that priests be men without wives (73–79);

4. to recognize the chrism of confirmation only if a bishop performs the ceremony (80–100);

5. to recite the creed with a phrase added—*Filioque* (101–7).

[omit lines 108–99]

I could provide a myriad of arguments against this impious idea, but the rules of letter-writing do not permit it (200–204).

"These bishops [*episkopoi*] of the darkness (for they have declared themselves men of darkness [*episkotoi*]) have sowed this impiety . . ."

NB the continuation of *ad hominem* attacks and emotional language used at the beginning of Ep. 2. More of this sort of language precedes the paragraphs that now show how wrong these practices are (205–30).

1. Sabbath fasting is condemned by Apostolic Canon 64 (recte 66), repeated by Council in Trullo Canon 55 (231–42).

2. Clerics who leave their wives are condemned by Canon 4 of the Council of Gangra and Trullo 13, as well as by the Gospel of Matthew

19:6 ("What God has joined together, let no man separate") and the First Letter to the Corinthians 7:27 ("Are you married? Do not seek a divorce").

3. and 4. Their errors regarding the first week of Lent and chrism are so obviously impious that they need no canonical refutation (269–72).

5. The blasphemy against the Spirit "would subject them to a thousand anathemas even if none of the other aforementioned things were dared" (273–76).

Comparison of Chapter Numbering in Various Manuscripts

Abbreviations

Vat. gr. 2195 Hergenroether's edition; based on Vatican, Biblioteca Apostolica Vaticana, MS Vaticanus graecus 2195 (Column. XXXIV)

Pal. gr. 216 Vatican, Biblioteca Apostolica Vaticana, MS Palatinus graecus 216

Paris. gr. 1228 Paris, Bibliothèque nationale de France, MS ancien grec 1228

Vat. gr. 1923 Vatican, Biblioteca Apostolica Vaticana, MS Vaticanus graecus 1923 (based on Hergenroether's *apparatus criticus*)

Vat. gr. 2195	Pal. gr. 216	Paris. gr. 1228	Vat. gr. 1923
1			
2	[no numeral]	1	1
3	[no numeral]	2	2
4	[no numeral]	3	3
5	[no numeral]	4	4
6	[no numeral]	5	5

Vat. gr. 2195	Pal. gr. 216	Paris. gr. 1228	Vat. gr. 1923
7	[no numeral]	6	6
8	[no numeral]	7	7
9	8	8	8
10	[no numeral]	[no numeral]	[no numeral]
11	9	9	9
11, post verbum κράτος	10	10	10
11, post verbum ἐπικωμάσει	11	11	11
12	12	12	12
13	13	13	13
14	14	14	14
15	15	15	15
16	16	16	16
17	17	17	17
18	18	18	18
19	19	19	19
20	20	20	20
21	[no numeral]	[no numeral]	[no numeral]
22	[no numeral]	[no numeral]	[no numeral]
23	[no numeral]	[no numeral]	[no numeral]
24	[no numeral]	[no numeral]	[no numeral]
25	[no numeral]	[no numeral]	[no numeral]
26	[no numeral]	[no numeral]	[no numeral]
27	[no numeral]	[no numeral]	[no numeral]
28	[no numeral]	[no numeral]	[no numeral]
29	[no numeral]	[no numeral]	[no numeral]

Vat. gr. 2195	Pal. gr. 216	Paris. gr. 1228	Vat. gr. 1923
30	[no numeral]	[no numeral]	[no numeral]
31	21	21	21
32	22	22	22
33	23	23	23
34	24	24	24
35	25	25	25
36	26	26	26
37	space in text + large initial in marg, no numeral	27	27
38	20	28	28
39	[no numeral]	29	29
40	[no numeral]	30	30
41	[no numeral]	31	31
42	32	32	32
43	33	33	Hergenroether does not note
44	34	34	34
45	35	35	35
46	36	36	36
47	37	37	37
48	[no numeral]	38	38
49	1	1	1
50	2	2	2
51	3	3	3
51, ante τὸ Πνεῦμα	4	4	4
52	5	5	5
53	6	6	7

Vat. gr. 2195	Pal. gr. 216	Paris. gr. 1228	Vat. gr. 1923
54	7	7	8
55	8	8	9
56	9	9	10
56, ante Εἶπεν ἐκεῖνος	10	10	
57	[no numeral]	[no numeral]	11
57, ante Ἱερολογεῖται	11	11	
58	12	12	12
59	[no numeral]	[no numeral]	[no numeral]
60	[no numeral]	[no numeral]	[no numeral]
60, post ἀποτίκτουσα	[no numeral]	13	[no numeral]
61	[no numeral]	[no numeral]	39
61, ante Ἐι γεγέννηται	39	39	[no numeral]
62	40	40	40
63	41	41	41
64	42	42	42
64, ante Προσέχειν	[no numeral]	43	[no numeral]
65	[no numeral]	[no numeral]	[no numeral]
66	[no numeral]	[no numeral]	[no numeral]
67	1	1	1
68	2	2	2
68, ante καὶ τί τοῦτο;	3	3	3
69	4	4	4
70	5	5	5
71	6	6	6
72	7	7	7
73	8	8	8

Vat. gr. 2195	Pal. gr. 216	Paris. gr. 1228	Vat. gr. 1923
74	9	9	9
75	10	10	10
76	11	11	11
77	12	12	12
78	13	13	13
78, Post ἀφανισθεῆναι σκότος	14	14	14
78, Post ἀνομολεγεῖ ἐκπορεύεται τὸ Πνεῦμα	15	15	15
79	16	16	16
80	[no numeral]	[no numeral]	[no numeral]
81	[no numeral]	[no numeral]	[no numeral]
82	[no numeral]	[no numeral]	[no numeral]
83	19	19	19
84	20	20	20
85	[no numeral]	[no numeral]	[no numeral]
86	space in text + large initial in marg., no numeral	[no numeral]	[no numeral]
87	space in text + large initial in marg., no numeral	[no numeral]	[no numeral]
88	nothing	[no numeral]	[no numeral]
89	nothing	[no numeral]	[no numeral]
90	[no numeral]	[no numeral]	[no numeral]
91	[no numeral]	[no numeral]	[no numeral]
92	[no numeral]	[no numeral]	[no numeral]
93	[no numeral]	[no numeral]	[no numeral]

Vat. gr. 2195	Pal. gr. 216	Paris. gr. 1228	Vat. gr. 1923
94	[no numeral]	[no numeral]	[no numeral]
95	[no numeral]	[no numeral]	[no numeral]
96	[no numeral]	[no numeral]	[no numeral]

APPENDIX 3

Overlapping Passages of
Ep. 2 and the "Mystagogia"

Verbatim correspondences are in bold print.

Ep. 2, 115–17:

Διὰ τί δὲ καὶ ἐκπορευθείη τοῦ υἱοῦ τὸ πνεῦμα; **Εἰ γὰρ** ἡ ἐκ τοῦ πατρὸς ἐκπόρευσις τελεία (**τελεία δέ, ὅτι Θεὸς τέλειος ἐκ Θεοῦ τελείου**), τίς ἡ ἐκ τοῦ υἱοῦ ἐκπόρευσις, καὶ διὰ τί;

Mystagogia, 31:

Εἰ γὰρ (ὦ τί ἄν σέ τις προσείποι;) τοῦ Πνεύματος ἡ ἐκπόρευσις ἡ ἐκ τοῦ Πατρὸς **τελεία, τελεία δὲ ὅτι Θεὸς τέλειος ἐκ Θεοῦ τελείου**, τί ποτ' ἄν ἡ ἐκ τοῦ Υἱοῦ συνεισενέγκῃ;

Ep. 2, 122–31:

Σκόπει δὲ κἀκεῖνο, εἰ γὰρ **ἐν ᾧ τοῦ πατρὸς ἐκπορεύεται τὸ πνεῦμα ἡ ἰδιότης ἐπιγινώσκεται αὐτοῦ, ὡσαύτως δὲ καὶ ἐν ᾧ γεννᾶται ὁ υἱὸς ἡ τοῦ υἱοῦ, ἐκπορεύεται δέ, ὡς ὁ ἐκείνων λῆρος, καὶ τὸ πνεῦμα ἐκ τοῦ υἱοῦ, πλείοσιν ἄρα ἰδιότησιν διαστέλλεται τὸ πνεῦμα τοῦ πατρὸς ἤπερ ὁ υἱός.** Κοινὸν μὲν γὰρ πατρὶ καὶ υἱῷ ἡ ἐξ αὐτῶν τοῦ πνεύματος πρόοδος, ἰδία δὲ τοῦ πνεύματος ἥ τε ἐκ τοῦ πατρὸς

Mystagogia, 32:

Πάλιν δὲ εἰ **ἐν ᾧ τοῦ Πατρὸς ἐκπορεύεται τὸ Πνεῦμα, ἡ ἰδιότης ἐπιγινώσκεται αὐτοῦ, ὡσαύτως δὲ καὶ ἐν ᾧ γεννᾶται ὁ Υἱὸς, ἡ τοῦ Υἱοῦ· ἐκπορεύεται δὲ, ὡς ὁ ἐκείνων λῆρος, καὶ τὸ Πνεῦμα ἐκ τοῦ Υἱοῦ, πλείοσιν ἄρ' ἰδιώμασιν διαστέλλεται τὸ Πνεῦμα τοῦ Πατρὸς, ἤπερ ὁ Υἱός.** Ἡ μὲν γὰρ πρόοδος ἡ ἐκ τοῦ Πατρὸς, εἰ καὶ τὸ μὲν πρόεισι γεννητῶς, τὸ δὲ ἐκπορευτῶς, ἀλλ' οὖν ἐπίσης αὐτῶν

ἐκπόρευσις καὶ μὴν καὶ ἡ ἐκ τοῦ
υἱοῦ. **εἰ δὲ πλείοσιν διαφοραῖς
διαστέλλεται τὸ πνεῦμα ἤπερ ὁ
υἱός, ἐγγυτέρω ἂν εἴη τῆς
πατρικῆς οὐσίας ὁ υἱός ἤπερ τὸ
πνεῦμα· καὶ οὕτως ἡ Μακεδονίου
πάλιν κατὰ τοῦ πνεύματος**
παρακύψει τόλμα, τὸ ἐκείνων
ὑποδυομένη δρᾶμα καὶ τὴν σκηνήν.

ἐκάτερον ἀφορίζει τῆς πατρικῆς
ὑποστάσεως· ἀποδιαστέλλεται δὲ τὸ
Πνεῦμα καὶ δευτέρα διαφορᾷ, ἣν
αὐτῷ τὸ διπλοῦν τῆς ἐκπορεύσεως
προξενεῖ· **εἰ δὲ πλείοσι διαφοραῖς
διαστέλλεται** τοῦ Πατρὸς **τὸ
Πνεῦμα ἤπερ ὁ Υἱὸς, ἐγγυτέρω ἂν
εἴη τῆς πατρικῆς οὐσίας ὁ Υἱὸς,** καὶ
διπλῶν ὄντων ἰδιωμάτων τῶν
ἀφυριζόντων τὸ Πνεῦμα θατέρῳ
τούτων ὑποβεβηκέναι τοῦ Υἱοῦ τῆς
ὁμοφυοῦς πρὸς τὸν Πατέρα
συγγενείας τὸ ἰσότιμον
δυσφημηθήσεται Πνεῦμα, **καὶ
οὕτως ἡ Μακεδονίου πάλιν κατὰ
τοῦ Πνεύματος** ἀναδύσεται λύσσα,
τῆς ἐκείνου δυσσεβείας δι᾽ ἑαυτῆς
ἀνακαλουμένη τὸ ἥττημα.

Ep. 2, 139–40:

Ἀλλὰ καὶ εἰ μόνου πνεύματός ἐστι
τὸ εἰς ἀρχὰς ἀναφέρεσθαι
διαφόρους, πῶς οὐκ ἔστιν μόνου
πνεύματος τὸ πολύαρχον ἔχειν
ἀρχήν;

Mystagogia, 33:

Ἀλλὰ καὶ εἰ μόνου Πνεύματός ἐστι
τὸ εἰς ἀρχὰς ἀναφέρεσθαι
διαφόρους, πῶς οὐχὶ καὶ μόνου
Πνεύματος ἀκόλουθον λέγειν τὸ εἰς
πολύαρχον ἀναφέρεσθαι ἀρχήν;

Ep. 2, 141–44:

Ἔτι δέ, εἰ ἐν οἷς πατρὶ καὶ υἱῷ
κοινωνίαν ἐκαινούργησαν, τὸ
πνεῦμα τούτοις ἀποτειχίζουσιν,
πατὴρ δὲ κατ᾽ οὐσίαν υἱῷ, ἀλλ᾽ οὐ
κατά τι τῶν ἰδιωμάτων εἰς
κοινωνίαν συνάπτεται, τῆς κατ᾽
οὐσίαν ἄρα συγγενείας τὸ πνεῦμα
περιορίζουσιν.

Mystagogia, 34:

Ἔτι δέ, εἰ ἐν οἷς Πατρὶ καὶ Υἱῷ
κοινωνίαν οἱ πάντα θρασεῖς
ἐκαινούργησαν, τὸ Πνεῦμα τούτοις
ἀποτειχίζουσιν, Πατὴρ δὲ κατ᾽
οὐσίαν Υἱῷ, ἀλλ᾽ οὐ κατά τι τῶν
ἰδιωμάτων εἰς κοινωνίαν
συνάπτεται, τῆς κατ᾽ οὐσίαν ἄρα
πατρικῆς συγγενείας τὸ ὁμοούσιον
Πνεῦμα ὑπερορίζουσι.

Ep. 2, 160–65:

Τὸ πνεῦμα τοῦ υἱοῦ ἐκπορεύεται;
πότερον τὴν αὐτὴν ἐκπόρευσιν ἢ

Mystagogia, 35:

Τὸ Πνεῦμα τοῦ Υἱοῦ ἐκπορεύεται;
πότερον τὴν αὐτὴν ἐκπόρευσιν ἢ

τῆς πατρῴας ἀντίθετον; εἰ μὲν γὰρ
τὴν αὐτήν, πῶς οὐ κοινοῦνται αἱ
ἰδιότητες, αἷς καὶ μόναις ἡ τριὰς
τριὰς εἶναι καὶ προσκυνεῖσθαι
χαρακτηρίζεται; εἰ δὲ ἐκείνης
ἀντίθετον, πῶς ἡμῖν οὐ Μάνεντες
καὶ Μαρκίωνες τῷ ῥήματι τούτῳ
προκύπτουσιν, τὴν θεομάχον πάλιν
κατὰ τοῦ πατρὸς καὶ τοῦ υἱοῦ
γλῶσσαν προτείνοντες;

τῆς πατρῴας ἀντίθετον; εἰ μὲν γὰρ
τὴν αὐτήν, πῶς οὐ κινοῦνται [but
Hergenroether notes that elsewhere it
is κοινοῦνται] αἱ ἰδιότητες, αἷς καὶ
μόναις ἡ Τριὰς τριὰς εἶναι καὶ
προσκυνεῖσθαι χαρακτηρίζεται; εἰ
δὲ ἐκείνης ἀντίθετον, πῶς οὐ
Μάνεντες ἡμῖν καὶ Μαρκίωνες
πάλιν τῷ βλασφήμῳ οὕτω
συναναχορεύσουσι ῥήματι, τὴν
θεομάχον πάλιν κατὰ τοῦ Πατρὸς
καὶ τοῦ Υἱοῦ γλωσσαλγίαν
πλατύνοντες;

Ep. 2, 181–92:

Χωρὶς δὲ τῶν εἰρημένων, εἰ πᾶν ὅπερ
μή ἐστι κοινὸν τῆς
παντοκρατορικῆς καὶ ὁμοουσίου
καὶ ὑπερφυοῦς τριάδος ἑνός ἐστι
μόνου τῶν τριῶν, οὐκ ἔστι δὲ ἡ τοῦ
πνεύματος προβολὴ κοινὸν τῶν
τριῶν, ἑνὸς ἄρα ἐστὶν μόνου τῶν
τριῶν. πότερον οὖν ἐκ τοῦ πατρὸς
φήσουσιν ἐκπορεύεσθαι τὸ
πνεῦμα; καὶ πῶς οὐκ ἐξομόσονται
τὴν φίλην αὐτοῖς καὶ καινὴν
μυσταγωγίαν; εἰ δ' ἐκ τοῦ υἱοῦ, τί
μὴ κατ' ἀρχὰς ἐθάρρησαν αὐτῶν
ὅλην ἐκκαλύψαι τὴν θεομαχίαν, ὡς
οὐ μόνον τὸν υἱὸν εἰς τὴν τοῦ
πνεύματος προβολὴν ἐγκαθιστῶσιν,
ἀλλὰ καὶ τοῦ πατρὸς ταύτην
ἀφαιροῦνται; οἷς ἀκόλουθον δήπου
καὶ τὴν γέννησιν τῇ προβολῇ
συμμετατιθέντας μηδὲ τὸν υἱὸν ἐκ
τοῦ πατρός, ἀλλὰ τὸν πατέρα
τερατολογεῖν ἐκ τοῦ υἱοῦ
γεγεννῆσθαι· ἵνα μὴ τῶν
δυσσεβούντων μόνον, ἀλλὰ καὶ τῶν
μαινομένων ὦσιν πρωτοστάται.

Mystagogia, 36:

Ἐπὶ δὲ τοῖς εἰρημένοις εἰ πᾶν ὃ μή
ἐστι κοινὸν τῆς παντοκρατορικῆς
καὶ ὁμοουσίου καὶ ὑπερφυοῦς
τριάδος ἑνός ἐστι μόνου τῶν τριῶν,
οὐκ ἔστι δὲ ἡ τοῦ πνεύματος
προβολὴ κοινὴ τῶν τριῶν, ἑνὸς ἄρα
καὶ μόνου ἐπὶ τῶν τριῶν. πότερον
οὖν ἐκ τοῦ πατρὸς φήσουσιν
ἐκπορεύεσθαι τὸ πνεῦμα; καὶ πῶς
οὐκ ἐξομόσονται τὴν φίλην αὐτοῖς
καὶ καινὴν μυσταγωγίαν; εἰ δ' ἐκ
τοῦ υἱοῦ, τί μὴ κατ' ἀρχὰς εὐθὺς
ἐθάρρησαν ὅλον αὐτῶν ἐξεμέσαι
τὸν ἰόν, ἀλλὰ κατὰ μέρος
ἀναβλύζουσιν; ἐχρῆν γὰρ εἴπερ ἦσαν
πεποιηκότες αὐτῶν τῷ δυσσεβήματι
ἐξ ἀρχῆς ἀνομολογεῖν, ὡς οὐ μόνον
τὸν υἱὸν προβολέα τοῦ Πνεύματος
δογματίζουσιν, ἀλλὰ καὶ τὸν
Πατέρα τῆς προβολῆς
ἀπελαύνουσιν· οἷς ἀκόλουθον
δήπου καὶ τὴν γέννησιν τῇ
προβολῇ συμμετατιθέναι καὶ
συμμεταφέρειν, καὶ μηδὲ τὸν υἱὸν
ἐκ τοῦ πατρός, ἐκ δὲ τοῦ Υἱοῦ
τερατολογεῖν τὸν Πατέρα τὴν

γέννησιν ἔχειν, ἵνα μὴ μόνον τοὺς
ἠσεβηκότας ἐξ αἰῶνος κρύψωσιν,
ἀλλὰ καὶ τῶν μεμηνότων
ἐλέγχωνται μανικώτεροι.

Ep. 2, 169–74:

Mystagogia, 37:

Ἔτι δέ, εἰ ἐκ τοῦ πατρὸς ὁ υἱὸς
γεγέννηται, τὸ δὲ πνεῦμα ἐκ τοῦ
πατρὸς καὶ τοῦ υἱοῦ ἐκπορεύεται,
τίς ἡ καινοτομία τοῦ πνεύματος,
μὴ καὶ ἕτερόν τι αὐτοῦ
ἐκπεπορεῦσθαι; ὡς συνάγεσθαι
κατὰ τὴν ἐκείνων θεομάχον
γνώμην μὴ τρεῖς, ἀλλὰ τέσσαρας
τὰς ὑποστάσεις, μᾶλλον δ'
ἀπείρους, τῆς τετάρτης αὐτοῖς
ἄλλην προβαλλούσης, κἀκείνης
πάλιν ἑτέραν, μέχρις ἂν εἰς τὴν
Ἑλληνικὴν πολυπλήθειαν
ἐκπέσωσιν;

Ἔτι δέ, εἰ ἐκ τοῦ Πατρὸς ὁ Υἱὸς
γεγέννηται, τὸ δὲ Πνεῦμα ἐκ τοῦ
Πατρὸς καὶ τοῦ Υἱοῦ ἐκπορεύεται,
τίς ἡ καινοτομία τοῦ πνεύματος,
μὴ καὶ ἕτερόν τι αὐτοῦ
ἐκπορεύεσθαι, ὡς συνάγεσθαι κατὰ
τὴν θεοβλαβῆ γνώμην μὴ τρεῖς,
ἀλλὰ τέσσαρας τὰς ὑποστάσεις,
μᾶλλον δ' ἀπείρους, τῆς δὲ
τετάρτης αὐτοῖς ἄλλην πάλιν
προβαλλούσης, κἀκείνης ἑτέραν,
μέχρις ἂν καὶ τῆς Ἑλληνικῆς
ὑπερελάσωσι πολυθείας.

APPENDIX 4

Parallel Passages in
Ep. 291 and the "Mystagogia"

Ep. 291, 122–23:

τρέποιτο δὲ τὸ βλάσφημον εἰς τὰς
τῶν αἰτίων κεφαλάς

Mystagogia, 9:

τὸ βλάσφημον εἰς τὰς τῶν αἰτίων
τρέποιτο κεφαλὰς

Ep. 291, 124–26:

ἄλλως τε δέ, εἰ μὲν τελεία ἡ ἐκ τοῦ
πατρός ἐστιν ἐκπόρευσις, τίς ἡ χρεία
τῆς δευτέρας ἐκπορεύσεως, ἤδη τῆς
τελειότητος ἐκ τῆς πατρικῆς προόδου
καθορωμένης τῷ πνεύματι;

Mystagogia, 31:

Εἰ γὰρ (ὦ τί ἄν σέ τις προσείποι;) τοῦ
Πνεύματος ἡ ἐκπόρευσις ἡ ἐκ τοῦ
Πατρὸς τελεία, τελεία δὲ ὅτι Θεὸς
τέλειος ἐκ Θεοῦ τελείου, τί ποτ' ἂν ἡ
ἐκ τοῦ Υἱοῦ συνεισενέγκῃ;

Although this parallel is not verbatim,
the same argument is made with some
of the same vocabulary.
NB: this is one of the places where
Ep. 2 and *Mystagogia* agree verbatim.

Ep. 291, 379–82:

Τούτων οὕτως ἐχόντων, τῆς
Ῥωμαϊκῆς ἐκκλησίας τοῖς ἄλλοις
τέσσαρσιν ἀρχιερατικοῖς θρόνοις
ὁμοφώνου τε καὶ ὁμοσδόξου

Mystagogia, 70:

ἀλλ' οὖν εἴ τι παρηνέχθησαν
ἐνασχημονῆσαι, τοὺς εὐγνώμονας ἂν
τῶν τοῦ Νῶε παίδων ἐμιμησάμην,
καὶ ἀντὶ περιβολαίων τῇ σιωπῇ

καθεστώσης, πῶς οἱ τοῦ Χὰμ μιμηταὶ
τῶν πατέρων αὐτῶν, ὥς φασι, τὴν
ἀσχημοσύνην οὐκ ἐρυθρίωσιν
ἀνακαλύπτειν καὶ εἰς χλεύην πᾶσι
προτιθέναι;

μᾶλλον καὶ εὐγνωμοσύνῃ τὴν
πατρικὴν ἐπεκάλυψα ἀσχημοσύνην
οὐχὶ δ' ὥσπερ σὺ κατὰ τὸν Χὰμ
διεπραξάμην.

NB: I include this parallel story of
Ham and Noah not because the
vocabulary is the same—on the
contrary, because it is so different.
Although the two texts tell the same
story and draw the same parallel from
Ham to those who use the *Filioque*, the
wording of the passage barely
overlaps.

From this point, *Mystagogia* continues
at length: You are not only not hiding
your fathers' nakedness, but displaying
it, promulgating it, trying to get
everyone to follow them.

Ep. 291, 283–300:

Mystagogia, 72:

Πόσα δ' ἄν τις ὑπὲρ τῶν μακαρίων
ἀνδρῶν ἐκείνων εἴποι; πόσαι γὰρ
περιστάσεις πραγμάτων πολλοὺς
ἐξεβιάζοντο τὰ μὲν
παραφθέγξασθαι, τὰ δὲ πρὸς
οἰκονομίαν εἰπεῖν, τὰ δὲ καὶ τῶν
ἀπειθούντων ἐπαναγκασάντων, τὰ
δὲ καὶ ἀγνοίαι, οἷα δὴ περιολισθῆσαι
τὰ ἀνθρώπινα; ὁ μὲν γὰρ ἴσως
αἱρέσει μαχόμενος, ἄλλος τῇ
ἀσθενείᾳ συγκατιὼν των ἀκροατῶν,
ἄλλος ἄλλο τι διαπραττόμενος καὶ
τὸν καιρὸν ἔχων πολλὰ τῆς ἀκριβείας
καθυφεῖναι παρακαλοῦντα, ἐπὶ
τέλει μείζονι καὶ εἶπεν καὶ ἔπραξεν,
ἃ μήτε λέγειν ἡμῖν μήτε πράττειν
ἔξεστιν. Καὶ ἵνα τοὺς ἄλλους ἐάσω,
ἐννόει μοι τοῦ θαυμασίου Παύλου
καὶ διδασκάλου τῆς οἰκουμένης τὸν
ἁγνισμόν, τὸ ξυρᾶσθαι, τὸ γάλακτι
τρέφειν τοὺς ἀρτι καθισταμένους
πρὸς μάθησιν καὶ οὐ βρώματι·
κἀκεῖθεν ἐφεξῆς εἴ τις τῶν ἱερῶν
ἀνδρων τὸν χορὸν διέλθοι, ὅλον ἂν

Εἶπον οὓς σὺ λέγεις ταῦτα. Εἰ δὲ διά
τινα περίστασιν ἢ πρὸς Ἑλληνιστῶν
ἀντιφερόμενοι λύσαν ἢ

πρὸς ἄλλην αἱρετικήν διαμαχόμενοι
δόξαν ἢ τῇ τῶν ἀκροατῶν
συγκαταβαίνοντες ἀσθενείᾳ, ἢ πόσα
τοιαῦτα καθεκάστην ὁ ἀνθρώπινος
ἐπιδείκνυσι βίος·

ἀνθρώπου κατατρίψοι βίον τὰ
τοιαῦτα ἐξαριθμῶν καὶ γραφόμενος.
ἀλλὰ γὰρ εἴ τις τῶν τοιούτων λόγων
καὶ πράξεων τὴν ἀσθένειαν τῶν
ἀκροατῶν καὶ τὴν οἰκονομίαν τοῦ
λόγου τήν <τε> πρὸς τοὺς
ἀντιτεταγμένους μάχην περιελών,
γυμνὰ τῶν εἰρημένων καὶ ὡς δόγμα
προβάλλοι καὶ περιθάλποι, αὐτοὺς
ἐκείνους τοὺς τὰ τοιαῦτα καὶ
εἰπόντας καὶ πράξαντας εὑρήσει
κατ' αὐτοῦ τὴν δικάζουσαν ἀφιέντας
ψῆφον.

εἰ οὖν ἐκείνοις διά τι τούτων ἢ καὶ
διὰ πλείω τοιαύτην ἐκείνοις ἀφεῖναι
συνέπεσε φωνὴν, πῶς σὺ τὸ μὴ κατὰ
δογματικὴν ἐκείνοις ἔννοιαν
εἰρημένον, δόγμα καὶ νόμον ποιῶν
σαυτῷ μὲν ἀνοήθητον τὴν ἀπῶλειαν
ἐπάγεις, ἐκείνους δὲ συγκατασπᾷν
τῇ σῇ φιλονεικεῖς ἀπονοίᾳ;

NB: like the story of Ham and Noah
above, the ideas of these two passages
are the same, but differences in
vocabulary and expression are much
more obvious than similarities.

Divisions of the "Mystagogia"

Source 1 is in bold print.

Prologue, afterword, and chapters that look like transitions supplied by the compiler are italicized.

Material from Ep. 2 is underlined.

If a chapter is not bold, italic, or underlined, I have no well-founded guess about its provenance.

For each chapter, I have noted the addressee (either an ally who is assumed to share the author's opposition to the Filioque, an opponent who is assumed to be in favor of the Filioque, or "not explicit"), and any specific vocabulary that seems significant. In the latter category, I have noted occurrences of *mystagogia* and related words (see chapter 5, above, for discussion of this vocabulary). I have also noted which word or words a section uses for the proceeding, coming-forth, being-sent-forth, and so on, of the Spirit; and which word or words a section uses for cause or principle. Sometimes these matters of vocabulary suggest subdivisions of the text, and I wanted to make the information available to readers. Perhaps someone else can put the puzzle together more completely than I have done.

1. Prologue

    Addressee: an ally, re: "them heretics"

2. More prologue

    Addressee: an ally, re: "them heretics"

2. (Cont.) rhetorical questions that seem to introduce a section dealing with "the words of the Lord Himself."

Notable vocabulary: μυσταγωγέω
Addressee: an opponent, re: "you heretics"

3. But chapter 3 does not move on to "the words of the Lord himself"; instead it begins a theological discussion of terms and relations in the Trinity. If the Holy Spirit and the Son both come forth (*proagô*) from the Father—one by procession the other by begetting—and if the Spirit comes forth also from the Son, is it not necessary that the Son also come forth from the Spirit, and the Spirit be sender-forth (*paraktikon*) of the Son?

Vocabulary: forms of προάγω, προαγωγός, παρακτικός; προσλαμβάνω; αἴτιος
Addressee: not explicit

4. Dual cause and dual procession of the Spirit lead to composition and inequality of the Spirit.

Vocabulary: αἴτιος, προβολή, σύνθετος
Addressee: not explicit

5. Seems to introduce a section of references to the authority of Fathers and Councils.[1]

Vocabulary: μυσταγωγία
Addressee: an opponent, re: "you heretics"

6. The Spirit becomes both producer and produced, cause and caused.

Vocabulary: forms of προάγω, προαγόμενος; αἴτιος, αἰτιατός
Addressee: an ally, re: "them heretics"

7. Does the Spirit not proceed from the Father already perfect? What does he gain by proceeding from the Son?

Vocabulary: forms of προσλαμβάνω, πρόσληψις; σύνθετος
Addressee: not explicit

8. If the Father begets the Son, and the Spirit proceeds from the Son, of what is the Spirit the producer/sender-forth?

Vocabulary: προαγωγή
Addressee: not explicit

9. If the Spirit proceeds from the Son, the hypostatic properties fall, the persons are confused, Sabellianism rises again.

Vocabulary: ἰδίωμα, πρόσωπον, ὑπόστασις
Addressee: not explicit

10. It is a hypostatic property of the Father to have the Spirit proceed from him as cause, so when they say the Spirit proceeds also from the Son, they combine the Father's hypostatic property with the Son's and sever/distinguish/divide the Father's indivisible hypostatic property.

Vocabulary: ἰδίωμα, αἴτιος, ἰδιώτης
Addressee: an ally, re: "them heretics"

11. To posit two causes in the Trinity is to destroy the monarchy of God. This is polytheism, Hellenic error.

Vocabulary: αἴτιος
Addressee: an ally, re: "them heretics"? not entirely clear

12. If there are two causes in the Trinity, why not three, since that number appears more in the Godhead than two?

Vocabulary: αἴτιος, ἡ ἄναρχος καὶ ὑπεράρχιος ἀρχή = Father, ἰδίωμα
Addressee: not explicit

13. A chapter of lament.

14. Perhaps, a chapter that begins a new section: *"It is not difficult to see the magnitude of their impiety through the following. . . ."*

If the Son is made principle and cause, then there are two causes in the Trinity, one an uncaused cause, the other being a principle and at the same time reverting to a principle.

Vocabulary: ἀρχή, ἄναρχος, ἀρχόμενος, πρὸς ἀρχὴν ἀνατρέχουσαν; αἰτία
Addressee: an ally, re: "them heretics"

15. If the Father is the cause of those from him not by reason of nature but by reason of hypostasis, then to make the Son a cause makes the Son's hypostasis circumscribe the Father's. A worse doctrine than Sabellios's!

Vocabulary: αἴτιος, φύσις, ὑπόστασις
Addressee: not explicit

16. This impiety divides the Father's hypostasis into two—for either the person of the Son must share the Father's hypostasis or the Son perfects the Father's person—either way the Father's hypostasis is divided or imperfect.

Vocabulary: ὑπόστασις, πρόσωπον, φύσις, αἴτιος, μυστήριον
Addressee: not explicit

17. Begins with a lament, including allusions to the devil as the sower of weeds among the grain. Then moves into

If something is a property of two beings, then those two beings may be of the same nature. But if something is a property of two beings, but not a property of a third, then the third is of a different nature. Therefore, if the procession of the Holy Spirit is proper to the Father and to the Son, but not to the Spirit, then the Spirit is of a different nature than the other two persons—anathema!

Vocabulary: κυρίως ἴδιόν τινος; ἑτεροφυής, ὁμοφυής; ὁμοούσιος; ὑπόστασις

Addressee: an ally, re: "them heretics"

18. If the hypostatic property of the Father is changed into the hypostatic property of the Son, then the hypostatic property of the Son is changed into the hypostatic property of the Father, thus changing and transposing the characteristic properties of the hypostases, and then even the Father is begotten. Lament!

Vocabulary: τὸ ἴδιον, ἰδιότης, ἰδίωμα; ὑπόστασις

Addressee: an ally, re: "them heretics"

19. Re: all characteristics shared by more than one hypostasis in the Trinity. A property shared in this way is not a property of a hypostasis, but rather a property of the nature of the divinity. Therefore, if someone says that a property of the Father alone—the sending-forth of the Spirit—is also a property of the Son, they make that a property of the nature of the divinity, and that means that the Father's hypostasis is subsumed in the divine nature and the hypostases are destroyed.

Vocabulary: κυρίως ἴδιόν τινος, ἰδίωμα; ὑπόστασις; φύσις

Addressee: not explicit

20. Beginning of exegesis of Gospel passages about the Holy Spirit

Vocabulary: μυσταγωγέω, μυσταγωγία; αἴτιος

Addressee: some confusion here; the chapter switches from seeming to address an ally re: "them heretics" to addressing "you heretics"; μυσταγωγέω is used in both parts of the chapter

Chaps. 21–30 are about exegesis and addressed to "you heretics." The exegesis is of John 16:15b: "The Spirit will receive from mine. . . ."

Chaps. 21–30 are not numbered in various manuscripts, which then number Migne's chap. 31 as 21, 32 as 22, etc. See appendix 2, above, for details.

21. Exegesis of Jn 16:15.

Vocabulary: τὸ πρὸς οὐσίωσιν ἐκπορεύεσθαι

Addressee: an opponent, re: "you heretics"

22. Jn 16:15. Even children know the difference between "from me" and "from mine."

Addressee: an opponent, re: "you heretics"

23. Jn 16:15.

Vocabulary: μυσταγωγία

Addressee: an opponent, re: "you heretics"

24. Jn 16:15 and its context.

Vocabulary: μυσταγωγία, μυστήριον², διερμηνεύω

Addressee: not explicit

25. Jn 16:15 and its context.

Vocabulary: γνῶσις, ἀνακαλύπτω, μυσταγωγέω

Addressee: not explicit

26. Jn 16:15 and its context.

Vocabulary: ὁμοφυΐα

Addressee: not explicit

27. Jn 16:15 and its context. Still, in spite of the Lord's explicit teaching, the ancient enemy would have come along and sowed heresy, so Jesus tried to stop him by making it clear here: "Everywhere he preserves the consubstantiality, the identity of the nature, and the dignity of equal rank unadulterated." Each person in the Trinity glorifies the others.

Vocabulary: διδάσκειν καὶ φωτίζειν; τὸ ὁμούσιον καὶ ὁμοφυὲς καὶ τὸ τῆς ὁμοτιμίας ἀξίωμα; ἀποκαλύπτω; ἡ ἐκ τῆς θεογνωσίας αὐγή;

Addressee: not explicit

28. Jn 16:15 and its context.

Vocabulary: ἀποφαίνω, φωταγωγέω, ἔπισος, ὁμοούσιος, ὁμοφυΐα, ἰσοτιμία, μυσταγωέω

Addressee: not explicit

29. Jn 16:15b.

Vocabulary: ἀνακαλύπτω

Addressee: an opponent, re: "you heretics"

30. Summing up: What could be more brilliantly clear . . . ?

Vocabulary: More words of enlightening and revealing: e.g. λαμπρότερος, ἱερολογέω, ἐπίγνωσις. Some more theological vocabulary than in previous chapters: e.g. πρόσωπον, ἐνέργεια.

Addressee: an opponent, re: "you heretics"

31. A mixed chapter.

Starts out addressing "you heretics" in a way that carries on quite reasonably from chap. 30; illness and healing are used as analogies for heresy and the refutation of heresy.

Continues to address "you heretics" even as it moves into the section with close parallels (often verbatim) with Ep. 2; see appendix 3, above.

Vocabulary: ὑπόστασις

32. Much verbatim correspondence with Ep. 2; see appendix 3, above. Macedonios (pneumato-machianism) invoked.

Vocabulary: ἰδιότης, ἰδίωμα; ὑπόστασις, πρόοδος, οὐσία, ὁμοφυής, ἰσότιμος
Addressee: an ally, re: "them heretics"

33. Much verbatim correspondence with Ep. 2; see appendix 3, above.

Vocabulary: ἀρχὰι διάφοροι, πολύαρχος ἀρχῆς
Addressee: not explicit

34. Much verbatim correspondence with Ep. 2.

Vocabulary: οὐσία, ἰδίωμα, ὁμοούσιος
Addressee: an ally, re: "them heretics"

35. Much verbatim correspondence with Ep. 2. Mani and Marcion invoked (dualism/two gods).

Vocabulary: κοινοῦνται αἱ ἰδιότητες
Addressee: not explicit

36. Much verbatim correspondence with Ep. 2.

Vocabulary: ὁμοούσιος; προβολή, προβολεύς; μυσταγωγία
Addressee: an ally, re: "them heretics"

37. Much verbatim correspondence with Ep. 2.

Vocabulary: ὑπόστασις
Addressee: an ally, re: "them heretics"

End of correspondence with Ep. 2.

38. If the Son has his being-the-cause of the Holy Spirit from the Father, then he has something more than the Spirit does, and therefore the Spirit is inferior to the Son.

Vocabulary: αἴτιος, ἰσότιμος, ὁμοταγῶς, ὁμοτίμως
Addressee: an ally, re: "them heretics"

39. More about the heretical implications of positing two causes.

Vocabulary: αἴτιος, αἰτία
Addressee: an ally, re: "them heretics"

40. If the Son received from the Father the ability to be the cause of the Spirit, then why did he not pass on to the Spirit the ability to be the cause of some other entity.

Vocabulary: προέρχομαι, προάγω, ὁμοφυής, πρόοδος, ὑπόστασις
Addressee: may be opponent, but it is not clear

41. "That the Son is greater than the Spirit in relation to cause cannot be found in the holy Scriptures."

Vocabulary: φύσις, α ἴτιος, μυσταγωγέω
Addressee: not explicit

[I hypothesize that chap. 41 is a product of the author-compiler of the "Mystagogia" as we have it because it seems to be summing up what came before it: "the tongue that contends with God not only makes the Son greater than the Spirit in relation to cause, but also makes [the Spirit] farther from the nearness of the Father."

I am inclined to see it as a transition from whatever source gave us chaps. 38–40 to another source, but not yet back to Source 1.

One reason for seeing this as transition to yet another source is that it starts over: if the Spirit proceeds from the Son, there are two causes. . . .]

42. If the Son is a cause of the Spirit, we have two causes in the Trinity—an insult to both the first cause and the caused cause whom this idea is supposed to honor.

Vocabulary: αἴτιος, ἀρχῇ, αἰτιατός, προαγωγή
Addressee: not explicit

43. Double procession divides the Spirit and makes a fourth being in the Trinity.

Vocabulary: αἴτιος ἀναίτιος, αἴτιος αἰτιατός, ἀρχή
Addressee: an ally, re: "them heretics"

44. More about what being a "composed" being means: comparison to monsters such as centaurs.

Vocabulary: αἴτιος, ἀτελὲς δὲ καὶ ἡμίτομον ἢ σύνθετον [το Πνεῦμα]
Addressee: not explicit

45. If the Spirit is one properly and in a way that transcends nature, duality of cause is monstrous and impossible.

Vocabulary: τὸ Πνεῦμα καὶ ὑπερφυῶς τε καὶ κυρίως ἕν
Addressee: not explicit

46. Summing up previous theological arguments: you ought to recognize that each person of the consubstantial Trinity has its own hypostatic properties. . . .

Vocabulary: πρόσωπον, ὁμοούσιος, φύσις, ὑπόστασις, ἰδίωμα
Addressee: an opponent, re: "you heretics" at the beginning of the chapter; then an ally, re: "them heretics" at the end

47. Several different ways of expressing the flaws in a theology of double procession.

Vocabulary: προβολεύς, προβολή, πρόβλημα; φύσις, ὑπόστασις, ἱερολογέω, θεολογέω, αἰτία, ἰδίωμα

Addressee: an opponent, re: "you heretics"

48. Scriptural exegesis—Gal 4:6: "God has sent the Spirit of his Son. . . ."

Vocabulary: μυσταγωγός, μυσταγωγέω

Addressee: an ally re: them heretics at the beginning; then an opponent, re: "you heretics" at the end

49. Paul never said that the Spirit proceeds from the Son.

Addressee: not explicit

50. Paul said, "the Spirit of His Son."

Addressee: an opponent, re: "you heretics"

51. And when Paul said, "the Spirit of His Son," he meant that the Spirit is of the same nature and essence, of the same glory and honor and lordship. There is unity according to essence, but the Son does not bring forth a hypostasis of like nature. Nor does Paul speak of a cause.

Vocabulary: ὁμοφυής, ὁμοούσιος, τῆς αὐτῆς δόξης καὶ τιμῆς καὶ κυριότητος, ὑπόστασις, οὐσία, αἰτία, αἴτιος, προάγω

Addressee: an opponent, re: "you heretics"

52. Note well: the Father is also said to be "of the Son." Is it because the Father is begotten by the Son? Obviously not. It is because he is homoousios with the Son. So, too, the Spirit is neither sent forth by the Son nor the sender-forth of the Son.

Vocabulary: θεολογέω, ὁμοούσιος, αἴτιος, προαγωγός, προάγω, αἰτιατός, προβολεύς

Addressee: an opponent, re: "you heretics"

53. So we say "the Spirit of the Son," but we also say, "the Spirit of the Father," "the Son of the Father," "the Father of the Son." We are talking about beings of the same substance. So when we say "the Spirit of the Son", we mean the Spirit is consubstantial with the Father and the Son, and of equal rank and honor. And that the Spirit and the Son both come forth from the Father before the ages.

Vocabulary: ἱερολογέω, ὁμοούσιος, ἐξ ἑνὸς καὶ ἀμερίστου αἰτίου πρὸ αἰώνων τε καὶ ὁμοταγῶς ἑκατέρῳ ἡ πρόοδος

Addressee: not explicit

54. Spirit "of the Son" does not mean (σημαίνει) the same thing as Spirit "proceeding from" the Son means (μυσταγωγεῖ).

Addressee: an opponent, re: "you heretics"

55. Argues for the consubstantiality of Father and Son, using the phrase "light from light." Does not seem to fit with chapters before and after it.

Vocabulary: θεολογέω, ὁμοούσιος

56. Continues the argument about what Paul really said versus what "you" say he said.

Addressee: an opponent, re: "you heretics"

57. The Spirit is also called "of wisdom," etc. Does that mean the Spirit "proceeds from" wisdom?

Vocabulary: ἱερολογέω
Addressee: an opponent, re: "you heretics"

58. More about the Spirit "of" various appellations.

Addressee: an opponent, re: "you heretics"

59. More of the same. Ends "How much time one could waste going through your madness in detail!"

Addressee: an opponent, re: "you heretics"

60. Begins "But [this] heresy also accuses itself thus . . . ; then claims that what has so far been argued is sufficient to persuade anyone who is not completely "given over to impiety" or completely superstitious. Yet the author will not omit further arguments: some may be cured by one cure, others by another, even if others will voluntarily remain ill because of "depravity of opinion" [διὰ μοχθηρίαν γνώμης].

61. Therefore, the following should not be omitted. To make the Spirit proceed from the Son is to make the Spirit a grandson.

Addressee: not explicit

62. The Father is the proximate cause of the Spirit and the Son. If the Son is also the cause of the Spirit, then the Father is the remote cause of the Spirit. So the Father is both proximate and remote cause? That can't be.

Vocabulary: Τὸ αὐτὸ ἂν αἴτιον ὁ Πατὴρ καὶ πόρρω καὶ προσεχὲς αἴτιον εἶναι τοῦ αὐτοῦ
Addressee: not explicit

63. Given: the begetting of the Son and the procession of the Spirit are simultaneous because there can be no before and after in the Godhead. So if the Spirit proceeds from the Son, it must do so at the same time as it proceeds from the Father. But a single hypostasis cannot have two causes unless that hypostasis is somehow divided.

Vocabulary: θεολογέω, αἴτιος, ὑπόστασις
Addressee: not explicit

64. Anything not common to all three persons is proper to only one of them. There is no time in the Godhead; therefore the Son must cause the Spirit to proceed at the same time as the Son himself is being begotten. The Son then becomes both producer and produced. Also, the Spirit would be both proceeding and begotten (with the Son).

Vocabulary: ὁμοφυΐα, προάγω

Addressee: not explicit

65. "Behold your sophistry and your abuse of the scriptures—into what a pit of error and destruction they have forced you. . . . But how much time must we spend on matters we have already accurately and in many ways refuted when we need also to refute some other thing devised by them from their frivolous thinking?"

The change of addressee seems to indicate a transitional chapter. In fact, chap. 66 does return to Source 1—the Scripture has been dispensed with, so chap. 66 can introduce. . . .

66. . . . what the Fathers said. Ambrose, Augustine, Jerome.

Addressee: an ally, re: "them heretics"

67. Continues discussion of Fathers.

Vocabulary: μυσταγωγία, θεολογέω

Addressee: not completely clear; probably an ally, re: "them heretics"

68. Continues discussion of Fathers, specifically Ambrose and Augustine. WHO insults them—the heretics who say they taught double procession or we who deny that they taught such a heresy?

Addressee: this chapter primarily addresses an opponent, re: "you heretics," but returns to "them heretics" in the last few sentences

69. St Paul is invoked: "Even if an angel from heaven . . ." teaches you another gospel (Gal 1:8). Ambrose and Augustine are mentioned.

Vocabulary: μυσταγωγία in the "you heretics" part of the chapter.

Addressee: this chapter begins addressing an ally, re: "them heretics," then addresses an opponent, re: "you heretics"

70. Comparison of "you heretics" to Ham, son of Noah, revealing his father's nakedness.

Addressee: an opponent, re: "you heretics"

71. You cite Augustine and Jerome. But how do we know that their writings have not been treated fraudulently?

Addressee: an opponent, re: "you heretics"

72. Maybe some father said something that sounds like double procession because he was either combating heresy or condescending to his audience. One must consider the context of his statements.

Addressee: an opponent, re: "you heretics"

73. An example of an apostle condescending to his audience: Paul in Athens and the altar to an "unknown god" (Acts 17:16–32).

Addressee: an opponent, re: "you heretics"

74. Paul also condescended to the Jews

Addressee: an opponent, re: "you heretics"

75. Clement of Rome, Dionysius of Alexandria, Methodios of Patara, others; Irenaeus, Hippolytus—all of their writings might be found to contain errors.

Addressee: an opponent, re: "you heretics"

76. A transitional, lamenting chapter.

Addressee: an opponent, re: "you heretics"

77. Basil of Caesarea condescended to the weakness of his flock.

Addressee: not explicit

78. Pope Damasus and the Second Ecumenical Council, Pope Celestine—all attest that the Spirit proceeds from the Father.

Addressee: an opponent, re: "you heretics"

79. Pope Leo the Great and the Fourth Ecumenical Council attest that the Spirit proceeds from the Father and anathematize anyone who alters their creed.

Addressee: not explicit

80. Continues to discuss Leo and the Fourth Ecumenical Council.

Addressee: not explicit

81. Exhortation: "Look, you blind men, and listen, you deaf men, you who live in the heretical West, whom the darkness holds. Gaze upon the ever-brilliant light of the Church and look at noble Leo—or rather give ear to the things which the trumpet of the Spirit sounds against you. Ashamed, fear at least your own father even if you fear no one else." Invocation of Pope Leo I, Ambrose of Milan, Augustine of Hippo.

Addressee: an opponent, re: "you heretics"

82. Pope Vigilius and the Fifth Council also attest that the Spirit proceeds from the Father and anathematize those who change this doctrine.

Addressee: not explicit

83. Pope Agatho and the Sixth Council preserved the creed without alteration.

Addressee: not explicit

84. Pope Gregory the Great and Pope Zacharias who translated Gregory's work into Greek defended the creed and opposed any alteration of it.

Addressee: not explicit

85. John the Baptist and the Prophet Isaiah attest that the Spirit proceeds from the Father. [It seems odd to have them here, rather than in Scripture section.]

Vocabulary: μυστατωγία

Addressee: an opponent, re: "you heretics"

86. Returns to Gregory, Zacharias, and other popes—their defense of an unchangeable creed.

Addressee: an opponent, re: "you heretics"

87. Recently Pope Leo III defended the unchanged creed by erecting inscribed shields (see chap. 5, above) with the creed inscribed on them.

Addressee: an opponent, re: "you heretics"

88. Leo III's successor Benedict III preserved the unchanged creed.

Addressee: not explicit

89. "My John" (Pope John VIII) and his successor Hadrian III also professed the unchanged creed.

Addressee: not explicit

90. *After a passage that may be transitional,* a laundry-list of Scriptural passages, arguing that none of these passages says that the Spirit proceeds from the Son.

Addressee: an opponent, re: "you heretics"

91. "Of the Son" does not mean "proceeds from the Son."

Addressee: not explicit

92. Same basic point as chap. 91.

Addressee: an opponent, re: "your heretics"

93. Isaiah 61:2 and Luke 4:18: "The Spirit of the Lord is upon me. . . ."

Addressee: an opponent, re: "you heretics"

94. A complex theological argument is introduced for the first time: if the Spirit proceeds from the Son inasmuch as the Son is homoousios with us humans, then your argument leads logically to the Spirit being homoousios with flesh. "What could be more ungodly . . . ?"

Vocabulary: Τὸ ἡμέτερον φύραμα, ὁμοούσιος ἡ ἀνθρωπίνη φύσις τῇ θεότητι, [Πνεῦμα] ὁμοούσιον πρὸ τῆς σαρκώσεως καὶ μετὰ τὴν σάρκωσιν

Addressee: an opponent, re: "you heretics"

95. "You have accused our shared Lord, slandered the noble Paul, risen in rebellion against the holy and ecumenical councils, and disparaged the Fathers." This chapter seems to be the logical conclusion of Source 1.

Addressee: an opponent, re: "you heretics"

96. A conclusion addressed to the same person as the preface, chaps. 1–2, above.

Addressee: an ally, re: "them heretics"

NOTES

1. There are some striking similarities here to the language of the Council of Nicea 787 and the documents of the Restoration of Orthodoxy 843. See Auzépy, "Manifestations."

2. Here and in the following chapters, the vocabulary echoes with words for knowledge, revelation, initiation, teaching. I have noted some of that vocabulary.

Primary Sources

Anastasius Bibliothecarius. *De Vitis Romanorum Pontificum.* PL 128.

Berno of Reichenau. *Libellus de quibusdam rebus ad missae officium pertinentibus.* PL 142:1055–79.

Epiphanius of Salamis. *Panarion.* Ed. Karl Holl. *Epiphanius.* Vols. 25, 31, 27 of *Die griechischen christlichen Schriftsteller der ersten drei Jahrhunderte.* Leipzig: J. C. Hinrichs, 1915, 1922, 1931–33. Rev. ed. of vols. 2 and 3. Ed. Jürgen Dummer. Berlin: Akadamie Verlag, 1980, 1985. Trans. Frank Williams, *The Panarion of Epiphanius of Salamis Book I.* Nag Hammadi and Manichaean Studies 35. Leiden: Brill, 1987; *Books II and III.* Nag Hammadi and Manichaean Studies 36. Leiden: Brill, 1994. Trans. of selected passages, Philip R. Amidon, *The 'Panarion' of St. Epiphanius, Bishop of Salamis.* Oxford: Oxford University Press, 1990.

Gouillard, J. "Le Synodikon de l'Orthodoxie." *Travaux et mémoires* 2 (1967): 1–316.

Hergenroether, Josef. *Monumenta graeca ad Photium eiusque historiam pertinentia.* Ratisbon: George Joseph Manz, 1869. Repr. Westmead: Gregg International, 1969.

Jenkins, R. J. H., B. Laourdas, and Cyril A. Mango. "Nine Orations of Arethas from Cod. marc. gr. 524." *Byzantinische Zeitschrift* 47 (1954): 1–40. Repr. in Jenkins, *Studies on Byzantine History of the 9th and 10th Centuries.* London: Variorum, 1970, art. 6.

John VIII, Pope. Letter to Emperor Basil I and His Sons. *Monumenta Germaniae Historica* (MGH). Available online at http://www.dmgh.de. Epp. 7, Epp. Karolini Aevi 5, Ep. 259, 228–30.

John the Deacon. "La cronaca veneziana del diacono Giovanni." In *Cronache Veneziane antichissime,* ed. Giovanni Monticolo, 59–171. Rome: Istituto storico italiano, 1890.

Leo I, Pope. Letter 28 to Flavian of Constantinople. PL 54:756–82; also ed. E. Schwartz, *Concilium Chalcedonense.* Vol. 1. Berlin: de Gruyter, 1933, 10–20; Eng. trans. C. L. Feltoe, *Select Letters and Sermons of Leo I.* Oxford: Oxford University Press, 1895, 38–43.

Mango, Cyril. *The Art of the Byzantine Empire 312–1453: Sources and Documents* [Eng. trans. of many passages related to Byzantine art]. Toronto: University of Toronto Press, 1986.

Mansi, Giovan Domenico. *Sacrorum conciliorum nova et amplissima collectio.* 53 vols. Paris: H. Welter, 1801–27.

Middle English Dictionary. Ed. Hans Kurath. 13 vols. Ann Arbor: University of Michigan Press, 1952–2001.

Nicholas I, Pope. Letter to Emperor Michael. MGH Epp. 6, Epp. Karolini Aevi IV, Ep. 88, 454–86.

Niketas Byzantios. *Works against Islam.* Ed. and German trans. Karl Förstel, *Niketas von Byzanz, Schriften zum Islam.* Würzburg: Oros, 2000.

Opus Caroli Regis adversus synodum (Libri Carolini). Ed. Ann Freeman. MGH Leg. 3, Conc. 2, supp. 1.

Patrologiae cursus completus [. . .] Series Graeca. Ed. Jacques-Paul Migne. 161 vols. Paris: Migne, 1857–66 (PG).

Patrologiae cursus completus [. . .] Series Latina. Ed. Jacques-Paul Migne. 221 vols. Paris: Migne, 1844–64 (PL).

Paulinus, Patriarch of Aquileia. *Concilium Forojuliense.* PL 99:283–302.

Photios, Patriarch of Constantinople. "Archiepiscopo Aquileiae." In *Epistulae et Amphilochia,* vol. 3, Ep. 291.

——. *Bibliotheca.* Ed. René Henry. *Bibliothèque.* 9 vols. Paris: Société d'éditions les belles lettres, 1959–77. Eng. trans. J. H. Freese, *The Library of Photius.* Transactions of Christian Literature, ser. 1, Greek Texts. London: SPCK, 1920. Eng. trans. of selected passages, N. G. Wilson, *Photius, the Bibliotheca: A Selection Translated with Notes.* London: Duckworth, 1994.

——. "Encyclica ad sedes orientales." In *Epistulae et Amphilochia,* vol. 1, Ep. 2.

——. *Epistulae et Amphilochia.* Ed. B. Laourdas and L. B. Westerink. 7 vols. Leipzig: Teubner, 1983–88.

——. *Logos peri tes tou agiou pneumatos mystagogias.* PG 102:279–396. Eng. trans. *"On the Mystagogy of the Holy Spirit," by Saint Photios, Patriarch of Constantinople.* Holy Transfiguration Monastery. Astoria, N.Y.: Studion, 1983.

——. *The Homilies of Photius, Patriarch of Constantinople.* Intro., trans., comm. Cyril Mango. Cambridge, Mass.: Harvard University Press, 1958.

——. *Lexicon.* Ed. Christos Theodoridis. 2 vols. (letters A–M). Berlin: de Gruyter, 1982, 1998.

Price, Richard, and Michael Gaddis, trans. *The Acts of the Council of Chalcedon.* 3 vols. Liverpool: Liverpool University Press, 2006.

Ratramnus of Corbie. "Contra Graecorum opposita romanam ecclesiam infamantium libri quatuor." PL 121:229–30.

Theodore of Stoudios. *Joanni Spathario.* Ep. 1, 17. PG 99, 961–64.

Theophylact of Ohrid. Προσλαλιά τινι τῶν ὁμιλητῶν περὶ ὧν ἐγκαλοῦνται Λατῖνοι [Response to one of his students regarding accusations against the Latins]. Ed. and

French trans., P. Gautier, *Théophylacte d'Achrida. Discours, traités, poésies. Introduction, texte, traduction et notes.* Corpus Fontium Historiae Byzantinae 26/1, 247–69. Thessaloniki: Association de recherches byzantines, 1980.

Secondary Sources

Afinogenov, Dmitry E. "The Great Purge of 843: A Re-examination." In *Leimôn: Studies Presented to Lennart Rydén on His Sixty-fifth Birthday,* ed. Jan Olof Rosenqvist, 76–91. Uppsala: Uppsala University, 1996.

Ahrweiler, Hélène. "Sur la carrière de Photius avant son patriarcat." *Byzantinische Zeitschrift* 58 (1965): 348–63.

Alexakis, Alexander. *Codex Parisinus Graecus 1115 and Its Archetype.* Washington, D.C.: Dumbarton Oaks, 1996.

——. "The *Epistula ad Marinum Cypri Presbyterum* of Maximos the Confessor (CPG 7697.10) Revisited: A Few Remarks on its Meaning and History." *Byzantinische Zeitschrift* 94 (2001): 545–54.

——. "The Greek Patristic *Testimonia* Presented at the Council of Florence (1439) in Support of the Filioque Reconsidered." *Revue des Études Byzantines* 58 (2000): 149–65.

Anastos, Milton V. *Aspects of the Mind of Byzantium: Political Theory, Theology, and Ecclesiastical Relations with the See of Rome.* Ed. Speros Vryonis, Jr., and Nicholas Goodhue. Aldershot: Ashgate/Variorum, 2001.

——. "Constantinople and Rome: A Survey of the Relations between the Byzantine and Roman Churches." In *Aspects of the Mind of Byzantium,* art. 8.

——. "The Papal Legates at the Council of 861 and Their Compliance with the Wishes of the Emperor Michael III." In *Harmos: Timetikos tomos ston Kathegete N. K. Moutsopoulo gia ta 25 chronia pneumatikes tou prosforas sto Panepistemio.* 2 vols., 1:185–200. Thessaloniki: Aristoteleio Panepistemio Thessalonikes Polytechnike Schole, Tmema Architektonon, 1990. Repr. in *Aspects of the Mind of Byzantium,* art. 6.

——. "The Transfer of Illyricum, Calabria and Sicily to the Jurisdiction of the Patriarchate of Constantinople in 732–33." *Studi bizantini e neoellenici* 9 (1957): 14–31.

Auzépy, Marie-France. "Manifestations de la propagande en faveur de l'orthodoxie." In *Byzantium in the Ninth Century,* ed. Brubaker, 85–99.

Ayres, Lewis. "Articulating Identity." In *Cambridge History of Early Christian Literature,* ed. Young et al., 414–63.

——. *Nicaea and Its Legacy: An Approach to Fourth-Century Trinitarian Theology.* Oxford: Clarendon Press, 2004.

Baker, D., ed. *The Orthodox Churches and the West.* Oxford: Blackwell, 1976.

Barber, Charles. *Figure and Likeness: On the Limits of Representation in Byzantine Iconoclasm.* Princeton: Princeton University Press, 2002.

———. "The Koimesis Church, Nicaea: The Limits of Representation on the Eve of Iconoclasm." *Jahrbuch der österreichischen Byantinistik* 41 (1991): 43–60.

Barnard, Leslie. "The Theology of Images." In *Iconoclasm*, ed. Bryer and Herrin, 7–13.

Barnes, Michael R., and Daniel H. Williams, eds. *Arianism after Arius: Essays on the Development of the Fourth Century Trinitarian Conflicts.* Edinburg: T&T Clark, 1993.

Bauer, Walter. *Rechtgläubigkeit und Ketzerei im ältesten Christentum.* 1st ed. Tübingen: Mohr, 1934.

———. *Rechtgläubigkeit und Ketzerei im ältesten Christentum.* 2nd ed. Tübingen: Mohr, 1964. Trans. Philadelphia Seminar on Christian Origins, ed. Robert A. Kraft and Gerhard Krodel, *Orthodoxy and Heresy in Earliest Christianity.* Philadelphia: Fortress Press, 1971. Online translation updated by Kraft, http://ccat.sas.upenn.edu/rs/rak/publics/new/BAUER00.htm. Accessed 22 June 2007.

Bishop, Jane Carol. "Pope Nicholas I and the First Age of Papal Independence." PhD diss., Columbia University, 1980.

Boyarin, Daniel. *Border Lines: The Partition of Judaeo-Christianity.* Philadelphia: University of Pennsylvania Press, 2004.

———. "Semantic Difference; or, 'Judaism'/'Christianity.'" In *The Ways That Never Parted*, ed. Reed and Becker, 65–85.

Brock, Sebastian. "Iconoclasm and the Monophysites." In *Iconoclasm*, ed. Bryer and Herrin, 53–57.

Brown, Peter. "A Dark-Age Crisis: Aspects of the Iconoclastic Controversy." *English Historical Review* 88 (1973): 1–34. Repr. in Brown, *Society and the Holy*, 251–301.

———. "Eastern and Western Christendom in Late Antiquity: A Parting of the Ways." In *The Orthodox Churches and the West*, ed. Baker, 1–24. Repr. in Brown, *Society and the Holy*, 166–95.

———. *Society and the Holy in Late Antiquity.* Berkeley and Los Angeles: University of California Press, 1982.

———. *The World of Late Antiquity from Marcus Aurelius to Muhammed.* London: Thames and Hudson, 1971.

Brown, T. S. *Gentlemen and Officers: Imperial Administration and Aristocratic Power in Byzantine Italy, A.D. 554–800.* London: British School at Rome, 1984.

Brubaker, Leslie. "Byzantine Art in the Ninth Century: Theory, Practice and Culture." *Byzantine and Modern Greek Studies* 13 (1989): 23–93.

———, ed. *Byzantium in the Ninth Century: Dead or Alive? Papers from the Thirtieth Spring Symposium of Byzantine Studies, Birmingham, March 1996.* Aldershot: Ashgate, 1998.

———. "Icons before Iconoclasm?" In *Morfologie sociali e culturali in europa fra tarda antichità e alto medioevo*, 2 vols. Settimane di studi del Centro italiano di Studi sull'alto medioevo 45, 2:1215–54. Spoleto: Centro italiano di studi sull'alto medioevo, 1998.

———. "*In the Beginning Was the Word:* Art and Orthodoxy at the Councils of Trullo (692) and Nicaea II (787)." In *Byzantine Orthodoxies*, ed. Louth and Casaday, 95–101.

———. *Vision and Meaning in Ninth-Century Byzantium: Image as Exegesis in the Homilies of Gregory of Nazianzus.* Cambridge Studies in Palaeography and Codicology 6. Cambridge: Cambridge University Press, 1999.

Bryer, Anthony, and Judith Herrin, eds. *Iconoclasm: Papers Given at the Ninth Spring Symposium of Byzantine Studies.* Birmingham: Centre for Byzantine Studies, University of Birmingham, 1977.

Callahan, Daniel. "The Problem of the 'Filioque' and the Letter from the Pilgrim Monks of the Mount of Olives to Pope Leo III and Charlemagne: Is the Letter Another Forgery by Adémar of Chabannes?" *Revue bénédictine* 102 (1992): 75–134.

Cameron, Averil. "Ascetic Closure and the End of Antiquity." In *Asceticism*, ed. Vincent L. Wimbush and Richard Valantasis, 147–51. New York: Oxford University Press, 1995.

———. "Blaming the Jews: The Seventh-Century Invasions of Palestine in Context." *Travaux et mémoires* 14 (2002): 57–78.

———. "Byzantium and the Past in the Seventh Century: The Search for Redefinition." In *The Seventh Century*, ed. Fontaine and Hillgarth, 250–76. Repr. in Cameron, *Changing Cultures*, art. 5.

———. *Changing Cultures in Early Byzantium.* Aldershot: Variorum, 1996.

———. *Christianity and the Rhetoric of Empire: The Development of Christian Discourse.* Berkeley and Los Angeles: University of California Press, 1991.

———. "Disputations, Polemical Literature and the Formation of Opinion in the Early Byzantine Period." In *Dispute Poems and Dialogues in the Ancient and Medieval Near East*, ed. G. J. Reinink and H. L. J. Vanstiphout, 90–108. Orientalia Lovaniensia Analecta 42. Louvain: Uitgeverij Peeters, 1991. Repr. in Cameron, *Changing Cultures*, art. 3.

———. "Education and Literary Culture." In *Cambridge Ancient History.* Vol. 13, *The Late Empire, A.D. 337–425*, ed. Cameron and Peter Garnsey, 665–707. Cambridge: Cambridge University Press, 1998.

———. "Eustratius' *Life* of the Patriarch Eutychius and the Fifth Ecumenical Council." In *Kathegetria*, ed. Chrysostomides, 225–47. Repr. Cameron, *Changing Cultures*, art. 1.

———. "How to Read Heresiology." *Journal of Medieval and Early Modern Studies* 33 (2003): 471–92.

———. "Jews and Heretics—A Category Error?" In *The Ways That Never Parted*, ed. Reed and Becker, 345–60.

———. "The Language of Images: The Rise of Icons and Christian Representation." In *The Church and the Arts*, ed. D. Wood, 1–42. Repr. in Cameron, *Changing Cultures*, art. 12.

———. *The Mediterranean World in Late Antiquity, AD 395–600.* London: Routledge, 1993.

———. "Models of the Past in the Late Sixth Century: The Life of the Patriarch Eutychius." In *Reading the Past in Late Antiquity*, ed. Clarke, 205–23. Repr. in Cameron, *Changing Cultures*, art. 2.

———. "Texts as Weapons: Polemic in the Byzantine Dark Ages." In *Literacy and Power in the Ancient World*, ed. Alan K. Bowman and Greg Woolf, 198–215. Cambridge: Cambridge University Press, 1994.

———. *The Use and Abuse of Byzantium: An Essay on Reception.* Inaugural Lecture, King's College London, 15 May 1990. London: The School of Humanities, King's College London, 1992.

Chazelle, Celia. Review of Ann Freeman, ed., *Opus Caroli Regis (Libri Carolini)*, MGH *Conc. 2, Supplementum* (Hanover, 1998). *The Medieval Review* 1999: http://name. umdl.umich.edu/baj9928.9912.004. Accessed 25 June 2007.

La chiesa greca in Italia dall'VIII al XVI secolo. Atti del convegno storico interecclesiale (Bari, 30 Apr.–4. Magg. 1969), 3 vols. Italia sacra 20–22. Padua: Editrice Antenore, 1973.

Chrysos, Evangelos. "The Synodal Acts as Literary Products." In *L'Icone dans la théologie et l'art*, 85–93. Chambesy: Éditions du centre orthodox du patriarcat oecuménique, 1990.

Chrysostomides, Julian, ed. *Kathegetria: Essays Presented to Joan Hussey.* Camberley: Porphyrogenitus, 1988.

Clarke, G., ed. *Reading the Past in Late Antiquity.* Canberra: Australian National University Press, 1990.

Coakley, Sarah, and David A. Pailin, eds. *The Making and Remaking of Christian Doctrine: Essays in Honour of Maurice Wiles.* Oxford: Clarendon Press, 1993.

Cohen, Shaye J. D. *The Beginnings of Jewishness: Boundaries, Varieties, Uncertainties.* Berkeley and Los Angeles: University of California Press, 1999.

———. *From the Maccabees to the Mishnah.* 2nd ed. Louisville, Ky.: Westminster John Knox Press, 2006.

Constable, Giles. "Forgery and Plagiarism in the Middle Ages." *Archiv für Diplomatik* 29 (1983): 1–41.

Cormack, Robin. "Women and Icons and Women in Icons." In *Women, Men and Eunuchs*, ed. James, 24–51.

———. *Writing in Gold.* Oxford: Oxford University Press, 1985.

Corrigan, Kathleen. *Visual Polemics in Ninth-Century Byzantine Psalters.* Cambridge: Cambridge University Press, 1992.

Croke, Brian. "Justinian's Constantinople." In *Cambridge Companion to the Age of Justinian*, ed. Maas, 60–86.

Dagron, Gilbert. "Aux origines de la civilisation byzantine: Langue de culture et langue d'état." *Revue historique* 489 (1969): 29–76.

———. "L'Église et la chrétienté Byzantines entre les invasions et l'iconoclasme (VIIe–début VIIIe siècle)." In *Histoire du christianisme*, ed. Mayeur et al., 4:7–91.

———. "L'Église et l'État (milieu IXe–fin Xe siècle)." In *Histoire du christianisme*, ed. Mayeur et al., 4:167–240.

———. *Empereur et prêtre. Étude sur le "césaropapisme" byzantin.* Paris: Éditions Gallimard, 1996. Trans. Jean Birrell, *Emperor and Priest: The Imperial Office in Byzantium.* Cambridge: Cambridge University Press, 2003.

———. "L'iconoclasme et l'établissment de l'Orthodoxie (726–847)." In *Histoire du christianisme*, ed. Mayeur et al, 4:93–165.

Darrouzès, Jean. "Les documents byzantins de XIIe siècle sur la primauté romaine." *Revue des Études byzantines* 23 (1965): 42–88.

Dendrinos, Charalambos, et al., eds. *Porphyrogenita: Essays in Honour of Julian Chrysostomides*. Aldershot: Ashgate, 2003.

Dölger, Franz Josef, and P. Wirth. *Regesten der Kaiserurkunden des oströmischen Reiches von 565–1453*. Vol. 1, *Regesten von 565–1025*. Munich, 1924. Repr. Hildesheim: H. A. Gerstenberg, 1976.

Dvornik, Francis. *Byzantium and the Roman Primacy*. New York: Fordham University Press, 1966.

——. *The Photian Schism: History and Legend*. Cambridge: Cambridge University Press, 1948. Repr. 1970.

Ehrman, Bart. *The Orthodox Corruption of Scripture: The Effect of Early Christological Controversies on the Text of the New Testament*. Oxford: Oxford University Press, 1993.

Ekonomou, Andrew J. *Byzantine Rome and the Greek Popes: Eastern Influences on Rome and the Papacy from Gregory the Great to Zacharias, A.D. 590–752*. Lanham, Md.: Lexington/Rowman & Littlefield, 2007.

Elm, Susanna. "The Diagnostic Gaze. Gregory of Nazianzus' Theory of Orthodox Priesthood in his Orations 6 *De pace* and 2 *Apologia de fuga sua*." In *Orthodoxie, Christianisme, Histoire*, ed. Elm et al., 83–100.

Elm, Susanna, Éric Rebillard, and Antonella Romano, eds. *Orthodoxie, Christianisme, Histoire: Orthodoxy, Christianity, History*. Rome: École française de Rome, 2000.

Fine, John V. A., Jr. *The Early Medieval Balkans: A Critical Survey from the Sixth to the Late Twelfth Century*. Ann Arbor: University of Michigan Press, 1983.

Fontaine, J., and J. N. Hillgarth, eds. *The Seventh Century: Change and Continuity*. London: Warburg Institute, 1992.

Freeman, Ann. "Carolingian Orthodoxy and the Fate of the Libri Carolini." *Viator* 16 (1985): 65–108.

Gager, John G. *Kingdom and Community: The Social World of Early Christianity*. Englewood Cliffs, N.J.: Prentice-Hall, 1975.

——. *The Origins of Anti-Semitism: Attitudes toward Judaism in Pagan and Christian Antiquity*. New York: Oxford University Press, 1983.

Gay, Jules. *L'Italie méridionale et l'empire byzantin depuis l'avènement de Basil Ier jusqu'a la prise de Bari par les Normands*. Bibliothèque des Écoles Françaises d'Athénes et de Rome 90. Paris: A. Fontemoing, 1904.

Gero, Stephen. *Byzantine Iconoclasm during the Reign of Constantine V*. Corpus Scriptorum Christianorum Orientalium Subsidia 52. Louvain: CSCO, 1977.

——. *Byzantine Iconoclasm during the Reign of Leo III*. Corpus Scriptorum Christianorum Orientalium Subsidia 41. Louvain: CSCO, 1973.

Giannoni, Carl. *Paulinus II, Patriarch von Aquileia: Ein Beitrag zur Kirchengeschichte Österreichs im Zeitalter Karls des Grossen*. Vienna: Mayer, 1896.

Gibson, E. Leigh. "Jewish Antagonism or Christian Polemic: The Case of the *Martyrdom of Pionius*." *Journal of Early Christian Studies* 9 (2001): 339–58.

———. "The Jews and Christians in the *Martyrdom of Polycarp*: Entangled or Parted Ways?" In *The Parting of the Ways*, ed. Reed and Becker, 145–58.

Gordillo, M. "Photius et Primatus Romanus. Num Photius habendus sit auctor opusculi 'Pros tous legontas os e Rome thronos protos'?" *Orientalia Christiana Periodica* 6 (1940): 5–39.

Gouillard, J. "Nouveaux témoins du Synodicon de l'Orthodoxie." *Annalecta Bollandiana* (1982): 459–62.

Grabar, André. *L'iconoclasme byzantin*. Paris: Collége de France, 1957.

Gray, Patrick T. R. "Covering the Nakedness of Noah: Reconstruction and Denial in the Age of Justinian." *Byzantinische Forschungen* 24 (1997): 193–206.

———. *The Defense of Chalcedon in the East*. Leiden: Brill, 1979.

———. "Forged Forgeries: Constantinople III and the Acts of Constantinople II." In *Abstracts of Papers, Byzantine Studies Conference, 31st, 2005*, 90. Atlanta: Byzantine Studies Conference, 2005.

———. "The Legacy of Chalcedon: Christological Problems and Their Significance." In *Cambridge Companion to the Age of Justinian*, ed. Maas, 215–38.

———. "Neochalcedonianism and the Tradition: From Patristic to Byzantine Theology." *Byzantinische Forschungen* 8 (1982): 61–70.

———. "'The Select Fathers': Canonizing the Patristic Past." *Studia Patristica* 23 (1989): 21–36.

Grumel, Venance. *Les regestes des actes du Patriarcat de Constantinople*. Vol. 1, fasc. 2–3, *AD 715–1206*. 2nd ed., ed. Jean Darrouzès. Paris: Institut français d'études byzantines, 1989.

Guillou, André. "Cultura, insegnamento e ricerca in istoria. Un esempio: l'Italia bizantina." *Quaderni medievali* 2 (1976): 154–61. Repr. in *Culture et Société*, art. 16.

———. *Culture et Société en Italie Byzantine (VIe–XIe s.)*. London: Variorum, 1978.

———. "Grecs d'Italie du Sud et de Sicile au moyen âge: Les moines." *Mélanges d'archéologie et d'histoire* 75 (1963): 79–110. Repr. in *Studies on Byzantine Italy*, art. 12.

———. "Italie méridionale byzantine ou Byzantins en Italie méridionale?" *Byzantion* 44 (1974): 152–90. Repr. in *Culture et Société*, art. 15.

———. *Studies on Byzantine Italy*. London: Variorum Reprints, 1970.

Haldon, John. *Byzantium in the Seventh Century: The Transformation of a Culture*. Cambridge: Cambridge University Press, 1990.

Haldon, John, and Leslie Brubaker. *Byzantium in the Iconoclast Era (ca. 680–850): The Sources; An Annotated Survey*. Aldershot: Ashgate, 2001.

Hamilton, Bernard. "The City of Rome and the Eastern Churches in the Tenth Century." *Orientalia christiana periodica* 27 (1961): 5–26.

Haugh, Richard. *Photius and the Carolingians: The Trinitarian Controversy*. Belmont, Mass.: Nordland, 1975.

Hergenroether, Josef. *Monumenta graeca ad Photium eiusque historiam pertinentia*. Ratisbon: Georg Joseph Manz, 1869. Repr. Westmead: Gregg International, 1969.

———. *Photius Patriarch von Konstantinopel. Sein Leben, seine Schriften und das griechische Schisma.* 3 vols. Regensburg: Georg Joseph Manz, 1867. Repr. Darmstadt: Wissenschaftliche Buchgesellschaft, 1966.

Herrin, Judith. "The Context of Iconoclast Reform." In *Iconoclasm*, ed. Bryer and Herrin, 15–20.

———. *The Formation of Christendom.* Princeton: Princeton University Press, 1987.

———. "Women and the Faith in Icons in Early Christianity." In *Culture, Ideology and Politics*, ed. Samuel and Jones, 56–83.

Hunger, Herbert. *Graeculus Perfidus. Italos Itamos. Il senso dell'alterità nei rapporti greco-romani ed italo-bizantini.* Rome: Unione internazionale degli istituti di archeologia storia e storia dell'arte in Roma, 1987.

James, Liz, ed. *Women, Men and Eunuchs: Gender in Byzantium.* London: Routledge, 1997.

Jugie, M. "Le culte de Photius dans l'Église byzantine." *Revue de l'orient chrétien*, ser. 3, 3 (1922–23): 105–22.

Karlin-Hayter, Patricia. "Gregory of Syracuse, Ignatios and Photios." In *Iconoclasm*, ed. Bryer and Herrin, 141–45.

———. "Methodios and His Synod." In *Byzantine Orthodoxies*, ed. Louth and Casaday, 55–74.

Khazdan, Alexander, et al., eds. *The Oxford Dictionary of Byzantium.* Oxford: Oxford University Press, 1991.

Khoury, Adel-Théodore. *Polémique byzantine contre l'Islam (VIIIe–XIIIe s.).* Leiden: Brill, 1972.

———. *Les théologiens byzantins et l'Islam. Textes et auteurs (VIIIe–XIIIe s.).* Louvain: Nauwelaerts, 1969.

Kolbaba, Tia. *The Byzantine Lists: Errors of the Latins.* Urbana: University of Illinois Press, 2000.

———. "Latin and Greek Christians." In *The Cambridge History of Christianity.* Vol. 3, *c. 600–c. 1100*, ed. Thomas F. X. Noble and Julia M. H. Smith, 213–29. Cambridge: Cambridge University Press, 2008.

———. "The Legacy of Humbert and Cerularius: The Tradition of 'The Schism of 1054' in Byzantine Texts and Manuscripts of the Twelfth and Thirteenth Centuries." In *Porphyrogenita*, ed. Dendrinos et al., 47–61.

Laurent, Vitalien. "L'Eglise de l'Italie méridionale entre Rome et Byzance à la veille de la conquête normande." In *La chiesa greca*, 1:14–20.

Le Boulluec, Alain. *La notion d'hérésie dans la littérature grecque IIe–IIIe siècles.* 2 vols. Paris: Études augustiniennes, 1985.

Lemerle, Paul. *Le premier humanisme byzantin; notes et remarques sur enseignement et culture à Byzance des origines au Xe siècle.* Paris: Presses universitaires de France, 1971.

Lim, Richard. *Public Disputation, Power, and Social Order in Late Antiquity.* Berkeley and Los Angeles: University of California Press, 1995.

Loud, Graham A. "Byzantine Italy and the Normans." *Byzantinische Forschungen* 13 (1988): 215–33.

Louth, Andrew, and Augustine Casaday, eds. *Byzantine Orthodoxies: Papers from the Thirty-sixth Spring Symposium of Byzantine Studies.* Aldershot: Ashgate, 2006.

Lyman, J. Rebecca. "The Making of a Heretic: The Life of Origen in Epiphanius' Panarion 64." *Studia Patristica* 31 (1997): 445–51.

Ma, J., and N. Van Deusen. *Alexander's Revenge: Hellenistic Culture through the Centuries.* Reykjavik: University of Iceland Press, 2002.

Maas, Michael, ed. *The Cambridge Companion to the Age of Justinian.* Cambridge: Cambridge University Press, 2005.

Macquarrie, John. "Doctrinal Development: Searching for Criteria." In *Making and Remaking,* ed. Coakley and Pailin, 161–76.

Mango, Cyril. "Byzantine Literature as a Distorting Mirror." Inaugural Lecture, University of Oxford, 1975.

——. "The Liquidation of Iconoclasm and the Patriarch Photios." In *Iconoclasm,* ed. Bryer and Herrin, 133–40.

Markus, Robert A. *The End of Ancient Christianity.* Cambridge: Cambridge University Press, 1990.

——. "Social and Historical Setting." In *Cambridge History of Early Christian Literature,* ed. Young et al., 399–413.

Martini, E. *Catalogo di manoscritti greci esistenti nelle biblioteche italiane.* Vol. 2, *Catalogus codicum graecorum qui in Bibliotheca Vallicellana Romae adservantur.* Milan: Ulrico Hoepli, 1902.

Mayeur, Jean-Marie, et al., eds. *Histoire du christianisme des origins à nos jours.* Vol. 4, *Évêques, moines et empereurs (610–1054).* Paris: Desclée, 1993.

Mercati, Ioannes, and Pius Franchi de' Cavalieri. *Codices Vaticani Graeci.* Vol. 3, codd. 604–866. Vatican City: Biblioteca Apostolica Vaticana, 1950.

Meyendorff, John. *Byzantine Theology. Historical Trends and Doctrinal Themes.* New York: Fordham University Press, 1974.

Moore, R. I. *The Formation of a Persecuting Society: Power and Deviance in Western Europe 950–1250.* Oxford: Blackwell, 1987.

Mullett, Margaret. "The 'Other' in Byzantium." In *Strangers to Themselves,* ed. Smythe, 1–22.

Mullett, Margaret, and Dion Smythe. *Alexios I Komnenos, I, Papers.* Belfast Byzantine Texts and Translations 4.1. Belfast: Belfast Byzantine Enterprises, 1996.

Murphy, F. X., and P. Sherwood. *Constantinople II et Constantinople III.* Paris: Orante, 1974.

Nichols, Aidan. *Rome and the Eastern Churches: A Study in Schism.* Edinburgh: T&T Clark, 1992.

Noble, Thomas F. X. *The Republic of St. Peter: The Birth of the Papal State, 680–825.* Philadelphia: University of Pennsylvania Press, 1984.

Norris, Richard A., Jr. "Articulating Identity." In *Cambridge History of Early Christian Literature,* ed. Young et al., 71–90.

Noyé, Ghislaine. "Byzance et Italie méridionale." In *Byzantium in the Ninth Century*, ed. Brubaker, 229–43.

Olster, David. *Roman Defeat, Christian Response, and the Literary Construction of the Jew.* Philadelphia: University of Pennsylvania Press, 1994.

Pailin, David A. "The Supposedly Historical Basis of Theological Understanding." In *Making and Remaking*, ed. Coakley and Pailin, 213–37.

Papadakis, Aristeides. *Crisis in Byzantium: The 'Filioque' Controversy in the Patriarchate of Gregory II of Cyprus (1283–1289).* New York: Fordham University Press, 1984.

Papadakis, Aristeides, and John Meyendorff. *The Christian East and the Rise of the Papacy: The Church 1071–1453 A.D.* Crestwood, N.Y.: St. Vladimir's Seminary Press, 1994.

Pazdernik, Charles. "Justinianic Ideology and the Power of the Past." In *Cambridge Companion to the Age of Justinian*, ed. Maas, 185–212.

Pegg, Mark. *The Corruption of Angels: The Great Inquisition of 1245–1246.* Princeton: Princeton University Press, 2001.

Pelikan, Jaroslav. *The Christian Tradition.* Vol. 2, *The Spirit of Eastern Christendom 600–1700.* Chicago: University of Chicago Press, 1974.

Peri, Vittorio. "Il simbolo epigrafico di S. Leone III nelle basiliche romane dei SS. Pietro e Paolo." *Rivista de Archeologia Christiana* 45 (1969): 191–221.

Pohl, Walter. "Telling the Difference: Signs of Ethnic Identity." In *Strategies of Distinction*, ed. Pohl and Reimitz, 17–69.

Pohl, Walter, and Helmut Reimitz, eds. *Strategies of Distinction: The Construction of Ethnic Communities, 300–800.* Leiden: Brill, 1998.

Pourkier, Aline. *L'hérésologie chez Epiphane de Salamine.* Paris: Beauchesne, 1992.

Ramseyer, Valerie. *The Transformation of a Religious Landscape: Medieval Southern Italy, 850–1150.* Ithaca: Cornell University Press, 2006.

Rando, Daniela. *Una chiesa di frontiera. Le istituzioni ecclesiastiche veneziane nei secoli VI–XII.* Bologna: Il Mulino, 1994.

Rapp, Claudia. "A Medieval Cosmopolis: Constantinople and Its Foreign Inhabitants." In *Alexander's Revenge*, ed. Ma and Van Deusen, 153–72.

Reed, Annette Yoshiko, and Adam H. Becker. "Introduction: Traditional Models and New Directions." In *The Ways That Never Parted*, ed. Reed and Becker, 1–33.

——, eds. *The Ways That Never Parted: Jews and Christians in Late Antiquity and the Early Middle Ages.* Tübingen: Mohr Siebeck, 2003.

Rubenstein, Richard R. *When Jesus Became God: The Struggle to Define Christianity during the Last Days of Rome.* New York: Harcourt Brace, 1999.

Runciman, Steven. *The Eastern Schism: A Study of the Papacy and the Eastern Churches during the Eleventh and Twelfth Centuries.* Oxford: Clarendon Press, 1955.

Sahas, Daniel. "'Holosphyros?' A Byzantine Perception of 'The God of Muhammad.'" In *Christian-Muslim Encounters*, ed. Yvonne Yazbeck Haddad and Wadi Zaidan Haddad, 109–25. Gainesville: University Press of Florida, 1995.

Samuel, Raphael, and Gareth Stedman Jones, eds. *Culture, Ideology and Politics: Essays for Eric Hobsbawm.* London: Routledge and Kegan Paul, 1982.

Sanders, Jack T. *Schismatics, Sectarians, Dissidents, Deviants: The First One Hundred Years of Jewish-Christian Relations.* Valley Forge: Trinity Press International, 1993.

Sansterre, Jean-Marie. *Les moines grecs et orientaux à Rome aux époques byzantine et carolingienne (milieu du VIe s.–fin du IXe s.).* Brussels: Palais des academies, 1983.

———. "La parole, le texte et l'image selon les auteurs byzantins des époques iconoclaste et posticonoclaste." In *Testo e imagine nell'alto medioevo,* 197–240. Settimane di studio del Centro italiano di Studi sull'alto medioevo 41. Spoleto: Centro italiano di studi sull'alto medioevo, 1994.

Shepard, Jonathan. "Aspects of Byzantine Attitudes and Policy towards the West in the Tenth and Eleventh Centuries." *Byzantinische Forschungen* 13 (1988): 67–118.

Sillett, Helen Marie. "Culture of Controversy: The Christological Disputes of the Early Fifth Century." PhD diss., University of California, Berkeley, 1999.

Simon, Marcel. *Verus Israel: A Study of the Relations between Christians and Jews in the Roman Empire 135–425.* Trans. H. McKeating. New York: The Littman Library of Oxford University Press, 1986.

Smith Mahlon H. III. *And Taking Bread . . . Cerularius and the Azyme Controversy of 1054.* Paris: Éditions Beauchesne, 1978.

Smythe, Dion C. "Alexios I and the Heretics: The Account of Anna Komnene's *Alexiad.*" In *Alexios I,* ed. Mullett and Smythe, 232–59.

———. ed. *Strangers to Themselves: The Byzantine Outsider.* Society for the Promotion of Byzantine Studies Publications 8. Aldershot: Ashgate/Variorum, 1998.

Sode, Claudia. *Jerusalem, Konstantinopel, Rom. Die Viten des Michael Synkellos und der Brüder Theodoros und Theophanes Graptoi.* Stuttgart: Franz Steiner, 2001.

Sotinel, Claire. "Emperors and Popes in the Sixth Century: The Western View." In *Cambridge Companion to the Age of Justinian,* ed. Maas, 267–90.

Speck, Paul. "Further Reflections and Inquiries on the Origins of the Byzantine Renaissance, with a Supplement: The Trier Ivory and Other Uncertainties." In Speck, *Understanding Byzantium,* 179–204. Trans. of "Weitere Überlegungen und Untersuchungen über die Ursprünge der byzantinischen Renaissance, mit einem Nachtrag: Das Trierer Elfenbein und andere Unklarheiten." In *Varia II,* Poikila Byzantina 6, 252–83. Bonn: Habelt, 1987.

———. "Die griechischen Quellen zur Bekehrung der Bulgaren und die zwei ersten Briefe des Photios." In *Polupleuros Nous. Miscellanea für Peter Schreiner zu Seinem 60. Geburtstag,* 342–59. Munich: K. G. Saur, 2000.

———. *Ich bin's nicht, Kaiser Konstantin ist es gewesen. Die Legenden von Einfluss des Teufels, des Juden und des Moslem auf den Ikonoklasmus.* Poikila byzantina 10. Bonn: Habelt, 1990.

———. "The Origins of the Byzantine Renaissance." In Speck, *Understanding Byzantium,* 143–62. Trans. of "Die Ursprünge der byzantinischen Renaissance." In *17th International Byzantine Congress, Major Papers,* 555–76. New Rochelle, N.Y.: Caratzas, 1986.

———. *Understanding Byzantium: Studies in Byzantine Historical Sources.* Ed. and trans. Sarolta Takács. Aldershot: Ashgate 2003.

Stein, Dietrich. *Der Beginn des byzantinischen Bilderstreites und seine Entwicklung in die 40er Jahre des 8 Jahrhunderts.* Munich: Institut für Byzantinistik und Neugriechische Philologie der Universität, 1980.

Trapp, Erich. "Gab es seine byzantinische Koranübersetzung?" *Diptycha* 2 (1980/81): 7–17.

Treadgold, Warren. *The Nature of the "Bibliotheca" of Photius.* Washington, D.C.: Dumbarton Oaks, 1980.

Trompf, G. W. "Church History as Non-Conformism: Retributive and Eschatological Elements in Athanasius and Philostorgius." *Byzantinische Forschungen* 24 (1997): 11–33.

Von Falkenhausen, Vera. *La dominazione bizantina nell'Italia meridionale dall IX all'XI secolo.* Bari: Ecumenica Editrice, 1978.

White, Lynn Townsend, Jr. *Latin Monasticism in Norman Sicily.* Cambridge, Mass.: Mediaeval Academy of America, 1938.

Wilson, Nigel. *Scholars of Byzantium.* Rev. ed. London: Duckworth, 1996.

Wood, Diana, ed. *The Church and the Arts.* Studies in Church History 28. Oxford: Blackwell, 1992.

Wood, Ian. "Conclusion: Strategies of Distinction." In *Strategies of Distinction,* ed. Pohl and Reimitz, 297–303.

Young, Frances. "Christian Teaching." In *Cambridge History of Early Christian Literature,* ed. Young et al., 464–84.

Young, Frances, Lewis Ayres, Andrew Louth, eds. *The Cambridge History of Early Christian Literature.* Cambridge: Cambridge University Press, 2004.

INDEX

Typeset in 10/13 New Baskerville
Designed and composed by Heather M. Padgen
Manufactured by Thomson-Shore, Inc.

Medieval Institute Publications
College of Arts and Sciences
Western Michigan University
1903 W. Michigan Avenue
Kalamazoo, MI 49008-5432
http://www.wmich.edu/medieval/mip